THE COMPLETE BOOK · OF FISHING

THE
COMPLETE
BOOK OF
FISHING

A

GUIDE TO FRESHWATER SALTWATER & BIG-GAME FISHING

FOREWORD BY

A. J. McCLANE
EDITED BY KEITH GARDNER

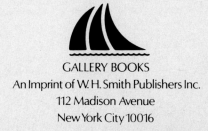

GALLERY BOOKS
An Imprint of W. H. Smith Publishers Inc.
112 Madison Avenue
New York City 10016

*The publishers would like to
dedicate this book to
Captain Joseph Masone
and the crew of the Debra.*

First published in 1987
by Octopus Books Limited
59 Grosvenor Street,
London W1X 9DA

This edition published in 1987
by Gallery Books

An imprint of W.H. Smith Publishers Inc.
112 Madison Avenue
New York, New York 10016
Reprinted 1988
© Bookbourne Limited 1987

ISBN 0 8317 1565 0

Printed by Mandarin Offset
in Hong Kong

FOREWORD BY A. J. McCLANE

It has been estimated that published fishing books outnumber the total printed on all other sports combined. This I can certainly believe. I have read literally thousands of books on fishing and written no less than eighteen myself. A few decades ago it was possible in any given year for me to fish in half-a-dozen countries (some of which no longer exist!), write a monthly fishing column for *Field & Stream* magazine, write all or most of a new fishing book, and still find time to read almost everything on the subject published in English.

Those days are gone forever. The exponential curve of population growth has produced a geometric progression of fishing authors. Nowadays, to keep up would require a speed-read addict functioning in a haze of amphetamines, as few volumes cover every discipline of angling.

To what source, then, can the beginner turn if he wants to learn about modern angling techniques as they are practised today? Somewhere within *The Complete Book of Fishing* almost every reader will find those words or pictures that will set him on the right path, whether it is in the aesthetically elegant practice of fly fishing, or the physically demanding sport of big-game fishing. In these pages even most veteran anglers will learn than there are new ramifications of the art that they have not yet explored. To the extent that any body of knowledge can ever be 'complete', this volume is indeed the ultimate modern work of reference, worthy of every angler's bookshelf.

A. J. McClane

CONTENTS

INTRODUCTION BY KEITH GARDNER OF FISHING WORLD

One picture is *not* worth a thousand words: a bad picture is worthless and a thousand ill-chosen words are stupefying. With *The Complete Book of Fishing* you hold in your hands an outstanding example of state-of-the-craft communication for pedagogical means, the very latest in teaching techniques. Its function is to present in vivid and succinct form the way Anglo-Saxons fish for sport. Other breeds with other laws may be absolutely whiz-bang at skiing, scuba-diving, kick-fighting and hockey, but all the world follows the English-speaking folk when angling.

Logically, an English-derived behavioral set should be irrelevant to Japanese, but they are dedicated fly-fishermen, or to Spanish-speaking peoples, though they have made a cult of wingshooting. But logic has little to do with it. Perhaps cultural acquisitions are controlled by the pineal glands of men and women. The pineal is the ductless gland that sits in your brain (presumably for a reason) and performs functions utterly unknown to our sciences. If this book fails to make your ductless glands oozy, perhaps you should try billiards.

Permit me, as one who has been there, to tell you how to read the five sections of the text that follows.

TACKLE

Homo ludens, the player, must be preceded by *Homo faber*, the maker. Every sport needs its tools, and TACKLE is the tools of fishing. There are 22 chapters specific to every aspect of this nice stuff. Since this is a reference work, devoted to scope rather than detail, you can follow up any element of TACKLE that intrigues you. Whole books for instance, and quite a few of them, have been devoted to hooks, the very essence of angling. Read or scan through this chapter, then go back and dwell on whatever has twigged your fancy, which will change with time, because *you* do.

BAIT

The efficacy of baiting your angle with something that smells like animal protein is indisputable, yet artificial lures are a growth industry which attracts Harvard MBA's and London School of Economics graduates. Some manufacturers in this field rarely fish, on the same grounds that criminal lawyers seldom commit crimes: their interest in the subject is largely satisfied by making money off those who do. The Wisdom of the Ages is to begin fishing BAIT to learn the ways of fishes, move on to artificial lures such as spoons and spinners and plugs, and then attempt fly-fishing (but only if you have a true vocation, and aren't some sort of nasty little *arriviste* given to puttin' on airs).

FISH SPECIES

In this section you will find 26 chapters covering more than 60 popular sport fishes, fresh- and saltwater, on both sides of the North Altantic Ocean. The coverage is zoological: the physiological eccentricities of each SPECIES, their behavior, habitats, distribution and favorite foods. You are also advised which tackle and techniques to use for them. Note that some of these fish would cost a fortune on the menus of posh restaurants, while others would be unacceptable to a judicious dung-fly. Some are extremely wary and fascinating to beguile, then on the hook are almost devoid of wriggle. Others will gobble any bait, then make you sweat to boat them, and thank you for doing so by trying to take your leg off (at times they succeed!).

TECHNIQUES

These are simply how you go about manipulating TACKLE. Read about the TECHNIQUES and TACKLE appropriate to the fish you are likely to have first crack at, if you are a neophyte, or next crack if you are not. Remember that on the tennis court you are using the same ball, racquet, net and strokes as the latest winner at Wimbledon or Forest Hills. TECHNIQUES are the Art of fishing.

READING THE WATER

Everyone is susceptible to the charms of Conan Doyle's marvelous Victorian thinking-machine, Sherlock Holmes, the biological supercomputer. The particular type of thinking at which he excelled is called induction, or deduction; its practitioners see the obvious, and infer the hidden. The reflective/refractive indices of the meniscus, the top of the water column, dictate that human vision, even with polarizing aids, will see mere glimpses of what takes place below. Thus we have READING THE WATER, which is to infer from superficial telltales the underlying reality. If you think that Holmes, from calluses on a man's hand, could deduce the work that caused them only in fiction, then think again, angler. Successful physicians, psychiatrists and politicians have built careers on evidence less obvious than that. I can think of four different reasons for one tiny bubble of gas to rise to the surface: two animal, one vegetable and one mineral. That is an essentially stillwater inference made by an angler who much prefers to fish in torrents, where bubbles are numbered in the billions!

Consider that a stream trout, with one eye, can fix his position in the current by looking at a subsurface rock, while another fovea of that same eye focuses on a bankside tree behind which you are hiding. At the same time, with the two foveae of his other eye, he can sharply see both a near sunken and a distant floating insect. You are behind the tree because the rock he is taking a bearing from creates a pressure wave that very slightly bumps the surface a few feet downcurrent from its position in the streambed. You think that if he is anywhere, he is there. Read the nine chapters of READING THE WATER, slowly, then do it again.

Fish were (and are) the world's first vertebrates, and therefore precede mammals in the chain of life. We fish for our ancestors, whose capabilities and traits are embodied within us, either implicitly or obviously. Fish can be categorized on many bases, one of which is the tripartite organization of their pineal glands. Some fish are positively phototactic and have a clear spot in their cranial roof that allows electromagnetic radiation to freely strike the gland. Some, such as the salmonids, can vary their reaction to light through the movement of chromatophores that permit or restrict the entrance of radiation. A third category of fish are negatively phototactic. They have opaque skulls that admit no light to the gland.

Some questions should be posed. Did (and do) pineal glands struck by electro-magnetic radiation see visible light, or some other portion(s) of the spectrum? Have they become partly vestigial, and useless as organs of radiation perception, because that capability has been superseded by the hard, focused light from the eyes? Or was the development of opaque skulls evolutionarily retrograde, one of those curses that can bring ruin to entire classes, such as Class Dinosauria? Why are the ductless, or endocrine, glands so mysterious? What is pineal vision? Who is hiding something from us?

When it is a long time between bites, and a fisherman's wits have been dulled by bucolic scenery, and by quiet sylvan noises at the edge of perception (such as a million insects chewing a million blades of grass) and you have lost the hard focus that comes only from civilization, then your mind may blither off into vagrant speculations like these, asking unanswerable questions, wasting time, making a fool of yourself – but thank God it is in private, in silence, where no one else can know what you are really like and make fun of you!

Keith Gardner

TACKLE

Over the past couple of decades, the fishing tackle industry has consistently been among the first to make widespread use of new materials, first fiberglass and then other composites, most successfully those based on graphite. These light, strong materials now form the basis of many rods, reels and other items. The performance of tackle made from them is often so good that some people are tempted to claim that there is now little scope for any further worthwhile improvement. But to make such a claim would be foolish; technology generally is developing at a steadily increasing rate, and there is no reason to believe that its progress won't continue to have an impact on angling.

The tackle industry is now more international than ever before. Japanese manufacturers, perhaps predictably, are now a major force in the market, and European and American companies are not just exporting products designed originally for their domestic markets, they're also producing items intended specifically for export. For instance, American firms are making rods, such as carp and other specialist rods, for the European market, while European companies produce reels and other items designed primarily for sale in the USA.

The most obvious differences between North American and European angling practices are found in freshwater fishing. Baitcasting and spinning with artificial lures constitute by far the largest part of American freshwater sport, perhaps 90 percent of it; in Europe, the situation is almost completely the opposite. For example, probably less than 10 percent of British freshwater anglers regularly fish with artificial lures.

This state of affairs gives anglers on both sides of the Atlantic plenty of scope for trying out techniques which are new to them. For instance, the sheer delight of flipping out a lure with an American baitcasting outfit is an experience sadly unknown to the vast majority of British anglers, who have yet to appreciate the pleasure of fishing with these short, light rods and tiny multiplying reels.

The situation is changing, although so far only slowly, as more and more British anglers, especially pike fishermen, are getting into the American lure scene. Conversely, some British methods, such as static deadbaiting for pike, and ledgering with electronic bite alarms for bottom-feeding species, are catching on in the USA. As increasing numbers of anglers are crossing the Atlantic for fishing holidays, and trying the local techniques, these trends are likely to continue.

Another American technique that could be used to great advantage on many British waters is downrigger trolling. This method, used in conjunction with fish-locating sonar, would transform the angling scene on large, deep British lakes, lochs and reservoirs.

Some of the more recent developments in angling tackle (and techniques) have come about because of changing attitudes more than through technical progress alone – anglers have become more conservation-minded. Modern attitudes to conservation originated largely in America, but soon gained ground in Europe as well. Anglers began to understand that the need to preserve fish stocks would not, in the long term, be met by simply imposing a close season while fish are spawning, or by artificial restocking. In America, the catch-and-release approach is steadily gaining ground, while in countries such as Britain, where the pressure on fish stocks is much greater, a new breed of specialized tackle items has been developed.

For instance, large, lightweight landing nets, made from soft, knotless netting, are replacing the gaff as the means of landing fish. Increasingly, it's only large fish designed for the table, such as salmon and various sea fish, which are gaffed. The others are caught and returned with as little injury as possible.

For freshwater anglers who want to retain their fish for a short time, to allow for photographing or weighing them, soft nylon keep sacks were introduced. Fish will lie perfectly still in these black sacks, which are also ideal for keeping species like pike and carp quiet prior to release. There are also unhooking mats, a great idea, which protect large fish from injury such as lost scales as they flap about while they're being unhooked.

This chapter describes the main types of tackle, such as rods and reels, that are used in freshwater and saltwater angling. The individual makes and models illustrated are but a very small sample of the vast range available; further information on these products can be obtained from the manufacturers and distributors listed at the back of the book.

BIG GAME TACKLE

The straight butt of the Daiwa CB 80FT and the curved butt of the Hardy Atlantic Canada. To comply with IGFA rules, the butt of a big game rod must not exceed 27 inches; if the butt is curved, the length is measured in a straight line from end to end across the curve.

To stand up to the rigors of the rough, tough sport of big game fishing, the tackle has to be of the best available design and quality – inferior or untested tackle isn't trustworthy and often breaks down under hard usage.

All big game fishing is done with multiplying reels, either star drag or lever drag types. The star drag system, which has a control knob that's turned by hand to increase or decrease the drag, may look old-fashioned but it works well and these reels are the basic workhorses of the sport.

There once were a number of American manufacturers producing star drag reels, but now only one – Penn – still does. These Penn Senator reels range in size from 4/0 up to the massive 16/0, the commonest being the 10/0, 12/0 and 14/0 models.

The lever drag reels, as their name implies, are operated by a smooth-acting lever which is pushed forwards to increase the drag or pulled backwards to decrease it. These reels, which are widely used in big game

tournament fishing, are produced by a number of companies around the world. The top of the market includes the Hardy Zane Grey range (UK) and the Fin-Nor range from Tycoon Tackle (USA), which are highly sophisticated and correspondingly expensive. Also very good, but less costly, are the Penn Internationals and the lever drag reels from Everol (Italy) and Triton and Daiwa (Japan).

The reason for the popularity of the lever drag over the older star drag lies in its greater sensitivity. With lever drag, you can increase the drag tension slowly and accurately, whereas with the star drag its's easy to apply just a fraction too much drag which can result in a broken line. Lever drag reels are seldom cheap, although the Everol range cost little more than the Senator star drag reels, offering extremely good value for money.

Big game rods come in many styles and sizes, but when fishing for truly big game you need a rod in the IGFA 50,

A big game fisherman playing blue shark – a poor fighter – on relatively light tackle.

80 or 130-pound classes, or occasionally in the unlimited class. The line should be in the same class as the rod; unlimited class rods, for instance, are those which should be used with lines of over 130 pounds test.

The IGFA is the International Game Fishing Association, based in Fort Lauderdale, Florida, which sets all the rules for the sport, including general tackle specifications. Any rod bearing an IGFA class number will conform to the IGFA regulations – for instance, the rod tip must be at least 40 inches long, and the butt length mustn't exceed 27 inches. If the rod has a curved butt, the length is measured across the curve, rather than round it.

Big game rods are designed for hard work, and so most are fitted with a full set of roller guides, AFTCO and Fin-Nor being the most popular types. Japanese manufacturers are now produc-

ing non-roller 'turbo' guides which are lined with hard, low-friction materials such as silicon carbide or titanium, providing a good, lightweight alternative to bulky roller guides.

Reel seats should always be of the heavy-duty, hooded type, and the rod butt of anodized aluminum, but whether you have a straight or curved rod butt depends on your own personal preference.

The two rods shown here are the **Daiwa CB 80FT** (on the left) and the **Hardy Atlantic Canada**.

The reel on the right is a **Shakespeare Sigma 2960-900**, a star drag reel which can handle line of up to 150 pounds test. It weighs 62 ounces and has a retrieval ratio of 2.6:1.

These reels are the **Penn Senator** 14/0 star drag reel and the bronze-colo red **Everol Cairns** 14/0, which is a lever drag reel.

Nylon monofilament lines are the most popular type for big game fishing. Tough enough to withstand scuffing and even minor nicks, Mono has only one real disadvantage: stretch. Its inherent elasticity means that it acts as a great shock absorber, but it often stops the hook from being set solidly.

For shark and tuna, which normally gulp the bait back, this isn't too much of a disadvantage,

but with billfish the elasticity of the nylon often absorbs the strength of the strike and so the hook doesn't set in the bony jaw plates. This occurs mostly during fast water trolling with artificial lures.

The alternative to nylon is Dacron, a polyester fibre which is prestretched during manufacture. Dacron sets hooks solidly, but the slightest damage to the line will cause it to snap instantly when

tension is applied. The same thing happens if the line gets dragged across the back of another fish while tensioned. Because of this, Dacron is now used by only a few, highly experienced, big game anglers.

Whichever line you use, it should always be one which has an IGFA rating. The most popular nylon lines are Ande and Berkley Trilene.

Leaders for big game fishing

are almost always made from either heavy longliner's nylon or from braided or single-strand stainless steel wire. The normal strength of a big game trace is 300 to 500 pounds test, far heavier than the actual reel line. This is to soak up damage and severe punishment during the battle, and to allow a beaten fish to be pulled to within gaffing range. Under IGFA rules the leader must not exceed 30 feet in length.

CENTERPINS AND MULTIPLIERS

The centerpin is one of the simplest of all reels, but also one of the most difficult to use. Casting with the centerpin takes skill, especially over long distances, which is one of the main reasons for its dramatic decline in popularity after the easy-casting fixed spool reel was introduced to the mass market in the 1940s. Centerpins are still used by some anglers in the UK and Europe, but are unknown in the US and scarcely used in Canada.

The centerpin consists of a flanged drum which carries the line and revolves freely on a steel axle. Most have a ratchet mechanism and some also have a drag system, but it's the reel's free-running action and the way that it can be controlled simply by thumb pressure that are its main advantages.

Because the line winds directly onto the spool, instead of first passing over a bale arm, the centerpin gives extremely sensitive control over float tackle that is being allowed to drift smoothly downstream with the current. The line can be retrieved rapidly by giving the drum a series of sharp taps with the fingertips to spin it, or it can be wound in by using a handle fixed to the outer flange of the drum. The amount of line retrieved for each turn of the handle depends on the drum diameter: the larger the drum, the more line it will wind on with each revolution. Most centerpins have a drum diameter of three to six inches.

Most multipliers, on the other hand, have small-diameter drums which don't take up much line per revolution, but rapid retrieval is possible because the handle drives the drum via a gear mechanism. This gearing makes the drum turn more than once for each turn of the handle, which is why the reels are called multipliers. The gear ratio varies from one model to another, but it's usually between 2:1 and 4½:1.

Many multipliers, especially the smaller ones, are fitted with level wind mechanisms. These track the line from side to side across the drum as the handle is turned, so that the line is wound on neatly and evenly. Another feature of most small multipliers is a magnetic braking system which avoids the risk of overruns when casting. These allow the angler to make a long, powerful cast without having to worry about the drum continuing to

spin and spew out line after the terminal tackle has hit the water. Once the weight of the tackle is no longer pulling line from the spool, the magnetic brake brings it smoothly to a stop.

To minimize the possibility of line breakage when a fish is being played hard, multipliers have a slipping clutch or drag mechanism. This is adjusted, by means of a star-shaped knob or lever, so that the reel will only turn and give line when the line is pulled strongly, but not so strongly as to break it. When the drag is set correctly, the angler can confidently put maximum pressure on the fish.

Among the smallest of the multipliers are the little teardrop-shaped baitcasters. These fit snugly into the hand, allowing you to fish with two or three fingers in front of the rod trigger. This makes for comfortable all-day casting, to which reel manufacturers have further contributed by designing a smooth endplate without protruding

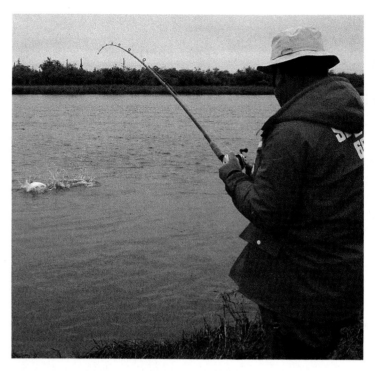

Above *The risk of line breakage is reduced if the drag mechanism of the reel is properly adjusted.*

Right *Applying gentle pressure to the rim of a centrepin will slow down the largest fish.*

RYOBI T-1
The Ryobi T-1 is a little baitcasting reel with a graphite body and a right-left convertible handle. The spool is mounted on ball bearings, and the gear ratio is 5.0:1. The reel has a level wind, and spool capacity is 120 yards of 14-pound test line.

DAIWA PT 15E
Apart from having all the mechanical features of a good-quality multiplier, the PT 15E is fitted with a micro-computer and liquid crystal display. The computer gives data on factors such as line strength, line capacity, casting distance, water depth, countdown depth and rate of retrieve.

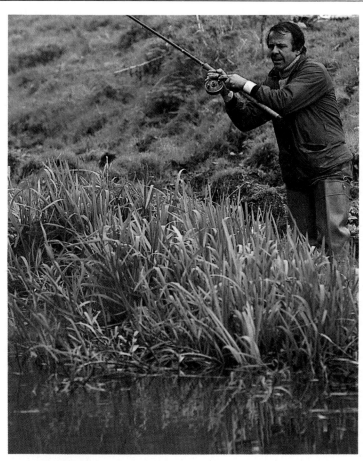

buttons and bearing caps. Another good feature of most of these reels is the thumb bar which disengages the spool for casting.

These baby multipliers can hold from 100 to 150 yards of 10 to 12 pounds test line, which means they can be used for catching fish as large as a pike or bass.

Larger multipliers, with a capacity of between 200 and 300 yards of 14 or 15-pound line, are useful for heavy baitcasting, light surfcasting and estuary fishing. These have the same sort of features as the little baitcasters, such as the magnetic cast control which is so beneficial to the long-distance beachcaster.

A much more rugged reel with a greater line capacity is needed for uptide fishing, light sea trolling or trolling large lakes with a downrigger. The reel should hold 250 to 300 yards of line of 15 to 18 pounds test or heavier.

A level wind is useful but not essential, but the spool must be strong, crushproof and corrosion-resistant, preferably of diecast aluminum. The handle should be a sensibly-sized torpedo shape, and instead of a thumb bar a positive-actioned gear lever which cannot be engaged accidentally is a must, as is a click or ratchet for when the reel needs to be left in free spool. A handy feature of some models is a lever drag control, which is a faster and more sensitive system than the star drag when you're controlling the run of a big fish.

Even larger reels are needed for offshore boat and wreck fishing when you're after the smaller pelagic species or big bottom feeders like rays, groupers, white sea bass or conger. These reels, up to around size 4/0 (the small end of the big game range), need both strength and durability to cope with the hard work of pirking, wrecking or trolling. The spool should be of brass or stainless steel to withstand the constriction of heavy nylon or wire lines, and the body reinforced with strong, chromed endplates.

A level wind isn't necessary, but a large line capacity is, if only to give a faster retrieve when the reel is full. Somewhere between 300 and 400 yards of 30 to 40-pound line should cope with most situations.

DAIWA SEALINE 27H
Designed specifically for saltwater boat fishing, the Sealine 27H has a gear ratio of 3.8:1 and a spool capacity of 370 yards of 10-pound line. The spool is mounted in stainless steel ball bearings and the spool and the side plates are of corrosion-resistant anodized aluminum.

ABU AMBASSADEUR 9000 CL
The 9000 CL is a heavy-duty saltwater multiplier for both beach and boat fishing, including trolling. The gear ratio is normally 4.2:1, but when a big fish is being played and the reel is heavily loaded, the ratio automatically shifts down to 2.5:1 to give a slower but more powerful retrieve.

FIXED SPOOL REELS

SHAKESPEARE SIGMA 2400-040
A lightweight, graphite-bodied reel with a rear drag, 4.8:1 retrieve ratio and a spool capacity of 230 yards of 8-pound line.

DAIWA PROCASTER ST-8000D
This alloy-bodied reel has a long, tapered spool to give great casting ability for surfcasting or saltwater spinning. The gear ratio is 4:1, and spool capacity is 290 yards of 15-pound line.

DAIWA 125M
The Daiwa 125M is a closed face reel which, unlike most other closed face reels, has its drag control at the rear rather than on the handle shaft. The reel has a graphite body and a 4.1:1 gear ratio, with spool capacity of 110 yards of 2-pound line.

The fixed spool or spinning reel opened up a whole new chapter in casting performance when it became widely available in the 1940s. It was said then that 'anyone can cast a long way with a fixed spool reel', and that statement still holds true today.

There are several different types of fixed spool reel, but they all work on the same basic principle. On the retrieve, the line is wound around the spool by a rotating bale arm. The spool doesn't revolve, but it does move up and down along the line of the rod to facilitate even line lay.

The spool needs to be almost full of line for best casting: line should fill the spool to just below the rim and be wound on firmly. Many anglers fail to appreciate this, and their casting deteriorates as the level of line on the spool drops due to wear.

Although the spool doesn't turn when the line is being retrieved, it does revolve to give line to a running fish. The spool turns under the control of a drag or slipping clutch, which can be adjusted so that the spool turns and gives line before the breaking point of the line is reached. An antireverse mechanism (some silent, some audible) prevents the handle from turning backwards when the spool is rotating.

Fixed spool reels are available in a variety of retrieve rates. A ratio of about 4:1, which will retrieve around 20 inches of line for each turn of the handle, is suitable for most purposes. However, many anglers prefer a 3:1 ratio (about 15 inches per turn) for spinning when they want to work the lure at a slow, steady rate, or a 6:1 ratio (30 inches per turn) for cranking in lures at high speed when after pelagic species in clear water.

The closed face reel is a type of fixed spool reel which doesn't have an exposed bale arm. The line passes through a hole in the

SHAKESPEARE SIGMA 2401-080
This large reel is made of a material called Whisker Titanium, which is light, tough and corrosion-resistant. To improve casting, the line can be loaded towards the rear of the spool instead of towards the front, and the Teflon spool lip reduces line friction.

RYOBI ML 3C
The Ryobi ML 3C is a medium-sized fixed spool reel for either freshwater or saltwater use. The body, spool and rotor are made of a ceramic/graphite composite material and the handle is made of graphite. The gear ratio is 4.5:1, and the spool capacity is 260 yards of 10-pound line.

completely-enclosed front face of the reel, and is wound round the spool by a rotating steel pin. During casting, this bale pin is disengaged from the line by finger pressure on the front face of the reel, or on some models by pressing a button at the rear.

Depending on the make, the drag control is either mounted on the handle shaft or at the rear. Most reels will only allow the spool to rotate and give line when the antireverse is on, but a few allow line to be given by back-winding.

Closed face reels are very efficient for light line fishing, but their use with lines in excess of 4 or 5 pounds test is not recommended. Far too much torque would be transmitted to such a sensitive machine when playing a

The fixed spool or spinning reel is ideal for float fishing and ledgering, as well as for spinning in both fresh and salt water.

heavy fish on such lines.

All the closed face reels and the smallest fixed spools will hold around 100 yards of between 2 and 4 pounds test line, and are ideal for jigging and lightweight float fishing and ledgering for species like perch, the smaller cyprinids and crappies.

For anything heavier, the medium sized fixed spool reels should be used. One reel and two interchangeable spools should cover all your needs: one spool with 100 to 150 yards of 5 or 6 pounds test, plus a deeper one holding 150 to 200 yards of 8 to 12 pounds test. The deeper spool should be crushproof, as the constriction of the line can be considerable when you're playing larger species such as carp, catfish, pike, salmon or big bass.

Lightweight graphite bodies, disengaging spools and rear drag levers are all useful on this type of reel, but most importantly the reel should be hard wearing and

free running, with a wide, deep spool for easy, long casting.

The largest fixed spool reels are those designed for surfcasting and estuary fishing. These should be corrosion-resistant (many aren't) for regular use in saltwater, and have wide, smooth-lipped spools capable of holding somewhere between 200 and 250 yards of 15 to 25 pounds test line.

More so than for any other type of fishing, beach reels need to be very smooth-running, so look for those whose spools turn effortlessly on ball or roller bearings.

A sensibly-sized, torpedo-shaped handle is essential for a good grip, and a sensitive, progressive drag (either front or rear) is a must for playing fast, hard-fighting fish. Spools with conical-shaped inners are preferable for long-distance casting, as are small, manually-operated bale arms which won't accidentally snap closed during a powerful cast.

FLOAT RODS

The modern float rod, made of hollow fiberglass or graphite-based composite materials, is an incredibly powerful and versatile tool despite its fragile looks – a good 13-foot graphite rod can weigh as little as 6 ounces.

When you're choosing a float rod, it's important to pick one with the right sort of action for the type of fishing you do. For instance, a soft, highly flexible rod will be next to useless if much of your fishing demands hitting quick bites.

To assess the action of a rod, hold it horizontally as you would when fishing, with your forearm along the handle, then lower the tip to about 12 inches from the floor. Try a smart upward strike, keeping your eye on the tip; if it dips and touches the floor, the action is too sloppy for float fishing and the rod should be rejected. With a stiff, fast-actioned rod, the tip shouldn't touch down on a strike when it's held only 6 inches from the floor.

If the rod passes this test, have the tackle dealer hold the tip-top guide at waist height while you slowly lift the rod upwards into a nice bend. You will then be able to see if the action is more or less confined to just the tip, the top section or the middle, or if it's completely all-through, which is preferable.

Other points to watch for when you're selecting a float rod include the number, height and type of guides, and the length and diameter of the handle. Guides of hard chrome stainless steel are very popular and usually stand a couple of seasons of hard use before starting to groove, but lined guides provide a significant reduction in friction and subsequent grooving and line wear.

Float rod guides should stand high off the blank to keep the line clear of the rod to minimize line slap and eliminate line stick during wet weather, and there should be one guide for every foot of overall rod length (although they will, of course, be placed at varying intervals, not simply every 12 inches).

The handle size is a more important part of float rod design than many anglers realize. Too many handles are too thick or too long, or both: a diameter of one inch is ideal for a firm grip, while a length of 22 to 24 inches is quite sufficient. There's little point in investing in an expensive 14-foot rod if its handle is so long that a foot of it sticks out behind your elbow when you're fishing; this reduces its effective length to 13 feet. As for the handle material, whether you choose cork or a synthetic material depends entirely upon your personal preference.

At the bottom end of the price range, 10 to 12-foot hollow glass rods are well-suited to general float fishing for bluegills, crappies and similar species. Being thicker in wall section and heavier than graphite rods, they are ideal for youngsters and beginners because the action is more progressive than superfast, which makes them easier to use.

Rods in the 12 to 15-foot range are now mostly made of graphite, often mixed with boron, silicon carbide or Kevlar. In general, the higher the proportion of graphite in the rod, the better it will perform. Flexing the rod in a mock strike is a good way to get an idea of how much graphite the rod contains. A sloppy rod which

Right *Playing a big carp on a long float rod. Made of lightweight composites, a 15-foot rod will weigh only about half a pound.*

The upper rod in this picture is a **Shakespeare 1835/390 President Super Match**. This three-piece, 13-foot graphite rod has a cork and Hyperlon handle, and is fitted with eighteen Fuji low-friction guides. The rod has a fast tip action, and weighs 8.6 ounces.

The rod in the centre is another **Shakespeare** model, an **1842/330 'O' Series**. Made of hollow fiberglass with a 28-inch Hyperlon handle, this three-section rod has a threaded tip guide to take swing, quiver or spring tips and so can be used for ledgering as well as float fishing.

doesn't return quickly won't have a very high percentage of graphite in its structure. Look for a rod with a snappy return and the sort of action which will best suit your requirements.

Pick a delicate tip action if you intend fishing for small species, and one which will bend right through to the middle and bottom sections if you're going to be angling for fish that weigh pounds, rather than ounces.

Overall, a rod of around 13 feet will generally suffice, but 14 and 15 foot float rods are very useful for fishing into exceptionally deep lakes and pits.

Whatever length of rod you choose, if it's a graphite rod don't fish near overhead power lines, or when there's lightning about. Graphite is an excellent conductor of electricity, and if your rod touches a power line you'll get a serious, even fatal, shock.

The **Daiwa WKM 14** rod is made of Whisker Kevlar, a composite material of silicon carbide and graphite reinforced with Kevlar. The 14-foot, three-piece WKM 14 weighs only 7.4 ounces and is fitted with fifteen Dynaflo guides and a comfortable, non-slip handle.

FLOATS

The floats shown here are used as follows:
Avons: in turbulent, fast-flowing water
Loafers: for grayling and chub fishing in fast-flowing rivers
Zoomers: weighted floats for casting long distances on still waters
Crystal wagglers: on still or slow waters
Sticks: for fishing close-in on rivers
Balsas: on medium to fast waters
Onions: on still waters
Crystals: on still or slow waters
Peacock wagglers: on still or moving waters
Polywags: on still or moving waters, especially in strong winds
Swingers: close-in fishing on rippled waters

| Avons | Loafers | Zoomers | Crystal wagglers | Sticks | Balsa | Onions | Crystals |

The float is one of the most sensitive and versatile bite indicators an angler could wish to use, and it not only gives excellent bite indication, it also allows the bait to be presented in a natural way.

Plastics, such as polycarbonates, dominate float production these days. Early floats were made from porcupine quills or the quills of bird feathers, with bodies of cork, elder pith or balsa if extra buoyancy was needed.

Of these materials, balsa is still used quite extensively, and for the 'waggler' type of floats a better material than peacock quills has yet to be found. There is, as yet, no synthetic material to match it for its combination of strength, lightness and buoyancy, although synthetics can always beat quill on price and availability.

Sarkansas reed, which has a buoyancy similar to that of peacock quill, is another natural material still used for making float stems, along with cane and balsa. To make a waggler float, a small metal eye is inserted into the bottom of the stem. For partially-weighted wagglers, a small brass or steel rod, with one end formed into an eye, is fitted into the stem.

In use, the reel line is passed through the eye of the waggler and the float is locked in position with a split shot or shots on the line at each side of the eye. Other types of float are fixed to the line by silicone rubber float bands at the top and bottom of the float. Despite the hundreds of different shapes and sizes of floats available, most of them fall into just one of two general groups: those fixed to the line at the bottom end only, usually through an eye, and those fixed at both the top and bottom ends by rubber bands.

The most popular of all the top and bottom fixed floats are the wire-stemmed balsa or cane stick-type floats. Used only in rivers, these floats allow you to drift the bait slowly downstream. You can hold back hard on the float so that it travels slower than the current, and the bait (usually maggots or casters) will swing forwards ahead of the float. These floats work most effectively at quite close range, certainly no further out than about 1½ rod lengths.

Thicker versions, balsa floats carrying more weight, are good in medium to fast water where the lighter ones are less effective.

Two other useful top and bottom fixed floats are the Avon and the loafer (or chub trotter). The Avon float has all its buoyancy concentrated in a balsa body immediately below the tip (also balsa). This allows it to ride evenly through turbulent water such as weir pools, and it can be held back to swing the bait upwards without being dragged off course.

Loafers are made from solid balsa or clear, hollow plastic. They are, in effect, shorter, squatter versions of the balsa float, being much thicker and carrying more weight so that they

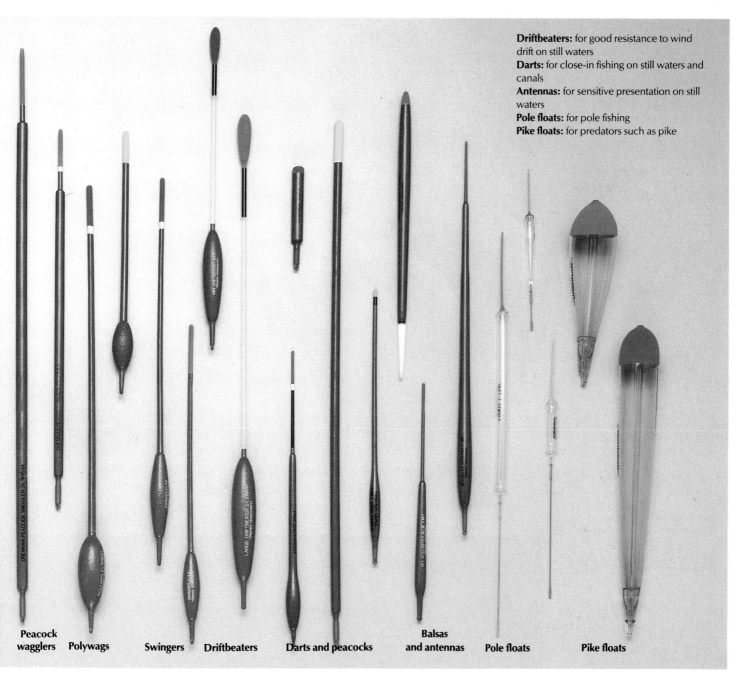

Driftbeaters: for good resistance to wind drift on still waters
Darts: for close-in fishing on still waters and canals
Antennas: for sensitive presentation on still waters
Pole floats: for pole fishing
Pike floats: for predators such as pike

Peacock wagglers **Polywags** **Swingers** **Driftbeaters** **Darts and peacocks** **Balsas and antennas** **Pole floats** **Pike floats**

hold steady in fast currents. Their thick tips are easily visible even when they're fished a long way downstream, and they're ideal for grayling or chub fishing in fast rivers.

The most versatile of all floats are the peacock quill wagglers, which are fixed bottom end only. A handful of peacock wagglers of various sizes would easily meet threequarters of all float fishing requirements, either in still or running water. They are locked on the line with split shot either side of the eye, and in running water they're always fished preceding the bait. If all the weight is concentrated around the float, very slow-moving swims can be fished well over depth so that the bait trundles along the

bottom very slowly, with just a couple of tiny shots down the line.

A peacock waggler works equally well with all the shots close to the hook, for fishing with the lift method. With all the shots down at the hook, the float is fixed to the line with a rubber float band.

The bodied peacock waggler allows you to cast further than with the waggler, because the extra buoyancy provided by its polystyrene body allows more shot to be used. As well as being useful for fishing distant swims, these floats are good in windy weather, but remember to sink the line well to avoid surface drift.

To facilitate quick, easy changing of all waggler style floats, use a rubber or plastic float

attachment. This threads onto the line just like the bottom of a float, and the float is simply pushed into it.

Darts are tiny, bulbous-bottomed floats with extra-fine tips, designed to indicate the tiniest of bites. They are good for fishing close-in in still water. Pole floats are also very small, sometimes with super-fine 'bristle' tips. They may be fixed bottom end only or top and bottom, and they work in just the same way as other floats. They are, however, much easier to control (which is why they're smaller) because the pole tip is positioned directly above, with as little line as possible between tip and float.

For float fishing at night, you

can use luminous elements which are glued to the float or attached to it by a length of tubing. Alternatively, battery-powered floats (which are more or less the same shape as a bodied waggler) are available.

Most floats used for live or deadbaiting for predators are cigar-shaped slider floats. The line either passes through an eye at the bottom of the float, or, if it's a tubed float, through a hole running right through the float from end to end.

Drift floats, which have little vanes or sails which catch the wind to take them and the bait (live or dead) out beyond casting distance, are useful for predator fishing from the bank on large waters.

FLY REELS

It is sometimes said that the reel is the least important item in the fly fishermen's tackle bag, the inference being that if it will hold line and revolve in both directions, it will be good enough.

Of course, it is possible to catch fish on a fly rod without using a reel at all, keeping the extra line and backing on a spool in your pocket, and feeding it out and retrieving it by hand as required.

Indeed, it's a common fallacy to think that you need a reel on your rod to make it balance properly, some anglers even claiming that a heavy reel is needed to balance a heavy rod. In fact, you get a better casting action if your rod is unencumbered by a reel at all, but it makes obvious sense to have a reel on a fly rod, and certainly on one for salmon. So although it may often be regarded as one of the less important items of tackle, it pays to use the best you can afford.

Instead of the old-fashioned, solid-construction reels of heavy brass, most reels are now made of lightweight materials which are cast with holes and slots to lighten them and give good ventilation to the backing line. Some are made from light metal alloys, while there are a few ultralight carbon fibre (graphite) models.

It's important to have a good check mechanism, and for the checkwork to be adjustable so that you can use your reel for either left or right hand wind, according to your preference. When set properly, the checkwork should offer more resistance to the line when it's going out than when it's being wound in. Some reels have an adjustable check so that varying degrees of resistance to a running fish may be selected or varied at will.

Typical of the more popular makes of fly reel are the Hardy Marquis series, the Bruce and Walker Expert, and the System Two reels made by Leeda tackle in England for the 3M company. The latter have a superb adjustable drag mechanism and the added bonus of being more resistant to salt water than most other reels. Perhaps the ultimate in fly reels are made in America by the Bogdan Reel Co. These

Right *A fly-caught salmon, and the rod and reel that it was taken on. The holes in the side of the spool of the reel make it lighter and ventilate the backing line.*

LEEDA SYSTEM TWO 1011

System Two

System TWO 1011
Scientific Anglers/3M
Made in England

MITCHELL 710

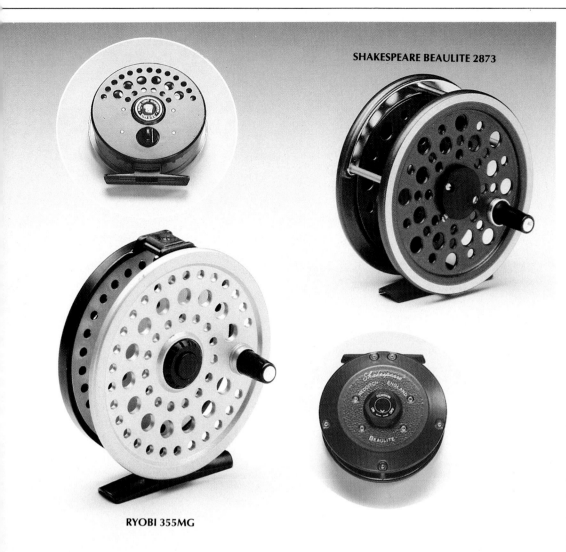

SHAKESPEARE BEAULITE 2873

RYOBI 355MG

The reels shown here are, from left to right, the Mitchell 710, the Leeda System Two 1011, the Ryobi 355MG and the Shakespeare Beaulite 2873.

The Mitchell 710 is an automatic reel. There is no handle, as the line is retrieved by a clockwork mechanism which turns the spool when the lever is operated. The mechanism is wound up as line is stripped from the reel, or by turning the ribbed black cover on the left hand face of the reel.

The Leeda System Two 1011 is a direct wind reel with a disc-brake drag system. Turning the drag control knob adjusts a pair of brake pads which act on a stainless steel disc on the spool.

The Ryobi 355MG is an ultralight (3 ounce) direct wind reel made of diecast magnesium. This metal is light and strong, but must be used only for freshwater fishing – salt or brackish water would quickly corrode it.

The Shakespeare Beaulite 2873 is also direct wind, with a wide 3½-inch spool and exposed rims, and is intended for use with single handed rods.

reels are fine examples of metal craftsmanship, but at several hundred dollars each they're not within everyone's budget.

Many manufacturers offer reels in differing retrieve ratios. The normal reel, which is excellent for general use, is the direct wind type where there is no gearing to alter the retrieve rate. Alternatively, you might prefer a geared multiplying reel. These are fine when retrieving line at the end of your cast, but they do tend to make it harder work to wind in a fish in play, so you may have to use pump-and-wind tactics as you would do when using fixed spool or multiplying spinning reels.

Their one great advantage is for the stillwater angler, who is accustomed to fish taking his fly as he strips in line during the retrieve. Some anglers, of course, never bother to get the line back onto the reel to cope with a fish in play, but if you want to do it, and quickly, then the multiplying fly reel does a better job than the standard.

A multiplying reel is also very useful for those situations when a fish runs hard and straight, then turns quickly and comes charging back at you. It's then important to be able to keep contact with your fish, and the multiplier enables you to do it more effectively than with a reel with a standard rate of retrieve.

Ideally, the size and type of reel you choose should be determined by the type of fish you're after and the length of your rod. A 15 foot salmon rod, for instance, may well need a 4-inch diameter reel so that it can accommodate a number 11 line and the 20 or 25 pound backing needed to cope with salmon of up to 30 pounds.

An 8-foot single handed trout rod, on the other hand, may need a reel of only 3 inches diameter (or less) to adequately hold a number 6 line and the appropriate 10 pound backing. Only rarely will a trout of less than 2 pounds get you down to the backing. But on those still waters where trout of double figures may be found, you'll need a medium-sized reel and something like a number 8 line and 12 pound backing.

Some manufacturers, such as Mitchell of France, make automatic reels which find favour with some anglers. The reels have a clockwork retrieve mechanism, which is actuated by a lever and can be overridden when a fish wants to run and take line.

In theory, when you're playing a fish you can just stand there with the lever pressed and let the line come in and out as the fish plays. In practice, some form of pumping is often needed, and if you're bringing a fish in from a long distance you may have to rewind the clockwork in order to complete the job.

The retrieve rate of automatic reels is typically 10 to 12 feet per second. Enthusiasts of automatic reels claim that they allow greater control over hooked fish than conventional models do.

As with any type of fly reel, when you're choosing an automatic model check that its spool will accommodate the sizes of line you expect to use, plus the required backing line. Another feature worth having is an interchangeable spool, which will save you having to change the whole reel when you want to switch to a different line.

FLY RODS

Fly rods, excluding salmon rods, range in length from the little 6½-foot brook rods up to 11½-foot models which give superb water command over still waters and large rivers. Apart from length, there are other factors to take into account when you're choosing a rod, for instance will you want a stiff-actioned rod for long-distance casting on lakes or reservoirs, or a softer-actioned one for delicate wet-fly fishing on small streams?

In general, there are three basic types of fly rod: those with a soft action to successfully cover water with shorter casts, and where you don't have to play very large fish; those with a stiff action, but which are not so long as to be too cumbersome for single handed use yet have enough power to double-haul a long line and to command big fish in play; and those rods of the maximum length for single handed use, and which have some ease of action for comfortable use but can still command a fish in play.

Although split cane was the

Fishing for brown trout in the well-oxygenated water below a small waterfall. Trout rods range in size from little 6½-foot single handed brook rods up to the 11½-foot models for fishing still waters and large rivers.

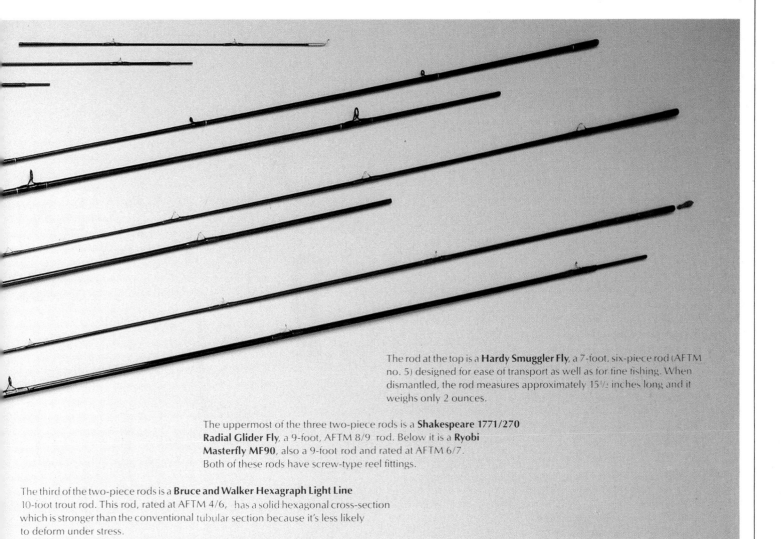

The rod at the top is a **Hardy Smuggler Fly**, a 7-foot, six-piece rod (AFTM no. 5) designed for ease of transport as well as for fine fishing. When dismantled, the rod measures approximately 15½ inches long and it weighs only 2 ounces.

The uppermost of the three two-piece rods is a **Shakespeare 1771/270 Radial Glider Fly**, a 9-foot, AFTM 8/9 rod. Below it is a **Ryobi Masterfly MF90**, also a 9-foot rod and rated at AFTM 6/7. Both of these rods have screw-type reel fittings.

The third of the two-piece rods is a **Bruce and Walker Hexagraph Light Line** 10-foot trout rod. This rod, rated at AFTM 4/6, has a solid hexagonal cross-section which is stronger than the conventional tubular section because it's less likely to deform under stress.

great rod-making material of bygone days, it's now rarely seen. Even the fiberglass rods so popular until recently tend to be regarded now as too heavy for prolonged use. Nowadays, there is nothing to beat graphite, and there has been a steady swing to this material since the mid Seventies. The snag with all tubular rods, however, even those made from graphite (and one that manufacturers have been reluctant to admit), is that when stressed to extremes, the tube assumes an oval shape and there's a sudden and dramatic loss of power and an increased risk of breakage.

One way of avoiding this problem is that used for the Bruce and Walker Hexagraph series. These have six graphite cores cemented together to form a solid section without being too heavy.

The longer the rod, the greater the area of water you will be able to command or cover, but don't forget that the advantages of extra length might be offset by drawbacks such as increased weight.

For instance, you can get a superb 11-foot rod which is very powerful and may even be used for salmon fishing. It might be the most useful rod for, say, up to a quarter of an hour at a stretch, but to fish with it all day making frequent casts might make you feel as though your arm's falling off. A delicate little rod, on the other hand, might be a joy to use but not give you the water command you need or deal adequately with very big fish.

Of course, it all boils down to the fact that, just as a golfer needs differing clubs, you will need a set of different rod actions and lengths to meet all your needs. For fishing on a small stream of little more than 25 feet wide, you would easily cope with a 7 to 8½-foot rod and still have more distance casting power than you're likely to need.

A river 45 feet wide, however, might well call for a rod of between 8½ and 10 feet. But if you want to limit yourself to only one rod for all types of fly fishing, including salmon, sea trout and

trout, you should choose a medium-action 10-footer.

If you want to fish on still waters, you have to decide whether you will spend the bulk of the time fishing from a boat or wading along the shore line: boat rods can be slightly less substantial than bank ones. Ideally, you should have access to a more powerful 9½ or 10-foot rod for bank fishing, but you should avoid those over-stiff devices which need the strength of a gorilla to flex them properly. They may be fine for the tournament caster who wants to throw a line into the next county, and who will only use it for a five minute session anyway, but they are not nice for prolonged fishing. Also bear in mind that the stronger and stiffer the rod, the stronger your leader will have to be to avoid breakage on the strike.

With all single handed rods it's preferable to have the reel fittings near the butt. Various fitments are available, and those that are the lightest are usually the best. Screw fittings offer greater

security than those with a friction hold, although you're unlikely to have a reel fall off whichever type you choose.

Despite the great variety of rod actions to suit different fishing situations, to some extent here is room for personal preference. It is usually said that a slightly stiffer-actioned rod is better for dry-fly fishing, and a soft-actioned rod is better for wet flies. But beware of any rod that is truly limp; these might be able to handle very light lines in calm conditions, but they often lack the stamina to cope with contrary winds and longer-than-average casts. Even though a fly rod shouldn't have too soft an action, when it's flexed it should have a good all-through action down into the butt. Tip-actioned rods with stiff butt sections have little use in fly fishing.

If you can afford it, get a rod in graphite by one of the more reputable manufacturers. There is much dumping of foreign over-production and these rods, while exceptionally cheap, may not represent very good value.

FRESHWATER HOOKS

Although they're often taken for granted, hooks are not only the essential point of angling tackle but also, in many ways, one of the most complicated. There is a hook, or a choice of hooks, for every angling need.

Hooks are made of carbon steel or stainless steel, and usually bronzed, blued, japanned or plated with nickel or cadmium. Until the 1980s, hooks were all about equal in terms of sharpness. Then a new process – called chemical etching – was introduced, first by Kamatsu and then by other manufacturers.

This method of sharpening the hook produces a point which is much sharper than that which can be obtained by any other process. This means that chemically-sharpened hooks will penetrate extremely easily, but it has been suggested that they're sometimes too sharp for soft-mouthed fish because they will actually cut their way out quicker than conventionally-sharpened hooks.

For freshwater fishing, double and treble hooks are used mostly on artificial lures, such as spinners and plugs, and for rigging live or dead fishbaits when fishing for predators such as pike.

The smallest sizes of single hook usually have flattened, spade-shaped ends, rather than eyed ends. For delicate presentation of baits to small fish, the spade end is superior to the eyed hook in the sizes from 12 down to 26, because it hangs well on the line and may be tied direct to a finer hook length. All sizes of spade end hook are available pre-tied to a short hook length which is easily knotted to the reel line. This saves you the trouble of whipping the hook to the line.

For presenting single tiny bloodworms or maggots, use a very fine wire hook of from size 16 to size 26, with a long, slightly reversed shank, a crystal bend (or a Limerick) and a chemically-sharpened point with a micro barb. Larger maggots or worms, or pairs of them, call for a hook with a thicker wire and a shorter shank. Sizes 12 to 20 should be strong enough for most fish up to about 3 pounds in weight. For a single maggot intended for a larger, more powerful species, or for presenting larger baits such as sweetcorn or small pieces of bread flake, a forged hook is needed.

Forged hooks have a flattened cross-section, as opposed to the round cross-section of the ordinary unforged wire hook, and size-for-size are much stronger.

Forged, eyed hooks of size 2 to size 12, with short shanks, round bends and small barbs, are ideal for general freshwater fishing with baits large and small. Hooks with medium-sized wires are suitable for most purposes, but where large fish are expected, or for fishing close to snags, use stronger hooks made from a heavier wire with a reversed, medium-length shank.

With heavy lines and for powerful fish such as carp and catfish, go for a black, forged hook with a long shank, a crystal bend and a whisker barb; sizes 1/0 down to 10 are most useful. For hooking small livebaits, or large bean or peanut baits, use a size 2 to 8 forged, bronzed hook with a long, reversed shank and a round bend.

Weedless hooks are worth using if you're fishing among thick weed. The incurving point of a weedless hook is shielded by a sprung wire guard which is fixed just below the eye. This guard prevents the hook from snagging on weeds, but when a fish bites, the guard wire is pushed towards the shank and the point and barb are exposed.

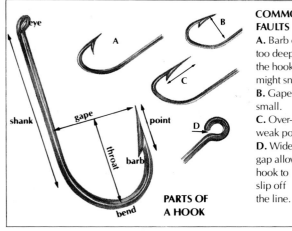

PARTS OF A HOOK

eye

shank

gape

throat

point

barb

bend

A

B

C

D

COMMON HOOK FAULTS

A. Barb cut too deep — the hook might snap.
B. Gape too small.
C. Over-long, weak point.
D. Wide eye gap allows hook to slip off the line.

Large treble

TREBLE HOOKS

Trebles are used on lures, and with live or deadbaits. For this, semi-barbless trebles are recommended – the barbed point holds the bait well, while the two barbless points are easier to unhook from the catch than barbed points are.

Semi-barbless treble

Small treble

DOUBLE EYE

The eye of a double hook is formed when the wire is bent double and brazed.

DOUBLE HOOKS

Double hooks with long shanks are used for tying salmon flies. The which-way double and VB-double types, whose two halves are back-to-back, are used in conjunction with trebles for live or deadbaiting.

VB-double hook

SPADE END

The spade end hook has a flattened end to its shank rather than an eye. It is superior to eyed hooks in sizes 12 to 26, because it hangs better on the line.

A

B

C

D

D

E

D

A Reversed curved point
B Long shank round bend
C Slightly reversed
D Crystal bend; large, med, small
E Round bend straight shank

READY-TIED HOOKS

Spade end hooks can be tied direct to the line or, for more delicate presentation, to a finer hook length. All sizes of spade end hook are available ready-tied.

Hooks shown larger than actual size

SCALE: circle represents ¼ inch (6 mm)

CRYSTAL BEND
The crystal bend is used with maggots and grubs.

SPROAT BEND
A rounded bend not un-like the Limerick in shape.

SNECK BEND
A strong and slightly angular pattern.

ROUND BEND
The wide gape makes this a good hook with worms.

TURNED DOWN EYE
The turned down eye is angled towards the point of the hook, and is intended to make the hook penetrate better on the strike.

TURNED UP EYE
The turned up eye is angled away from the point for good clearance between the shank and the point.

Turned down eye

Turned up eye

PLUG WITH TREBLE HOOKS
In freshwater fishing, treble hooks are most commonly used on artificial lures such as plugs and spinners.

TAPERED EYE
Because the shank end is tapered, the eye is smaller and neater.

Sliced shank

LOOPED EYE
The shank end is bent round and brazed flat against the shank.

HOLLOW POINT
The hollow point is ground into a pronounced concave shape between the tip of the barb and the tip of the point, to give the hook fast and clean penetration.

BARBLESS POINT
As the name suggests, the barbless point has no barb. The barbless point is easier to unhook than a barbed point, and makes a smaller, cleaner hole when it penetrates.

CURVED-IN POINT
The point curves in towards the shank. Although this narrows the gape, it makes it harder for the fish to dislodge the hook before the barb has penetrated.

STRAIGHT EYE
The straight or ring eye is in line with the shank, rather than being turned up or turned down.

LIMERICK BEND
The bend of the Limerick pattern is smoothly curved for most of its length, but the angle increases sharply and the wire straightens just before the barb.

FRESHWATER WEIGHTS

In most countries, all freshwater weights are made of lead, but since January 1987 the sale of most of the smaller types of lead weight has been banned in the UK. All split shot from size 6 up to and including swan shot, and all ledger weights up to and including 1 ounce, must now be made of non-toxic, lead-free materials.

The reason for this was the increasing number of swans found dead from lead poisoning, estimated at about 3000 a year at the time of the ban. Like other birds whose diet consists mainly of plants, swans must take grit into their gizzards to help crush the food before it can be digested, and in heavily-fished waters they were taking in small lost or discarded lead weights along with the gravel and tiny stones they need. The soft lead was easily broken down by the gizzards and digestive juices of the birds, and lead poisoning resulted.

Once the link between swan deaths and angling weights was established, the tackle industry began developing weights made from various lead-free materials, and a full range was available by the time the ban was introduced. The substitutes were often poor at first, but eventually split shot of almost the same size and weight as lead shot was developed, made of metal/polymer mixtures or tungsten alloys.

Lead-free dipsey sinkers are made from steel, brass or zinc, and are only a little larger than the old lead ones. In addition to the familiar pear shape, new versions, made of coated brass, have a screw-in swivel fitting. Once the swivel has been attached to the line, any of six different-sized sinkers can be quickly screwed on.

Freshwater sinkers are available in hole-through bullet shape (to thread on the line), coffin shape (to hold flat on the bottom and keep the bait static in running water) and the familiar dipsey bomb shape.

Bomb weights range from an eighth of an ounce up to 3 ounces. The size to use depends on how far you want to cast and, in running water, how much weight is needed to keep the bait on the bottom, either static or slowly moving. A slowly-moving bait can be very effective when you're fishing for those species which at times only show interest if the bait is on the move.

Simple ledger rigs can be made by pressing large shots onto a 6 to 10 inch length of mono of the same strength as the reel line. If a running ledger is needed, this nylon link should have a split ring or swivel at one end to slide on the reel line. A fixed ledger can be made by simply tying the end of the link to the bottom of the reel line's junction swivel.

Miniature ledgers are easily made by folding a 3-inch length of line in half and fixing on one or more large shots so that the fold in the line forms a tiny loop. This loop should be just big enough to slide freely along the reel line, but not so large as to be able to pass over the ledger stop. The stop, either a plastic ledger stop or an AA shot, should be fixed to the line between the hook and the ledger, at between 6 and 20 inches from the hook.

By adding one of these little ledgers to a lift-method float rig, you can convert it into a float ledger rig. The rig will cast much further because of the extra weight, but any bites will, of course, be registered by the float going under rather than lifting.

In float fishing, split shot is used for locking eyed floats in place on the line, for cocking floats, and to adjust the amount of float tip showing above the water.

Split shots are either round, the most popular shape, or slightly elongated – the 'mouse dropping' format. Sizes range from the tiny 'dust' shot (sizes 12 to 8) up through sizes 7 to 1, BB, AA and SSG (swan shot). Swan shot is so called because it's the size of shot (15 to the ounce) that was once used for shooting swans.

Always make sure that the line fits easily into the split of the shot, and use only gentle pressure to close the two halves onto the line until the shot holds firm. Never crunch it on with pliers, or line fracture will result. Also, especially with the larger sizes, open them slightly with your thumbnail before sliding them along and retightening when you're repositioning them.

With the arrival of lead-free weights came a new type, a tubed weight, available in several diameters and which can be cut to any length with a pair of scissors. A length of tube is simply threaded onto the line and locked in place by a tiny shot at each end. This type of weight is excellent for fishing tiny seed baits, such as hempseed, where fish often mistake round shot for the bait and give false bites.

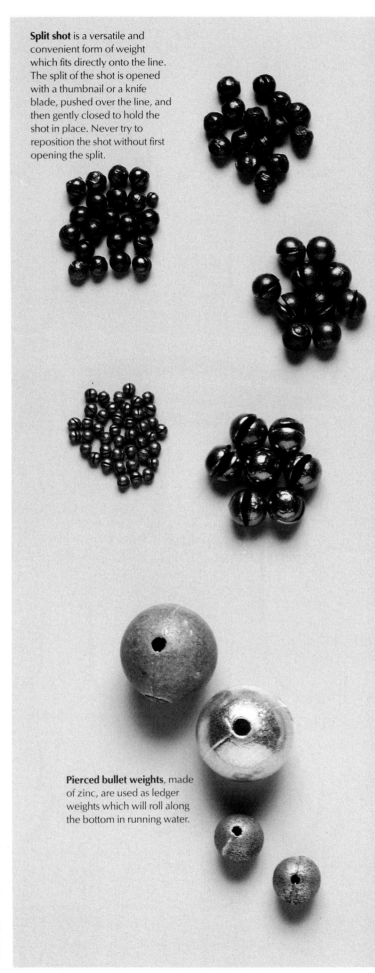

Split shot is a versatile and convenient form of weight which fits directly onto the line. The split of the shot is opened with a thumbnail or a knife blade, pushed over the line, and then gently closed to hold the shot in place. Never try to reposition the shot without first opening the split.

Pierced bullet weights, made of zinc, are used as ledger weights which will roll along the bottom in running water.

Dipsey sinkers, made of lead or of lead-free metals such as steel, zinc or brass, are the most popular ledger weights.

These **flat-bottomed ledger weights** are used mainly in carp fishing. Because of their shape, they rise quickly to the surface when retrieved.

Flexible tungsten shot is a thin tubing made of a polymer mixture containing tungsten. It can be used as an alternative to split shot for most purposes, and is less likely to snag than shot is.

The banana-shaped **Wye lead** with antikink swivel is used in conjunction with spinners and spoons.

Plummets are used to find the depth of the water. The hook is passed through the ring on the top and stuck into the cork base.

The **Jardine weight** is attached by wrapping the line around its body and through the wire spirals.

LANDING TACKLE

This Abu telescopic gaff, designed for landing trout and salmon, is just over 15 inches long when retracted and nearly 28 inches when it's fully extended. It weighs just 7 ounces, and when it's closed the point is protected by a spring guard.

A telescopic tailer from Hardy. When the tailer is retracted its length is 32 inches, and it extends to 40 inches. It weighs about 7¼ ounces.

This Hardy three-section telescopic gaff measures 44 inches long when extended and about 20 inches when it's retracted. It weighs 12 ounces.

Once a hooked fish has been played out, it should be landed or boated as quickly and efficiently as possible. If it's too big to be simply lifted out of the water, it can be netted, gaffed or tailed.

Landing nets range from the shallow pan nets, much used in the UK and Europe, which are little more than scoops for lifting out small fish taken on ultralight tackle, to the large specimen nets with rim diameters of 36 to 42 inches designed to engulf the largest pike or carp. Some anglers even use custom-built nets with 50-inch rims.

Most large nets nowadays have fiberglass frames instead of metal, the glass combining strength with lightness and durability, and the nylon mesh can have a drop of 3 feet or more. Once a big fish has been engulfed by this bag it has little chance of escape.

Trout anglers use a very different kind of landing net. This is normally a foldaway type with a telescopic handle, which can be hooked onto a belt to carry it until it's needed. Then the net's simply flipped open, and the frame locks into position ready for use.

Salmon anglers normally use fixed-frame nets which are made more manageable by having a handle which slides through the frame. This shortens the net and makes it easy to carry, and the handle can be quickly pulled out when it's needed.

When you're sea fishing from the shore or from a boat, you can use a fixed-frame net with a fixed handle. This is a very basic form of landing net, but it works well for small to medium-sized fish.

If you're fishing from a pier or jetty, though, a handled net's of little use, and you need a circular drop net which can be lowered and raised on a rope. The rim diameter should be at least 26 inches, but when big fish are known to be on the move, a 30 to 36-inch net is preferable.

The simplest form of gaff is a large hook lashed securely to a wooden handle, used for landing large fish such as salmon. Most salmon anglers, though, prefer a purpose-built.

The telescopic gaff, which can be carried clipped to a belt, is usually made of brass with a steel hook. The hook, with a gap of 2½ to 3 inches, is protected when not in use by a screw-on or slipover brass cover. Other salmon anglers

favor a fixed gaff head on a single-piece handle, which is carried slung over the back on a quick-release strap.

Often, though, you might prefer not to gaff a salmon in case the gaff point badly damages the meat. If you don't want to carry a net around, the alternative is to use a tailer, a neat device which operates on the same principle as a wire snare.

The tailer is a running noose of braided wire fastened to a metal handle. To use it, you pull the noose back to form a wide loop. When the salmon is completely exhausted, you slide the loop over its tail then pull the noose tight to lock it around the waist of the tail. This gives a hold which will never slip, but you must take care not to touch the fish's body or tail until the loop is in position. If you do, the fish might thrash around madly, break the line and escape.

For sea fishing, the most basic type of gaff is made by hammering a spiked gaff head into a hardwood handle and lashing it down so that it won't pull out. This sort of gaff normally has a 4 to 5-inch gap, and is used for fish of up to 100 pounds in weight.

If you're after larger fish, you

should use a breakaway gaff. This style of gaff has a head which is slotted rather than screwed into a handle. The lower section of the gaff head has a brazed lug to which is attached a 5-foot length of rigger wire, which in turn is shackled to a 30-foot length of strong, spliced rope.

Once a gaff head has been stuck into the fish, the handle is pulled clear, leaving the fish on wire and rope only. This style of gaff is essential for boating really large fish, or fish such as shark which are inclined to roll when they feel the gaff struck home. You can get gaff heads with or without barbs, but those with neat, folding barbs are useful, especially for tuna and billfish. These penetrate easily and cleanly, but hold well once they're in.

A version of the salmon tailer, but on a much larger scale, is often used for shark and other big game fish. Instead of having a handle, the wire noose is shackled to a heavy rope. Once it's over the tail of the fish, the wire is pulled tight and the fish is made fast to a cleat or corner post. With its tail immobilized, a big fish has little chance of escaping.

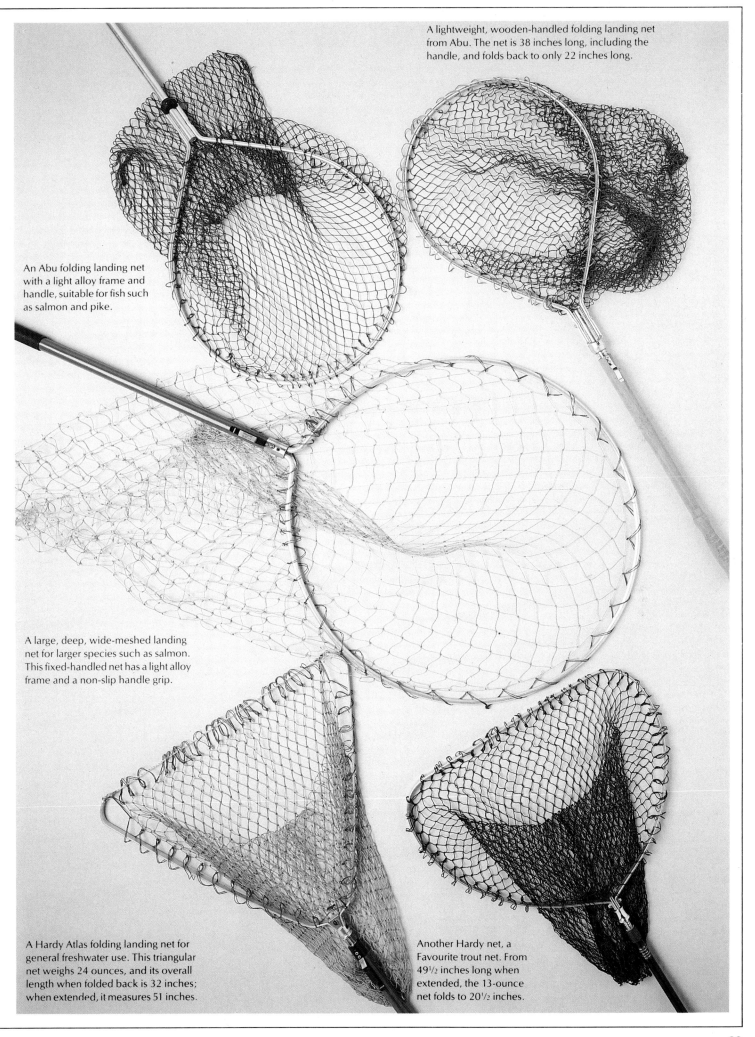

A lightweight, wooden-handled folding landing net from Abu. The net is 38 inches long, including the handle, and folds back to only 22 inches long.

An Abu folding landing net with a light alloy frame and handle, suitable for fish such as salmon and pike.

A large, deep, wide-meshed landing net for larger species such as salmon. This fixed-handled net has a light alloy frame and a non-slip handle grip.

A Hardy Atlas folding landing net for general freshwater use. This triangular net weighs 24 ounces, and its overall length when folded back is 32 inches; when extended, it measures 51 inches.

Another Hardy net, a Favourite trout net. From 49$\frac{1}{2}$ inches long when extended, the 13-ounce net folds to 20$\frac{1}{2}$ inches.

LEDGER AND SPECIALIST RODS

Ledger rods suitable for all-round freshwater bait fishing come in two basic formats, the standard type with a screw-threaded tip ring to take either a swing tip or a quiver tip, and those with a tapered quiver tip spliced directly into the tip.

Standard ledger rods have actions varying from fairly stiff to sloppy. With the stiffer-actioned rods, the rod tip will provide adequate bit indication when you're fishing in fast water, but when more sensitive indication is needed you should use a quiver tip screwed into the threaded tip guide. A threaded tip guide can be fitted to any rod that hasn't already got one.

The floppy or easy-actioned rod works well with a swing tip bite indicator, and unlike the stiff-actioned rod it won't cause the swing tip to wrap around the rod tip on the strike, which should be an easy pull-and-follow-through wrist action. Standard ledger rods are usually 9 to 10 feet long, and will handle a wide range of fishing situations in both still and running water.

Two-piece ledger rods, 10 to 12 feet long with built-in quiver tips, are another extremely versatile type of rod. Although they're generally used for river fishing, the quiver tip also provides good indication of shy bites in still waters. The graphite rods are lighter than fiberglass models and can be held comfortably for long periods, an important advantage when you're ledgering for fast-biting fish and you have to hold the rod rather than put it into rod rests.

The best of these rods remain quite rigid when fishing fast-flowing water, with only the flexible quiver tip moving to the pull of the current or of a biting fish. The rod handle should be short – only 20 inches or so – to maximize the length of the rod through which the action is developed, and the guides, especially if you're going to be playing large fish, should have hardened or lined centres.

Most specialist rods, for pike, carp or whatever, are classified according to their test curves as well as their lengths. The test curve is the amount of pull, measured on a spring balance, which is needed to bend the tip of the rod round into a quarter-circle. The resulting figure gives an indication of the range of line strengths that the rod will handle best. Lighter or heavier lines may be used, but the optimum strength of line for a particular rod can be calculated by multiplying the test curve, in pounds, by five or six. So a rod with a test curve of, say, 1 pound, will work best with a line of 5 or 6 pounds test, while a rod of 2 pounds test curve should be used with lines of 10 to 12 pounds test.

The higher the test curve, the more powerful the rod and the wider its range of uses. A 3-pounds test curve rod, capable of handling lines of between 15 and 18 pounds, would be a very powerful freshwater rod indeed, only really suitable for fishing large, wild waters where snaggy or rocky conditions or exceptionally large fish, or both, are expected.

Avon style rods of 11 or 12 feet and 1¼ pounds test curve (with a 6 to 7 pounds line) are perhaps the most versatile of all ledger rods. Those made of graphite have the ability to pick up line even when using a swimfeeder to present bait at distances of 50 to 60 yards, but they are still soft enough for close-range fishing.

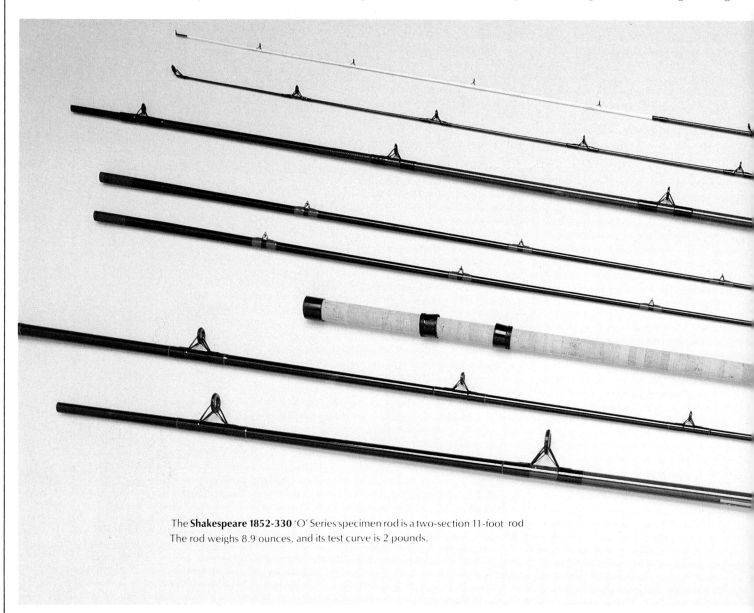

The **Shakespeare 1852-330** 'O' Series specimen rod is a two-section 11-foot rod
The rod weighs 8.9 ounces, and its test curve is 2 pounds.

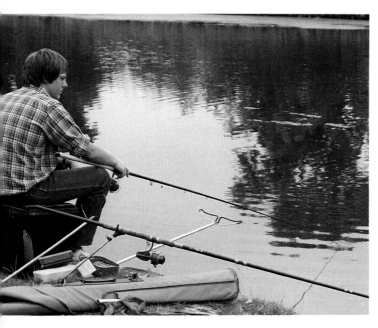

These rods were first developed for hooking and playing powerful fish on fast-flowing rivers, but they are also useful for light carp fishing both on the bottom or at the surface, as well as for float fishing for tench, plugging for chub, livebaiting for perch and all types of walleye bait fishing.

Specialist rods with a test curve of 1½ pounds and over are suitable for carp and pike fishing, and also for taking large eels and catfish. You should choose a rod which has enough power to handle the type and size of fish you expect to catch, and the conditions in which you are going to fish for it. A 1¾-pounds test curve rod will cope with most pike and carp fishing, but the rod action should be chosen carefully.

For instance, a powerful rod with a soft, all-through action would be useless for fishing at long range, say 70 yards or more.

Here a fast-taper, tip-action rod which can pick up this length of line is essential. On the other hand, using such a rod for large carp or pike only a few yards out from the bank would be asking for trouble. The only real elasticity in the outfit would be the line, and once that was exhausted, line breakage would be inevitable.

Most specialist pike and carp rods are available in lengths of 11 or 12 feet. Overall, the longer models are more versatile, but if most of your fishing is close-in, or from locations with overhanging trees, the shorter ones are advisable.

Always fix the rod together firmly by twisting the joints to ensure that the two halves are fully home, or the ferrule might split under heavy pressure. If the two sections are not properly fitted together, damage could result.

Above *Because most ledgering doesn't require constant manipulation of the bait, you can use rod rests and fish with more than one rod.*

The uppermost rod here is a **Ryobi AV110** John Wison rod. This 11-foot Avon-style rod is supplied with an alternative upper section which has a built-in quiver tip.

The rod in the centre is a **Daiwa 4195-10T** ledger rod, another rod offering a choice of normal or quiver-tip top section.

LINES AND LEADERS

Nylon monofilament is the standard line material for freshwater fishing and is extensively used in saltwater angling. Dacron and wire are essentially saltwater lines, rarely used in fresh water.

Wire traces, usually attached to the line by swivels, are used in both freshwater and saltwater angling.

Fishing lines fall into many categories apart from the obvious ones of freshwater, saltwater and fly lines. Some are designed for casting heavy terminal tackle, some have inbuilt weight to aid casting, others are designed to float, sink, or partially sink. Only experience can teach you which line is most suited to the job in hand.

Nylon monofilament line is available in a range of strengths from ¼-pound test up to 130-pound IGFA material. Nylon line is inherently stretchy, which gives it a useful ability to absorb the shocks of striking and playing. Sometimes, though, this elasticity is more of a hindrance than a help on the strike, as so much of the power of the strike can be lost in stretching the line that the hook won't be properly set.

Nylon lines normally give good service, but some anglers make the mistake of using the same line for several seasons. This is wrong, because the line will get worn during repeated use and so breakages and lost fish are more likely.

Exposure to bright sunlight also makes the line deteriorate, and can halve its strength in a remarkably short time – as little as a week, if the line's left lying in the sunlight.

Signs of serious line deterioration are discoloration, a dry feel, and a fine, white powder coming from the line itself. Any line showing these symptoms should be scrapped at once.

Dacron lines, made of a polyester fiber braided around a central core, are used mostly for sea fishing from boats, although salmon anglers sometimes use the lighter versions with multiplying reels for freshwater spinning. Dacron doesn't stretch under tension but the slightest damage can make it very likely to break.

Despite this, Dacron is an excellent line for boat fishing, and most Dacron lines are manufactured to International Game Fishing Association standards. Some brands of Dacron line appear to be of a softer weave than others; the harder lines are better. Berkley and Gudebrod lines are among the hard-braided Dacrons which perform well during intensive fishing.

Wire line, which was initially designed for trolling for smaller game fish, has been adapted for deep boat fishing for large, bottom feeding fish in strong tides. Being thinner in diameter and heavier in itself than nylon or Dacron lines, wire line helps the angler to keep the bait on the bottom with a minimum of additional weight.

There are three types of wire line: single-strand stainless steel, braided or multi-stranded stainless steel, and single-strand Monel metal (an alloy of copper and nickel plus small amounts of iron, manganese, silicon and carbon). The multi-strand steel is the nicest to use, but it has a tendency to fray rather quickly. The single-strand stainless steel kinks easily, and is liable to break at the point of kinking, but the Monel line, although thicker than the other two types, doesn't fray and seldom seriously kinks.

Fly lines are usually made of pvc-coated Dacron, and are produced in a vast range of sizes, tapers and ratings. The rating of the line should always be matched to that of the rod. All fly rods carry their AFTM (Association of Fishing Tackle Manufacturers) rating on the butt section, and this will tell you which rating of line is best for that particular rod.

For instance, a rod with a line rating of 6/7 will cast most efficiently with a number 6 or number 7 line. In general, the rod will perform better with the higher number, but the performance will also depend on the actual taper of the line.

Most fly lines are now made as double-tapered or as forward-tapered. Double-tapered (DT) lines are usually 90 feet long, and the last 10 feet or more of each end tapers down to form a fine line which lands delicately.

A forward-tapered line is tapered at one end only, instead of at both ends, but some 30 feet or so from the tip the line diameter is reduced sharply so that the last 40 feet is very fine; this means that the weight of the line is mainly in the first 30 feet. These forward-tapered or weight-forward (WF) lines are designed for casting long distances. As soon as the thick section of the line is airborne on the forward cast, the thin section of the line will shoot effortlessly through the rod guides.

Shooting heads are similar to weight-forward lines, but they don't have the fine shooting line after the forward section. Instead, they're knotted to a length of fine monofilament nylon which can be much longer than the shooting section of a weight-forward line, allowing more line to be shot during casting.

Fly lines are designed to float, sink quickly, sink slowly, or hang in the water at a predetermined depth. The latter type is known as an intermediate sinker, and it's useful when trout are feeding just below the surface. Some floating lines have a sinking tip section, which makes them good for creeping a nymph or shrimp imitation slowly over the bottom.

For very deep reservoir or lake fishing, lead-cored lines fished on specialist rods will get a wet fly down into the depths very

Fly lines, made in a great variety of sizes, tapers and ratings, are usually made of pvc-coated Dacron and classified according to the AFTM specifications. For best performance, the AFTM number of the line should match that of the rod.

The fly lines shown here are, from left to right – back row: floating line plus backing, ultrafast sinking line; front row: sink tip line, floating line, medium sinking line, neutral density line and 3-pound fly leader, floating line plus backing. Store your fly lines in loose coils in a cool, dark place, and use only cleaners specially formulated for fly line cleaning; detergent and solvents can damage the line.

rapidly.

When you're fishing for any freshwater species which has sharp teeth and strong jaws, such as pike, muskies or walleyes, it's essential to use a strong leader between the reel line and the hook or lure.

The leader should be made of a braided wire, such as Alasticum or Berkley Steelon, of 10 to 20 pounds test. For spinning, the leader should be about 12 inches long, with a size 10 swivel at one end for attachment to the reel line, and a snap at the other to take the lure. For live or deadbaiting, use a 20-inch leader, again with a size 10 swivel at one end, but with a hook fixed to the other end and perhaps another hook threaded onto the leader and free to slide along it. When you're mounting the bait, this sliding hook is locked in position on the leader by simply wrapping the leader around it a few times.

Leaders are used much more in saltwater fishing than in freshwater. For fish without teeth, plain nylon monofilament is adequate: flounder, weakfish and other small to medium-sized species call for a leader of 8 to 10 pounds test, while a 25 to 30-pound trace is strong enough for striped bass, pollack and similar fish.

For large fish, leaders made of either wire or heavy longliner's

mono are essential. The hardness of longliner's nylon, and the fact that it can be obtained in strengths of from 100 to 600-plus pounds test, makes it ideal for most types of big fish except shark.

100-pounds test nylon is heavy enough for giant skate and halibut, both of which can attain weights of over 200 pounds, but for catching big conger, groupers or other fish which live among sharp rocks or in wrecks, you need a leader that will withstand the damage that these habitats can inflict. For this reason you should use a 150-pound nylon leader whose extra thickness will help it to withstand any chafing and abrasion better than a 100-pound one would.

Fishing for giant tuna and billfish calls for mono leaders of 300 to 600 pounds test, and even a 1000-pound fish will do little damage to a leader made of this weight of hard nylon.

Heavy nylon is almost impossible to knot, but it can be crimped with the crimping sleeves used for wire traces. Under heavy pressure, though, the nylon can slip, so it's wise to double-crimp each end of a trace or leader.

Wire leaders come in several forms, the most popular (although not the best) being braided wire covered in a pro-

tective nylon sheath. For fish with large teeth, nylon-covered wire is useless. The nylon sheath will catch on the edge of a tooth, leaving the exposed wire to saw up and down over the tooth's edge. Once this sawing motion starts, a breakage is more or less inevitable, and for this reason nylon-covered wire should never be used for shark fishing.

Nylon-covered wire has one other drawback: water gets trapped inside the sheath and causes tiny rust spots on the wire. These spots are very difficult to see from the outside, and they rapidly weaken the wire strands until they snap under the lightest load. This problem has cost many anglers the fish of a lifetime.

For shark fishing, the best wire leaders are made of the stainless steel rigging wire used on small yachts. This wire is highly resistant to corrosion and strong enough to hold most sharks.

A shark leader should be made up in two equal sections, joined by a large, free-moving swivel. Hooked shark often spin or roll during the closing stages of the battle, so the swivel will help to stop the twisting fish from kinking the leader.

Stainless steel wire shark leaders are best made up at the chandler's, where the crimps can be put on by machine. Never leave any cut wire protruding

from the crimped sleeve, because when a fish is being gaffed the jagged wire can easily rip a man's hand.

The length of leader you use for saltwater fishing depends on the kind of fish you're after. For normal bottom fishing after flatfish, bass, cod and so on, use a leader of 3 to 8 feet. For big shark or conger, this can be reduced to 2 feet, while for big game fishing your leaders should conform to IFGA specifications.

Swivels are an essential part of any form of leader. Like hooks, swivels are produced in countless patterns, many of which are so poorly designed and made that they break under the minimum of pressure. The best general-purpose swivels are the Berkley range, made in the USA. These are produced in a wide range of sizes, from tiny freshwater patterns up to the 8-0 and 10-0 tuna and swordfish patterns.

For most saltwater work, size 1 or 1-0 Berkley barrel swivels are perfectly adequate, but for big shark, tuna, marlin and the like, size 6-0 or 8-0 should be used. For all trolling work, where swivels need to be exceptionally free-running, the ball bearing swivels produced by Sampo are the best available.

Some swivels incorporate a snap-on link to make leader or lure changing easy.

POLES

Pole fishing, one of the oldest and simplest forms of angling, gained a new lease of life in the 1960s with the introduction of fiberglass poles. These were not only lighter and cheaper than the cane poles then in use, but they could also be made much longer so that swims much further from the bank could be fished effectively with the deadly fixed line.

The first glass poles were telescopic, followed soon after by the more rigid, ferrule-less take-apart versions and more recently by the graphite models.

The take-apart poles, whether glass or graphite are always noticeably stiffer in action than the telescopic type because a very slow tamper can be maintained right throughout the spigoted sections. This is why all the top-class poles are of the take-apart type rather than telescopic.

Telescopic poles do have some advantages, though: they're a lot

cheaper, and the easy action is an advantage when you're playing a large fish at close range. With or without the use of shock elastic, there's far less chance of ripping the hook out or snapping the line with an easy-action telescopic pole. It just keeps bending.

Good-quality take-apart poles don't bend like that, which is why they're better for hitting tiny, fast bites and for delicate float control. Only the tip section, and in some cases the second section, actually bends. As some take-apart poles are over 40 feet long, they have to be rigid for most of their length to prevent them drooping under their own weight and being uncontrollably sloppy. This is less of a problem with telescopic poles, which are normally no more than about 22 feet long.

In the simplest method of pole fishing, the line is tied directly to a ring or nylon loop whipped to the pole tip. This is called the 'flick

tip' method, because it employs the natural flick of the finely-tapered, solid fiberglass pole tip. The flick tip method can be used for all types of pole fishing, except for presenting tiny baits on tiny hooks tied to gossamer lines of less than 1½ pounds test.

For this, a short (1 to 2 foot) length of shock-absorbing elastic is tied in between the pole tip and the line, or sometimes the tip is replaced by a springy metal crook to which the elastic is attached. Alternatively, a hollow crook may be used. The elastic passes right through the crook and the hollow second section of the pole, and is anchored at the lower end of the second section by a rubber grommet. The longer elastic stretches more than a short length tied to the tip, so it's better for absorbing the shocks of fighting a large fish.

Using some of the longer graphite poles of 25 feet or more

can be quite difficult for the beginner unless the butt end is reasonably slim and easy to grip, and the pole is stiff enough to be controllable in strong winds. Such poles are relatively expensive, and it's better to learn the basics of pole fishing with a cheaper glass or glass/graphite mix telescopic pole.

These inexpensive poles come in a variety of lengths from about 10 to 22 feet. Somewhere between 17 and 20 feet is a good starting length, because even cheap poles of this sort of length are quite manageable.

They're suitable for all forms of pole fishing, from controlling a float in a fast current to placing a jig out beyond margins thick with weeds or lily pads, and you can master all the basic skills with one before investing in something longer.

Shorter poles, 10 to 14 feet long, make good pond rods for

POLE TIPS
Crook tips fit onto the end of the second section of the pole. The shock elastic is looped into a notch near the end of the tip and held in place by the plastic sleeve.

The sections of a telescopic pole retract into the butt section which, like that of a take-apart pole, also serves as a protective tube for storage and transport.

youngsters and they're also much favoured by crappie fishermen for dabbling tiny marabou jigs and grubtails in awkward places among thick reedbeds.

When you're ready for a longer pole, go for the stiffness and lightness of a graphite take-apart model. Choose a length you can easily handle, rather than a longer one which retails at the same price but might not be as good. Many manufacturers offer butt extensions for their poles, so if you buy one that can be extended in this way, you can always add to it once you've got used to its 25 to 30-foot length.

Never use a pole anywhere near overhead power lines, or during a thunderstorm. Graphite is highly conductive, and damp fiberglass can conduct electricity through the surface moisture.

Right *Modern poles are light and easy to handle.*

SHAKESPEARE 1095/750 POLE
This take-apart, six-section pole is 25 feet long and weighs less than 2 pounds. For ease of transport the pole sections are stowed in the butt, which is only 59 inches long. The small butt diameter makes the pole easy to handle, and its stiff action means that it can cope with larger fish, and is more control-lable in strong winds, than a softer-actioned pole.

SHAKESPEARE 1051/700c OMNIPOLE
The Shakespeare 1051/700c Omnipole is a seven-section telescopic pole with a maximum length of 23½ feet.

POLE 1051/700c 7SECTIONS LENGTH 23.5FT-7.00M

ROD RESTS AND BITE INDICATORS

In those types of fishing where the bait may have to be left in the water for quite some time before a bite comes, it's easier to put the rod into some sort of holder or rest than to hold it in your hands. Rod rests are also essential if you're fishing with more than one rod.

Surfcasting often involves a long wait before a bite comes, and long surfcasting rods can be tiring to hold. The simplest type of beach rod rest is the single monopod, which has a U-shaped rod support at the top, a cup to hold the butt about 2 feet below it, and a pointed end which pushes easily into sand or other soft ground. Two-rod monopods are also available.

A beach tripod, which has three adjustable legs and a U-shaped head to hold the rod, is very stable and especially good on shingle beaches or concrete harbor walls. Because the butt rests on the ground, rather than in a cup, the rod is supported much higher up than it is with a monopod. As with the monopods, two-rod tripods are available.

Freshwater rods can be supported horizontally on a pair of rests pushed into the bank. The simplest of these rests is a steel or light alloy shaft, around 2½ feet long, with a V-shaped or U-shaped head to hold the rest. The rod can be put on two of these rests, but they're often used singly for the butt end only with a different type of rest at the front.

Front rest heads come in a variety of styles, from the wide, shallow U-shaped models to the 'keyhole' type which supports the rod without trapping the line. These rod rest heads are bought separately and screwed into fixed or telescopic shafts called bank sticks.

Telescopic bank sticks are adjusted to the required length, and held there by a thumb screw or a twist-and-lock collar. Good models are adjustable to lengths of 24 to 48 inches, which is useful when the bank is sloping. Most are made of plain or plastic-coated light alloy, and those with solid points are better than those with flat, pressed ends.

To support very long rods or poles, a U-shaped front rest is used in conjunction with a hook-shaped rear rest whose job is to stop the butt from tilting upwards rather than to support it. An alternative to this is the automatic pole rest made by Shakespeare. This has a rocker mechanism with the front rest at one end and a pair of hinged clamp jaws at the other. When the pole is put into the rest, its weight pushes the front rest downwards, bringing the rear jaws up to clamp around the pole. The jaws are automatically released when the pole is lifted.

When you're ledgering, particularly with the rod on rests, some form of bite indication is essential. The simplest indicator is, of course, the rod tip, which will give a sensitive enough indication when you're fishing in a fast river. Often, though, you need a more delicate indication of a fish mouthing the bait so that you can strike before the fish feels resistance and spits it out.

For this, a screw-in, tapered quiver tip is the answer, because it effectively extends the taper of the rod tip. Quiver tips screw into the threaded tip guide of a ledger rod, and come in test curves from light (1 ounce) for slow water to heavy (3½ ounce) for fast water. Made from solid glass or graphite, they range in length from 10 to 16 inches.

An alternative method is to use a swing tip. This is a straight, non-tapered cane or plastic stem with an eye at one end and a screw thread attached to the other by a silicone rubber hinge. The swing tip is screwed into the tip guide and the reel line passes through the eye. In use, the swing tip hangs at an angle of 45 degrees to the rod. When a fish takes the bait, it will feel almost no resistance until it's pulled the swing tip into line with the rod and it's beginning to pull line from the reel. A variation of this is the butt indicator, which clips to the butt a few inches in front of the rod handle instead of being screwed into the tip guide.

Another widely-used indicator, the spring tip, is a quiver tip pushed into a long, close-wound spring at its screw thread (rod) end. When it's pushed fully home into the spring, it functions just like a quiver tip; but when it's pulled gently out to the end of the spring, it pivots like a swing tip.

Other types of indicator which give a visual indication of a bite are those which are fastened to the line by a quick-release clip, and either rise or drop when the line is pulled. These include bobbins, monkey climbers and dropoff arms.

Shakespeare pole rest

Drennan 10½ inch swing tip

Drennan medium spring tip

Drennan quiver tip

The **Shakespeare 9404** automatic pole rest has a simple clamp mechanism, operated by the weight of the butt, which holds the pole firmly in place.

The two freshwater rod rests shown here are a **Kevin Nash Triprobe** and a **Keenets Aquarian** — both telescopic bank sticks — together with a pair of Drennan rest heads.

Kevin Nash Triprobe

Keenets Aquarian

Shakespeare Black Bass Beach Rest

The **Shakespeare 9405 Black Bass Beach Rest** is a lightweight alloy tripod with two rest heads wide enough to accommodate even the largest surfcasting rods.

A monopod beach rest, such as this **Shakespeare 9407 Black Bass Sand Spike**, has a strong, pointed end that can be pushed firmly into the sand.

Shakespeare Black Bass Sand Spike

Gardner dropoff indicator

Electronic bite indicators, such as this Gardner Bandit Buzzer, are battery-powered units which clip onto the rod rest and give an audible or visible indication when the line is pulled by a biting fish.

Gardner Windbeater monkey climber

Gardner Grease Monkey indicator

SALMON RODS

BRUCE AND WALKER HEXAGRAPH FLY ROD
The Bruce and Walker Hexagraph 14-foot, three-section salmon fly rod
This double handed rod has a compound taper and is rated at 10/12.

Salmon fishing in the UK and Europe differs from trout fishing in that you may need to spend part of the season with spinning tackle, rather than using fly tackle throughout as you would for Atlantic salmon angling in North America. The all-round salmon angler, then, may well opt for one or two spinning outfits and a similar number of fly outfits. A lot will depend on where and when you are going to fish: big rivers in early spring offer very different conditions to small spate rivers in summer, or any lake or impoundment you might want to fish from a boat.

Initially, you might be content to start off salmon fishing by concentrating on spinning, although it's not always the most productive method. For fishing small rivers, there's little to beat a 7½ or 8-foot graphite spinning rod with a medium-sized fixed spool reel and 8 pound test monofilament line.

Most rods of this length are single handed and don't need much effort when casting. They prove ideal for casting into little nooks and crannies in a small river, and the bait can be brought quickly under control and into action in the most likely-looking water. You might have to cast more accurately than you would with a longer, double-handed rod on a big river, but spinning on small rivers is tremendous sport and a very effective way of catching a few fish.

For spinning on bigger rivers, two double handed outfits worth considering are a 9½-foot rod with a fixed spool reel and 12 pound test line, which would be ideal for medium-sized rivers, and a stout 10-footer with a multiplying reel and 15 to 25 pound line for heavier baits of up to an

Above *Fishing for salmon in a fast-flowing river. Salmon are caught mostly on flies, but they are also taken on lures and prawns.*

The **Hardy Pall Mall Exclusive** is a four-piece salmon fly rod with a push-in extension handle. Made of graphite, this rod is 9½ feet long, excluding the extension handle, and is rated at AFTM 8/9.

ounce on large rivers.

The great feature of the multiplying reel is that it gives good control over the heavier baits — but use it with baits which are too light and you'll get frequent overruns and loss of casting distance. With the fixed spool reel, though, you'll get good casting distances with lighter baits, and perhaps a little more accuracy.

Screw reel fittings are ideal for all spinning rods, and it's important to have a large butt guide and good open bridge guides out to the tip. The large butt guide proves very useful with a fixed spool reel, where there may be a build up of friction as the line comes off the reel in wide spirals.

For fly fishing on small to medium-sized rivers you can use a single handed rod of 9½ or 10 feet and a number 7 line. On larger waters, a 12½ or 13-foot, double handed model with a number 9 line makes an ideal all-round salmon fly rod, but for the really heavy work, when you're fishing with large flies and lines of size 10 and upwards, you need a double handed rod of between 14 and 18 feet.

In mid season, where the water's low and clear, you can often use a good, medium-action 10-foot trout rod. This, in conjunction with a number 7 weight-forward floating line, will handle the smaller sizes of salmon fly (8s, 10s and 12s) very admirably.

It's important to remember that the longer and more powerful fly rods will need stronger terminal tackle to cope with the stress of playing a big fish. For early spring and late autumn you should rarely use leaders of less than 14 pounds test, and go to 20 pounds or more when using the large and heavy tube flies in the colder months. During the low water of summer, when fishing with shorter, single handed rods, there's little need to go stronger than 8 pounds test. This also frequently proves more than adequate when casting from a boat on still waters.

For much stillwater boat fishing it pays to use as long a rod as you can comfortably manage. For instance, a single handed, 11½-foot graphite rod will enable you to trip the fly over the waves and to bring it close into the boat before making your next cast. Very often, a salmon will take the fly just as you are about to retrieve for the next cast, unlike sea trout which are more likely to take your fly only following a long cast and a quick retrieve.

If you can afford it, for all-round salmon fishing you should go for at least two spinning outfits and two for the fly. For spinning, you should be able to handle most situations with a single handed 8-foot rod and a fixed spool reel, and a double handed 10-foot rod capable of being used both with a medium-sized fixed spool reel and with a multiplier.

For the fly fishing, a good choice would be a 15-foot, double handed graphite rod with a number 11 line, and a single handed, 10-foot rod carrying a number 7 line. As with trout rods, there are a variety of rod actions. Avoid tip-actioned rods like the plague, and only consider those with a steely through-action down to the butt and the ability to put great pressure on a strong fish. Remember, the rod has to serve two principal functions: it has to act as a spring when you're casting and as a lever when you're playing a fish.

SALTWATER HOOKS

With so many sizes and patterns of hooks on the market, it's essential to choose a selection of hooks that are properly suited to the type of fishing you intend to do.

For example, if you go fishing for flatfish, which have small, rather distorted mouths, you should use long-shanked, narrow-gape hooks. These are readily available, but like most hooks they need attention before use. With the exception of the chemically-sharpened hooks, you should regard every hook you buy as blunt. Before use, sharpen each hook on an oilstone or, if it's a big one, use a file first then finish off with a stone.

For larger shore-caught fish such as bass and cod, chemically-sharpened hooks such as the Kamatsu range are ideal. Available in sizes up to 4-0, these hooks are strong enough in the wire to resist bending or breaking under hard stress, and the round bend and short point makes them a near-perfect overall hook design. The same hooks can be used for rock fishing for medium-sized species, but when you're fishing in rocky waters you should check the fine hook point regularly for damage.

The fine-wire Kamatsu type of hook is good for fish of up to 10 or 15 pounds, but for larger species such as conger, tope or big cod, a more substantial hook is essential. One of the best and strongest readily-available patterns is the 4-0/6-0 O'Shaughnessy bronzed or stainless steel hook, a flat-forged, straight-eyed, no-nonsense iron which will retain its shape even during brutal usage. Again, these hooks should be carefully sharpened before and during use.

The O'Shaughnessy hooks are also ideal for most inshore boat fishing. Available in sizes up to 10-0, the most useful boat fishing sizes are 6-0 and 8-0, which can be used with whole or cut fish or squid baits. The beauty of these hooks is their strength; many sea hooks snap or distort in use, but the O'Shaughnessy is unlikely to.

Inexperienced anglers make the mistake of buying expensive rods, reels and lines, then using cheap, poor quality hooks. The best equipment in the world won't be much use if the hook lets you down. The worst sort of sea hooks are those with a point which is too long, fragile and curved, because such a point is likely to be too brittle to withstand hard use.

Careful choice of hook is even more important when you're fishing for really large fish. Even a small shark is a big fish which calls for a strong, well-shaped hook. Hook sizes suitable for shark and other large fish range from 8-0 to 16-0, the most widely-used sizes being 10-0, 12-0 and 14-0.

The best sort of hook for shark is a heavy, forged pattern with a straight eye and an offset point. Shark hooks with flat points lack the excellent penetration of the offset point. The beauty of the offset pattern is that when a fish is struck, the point of the hook is actually clear of the bait. With the flat style of hook, the bait often masks the hook point to such an extent that it doesn't always engage on impact.

Eye shape is also important. For shark fishing, a round eye is better than a needle eye because it allows the hook to swing freely on the trace loop so that the taking shark feels no unnatural stiffness as it mouths the dangling bait. Shark, like most big fish, can be cautious feeders, quick to reject any bait that arouses their suspicions.

Although they're not particularly good for shark fishing, flat, needle-eyed hooks are perfect for use with trolling lures such as Kona Heads. The offset hook is useless for this purpose because it causes the lure to twist in use, wrapping the skirt of the lure tightly around the shank and bend of the hook. Even when trolling a mounted natural bait the offset hook will tend to spin it, a movement that soon destroys the trace.

The flat-pointed hook is also excellent for fishing for big blue marlin, using a Kona head type of lure mounted on a two-hook rig with a stiff bar to hold the two hooks rigid.

Hooks are made of high-carbon steel or stainless steel wire. The wire is cut to length, the point is ground and the eye formed, and the barb is cut by a chisel. After this, the bend is formed and the eye is turned up or down (if required) and sometimes brazed to close the gap in it and make it stronger. The shaped hook is hardened and tempered, then cleaned. Finally, it may be blued, japanned or lacquered, or plated with bronze, nickel or cadmium, to protect it from corrosion. For added strength, the hook bend is often forged before tempering.

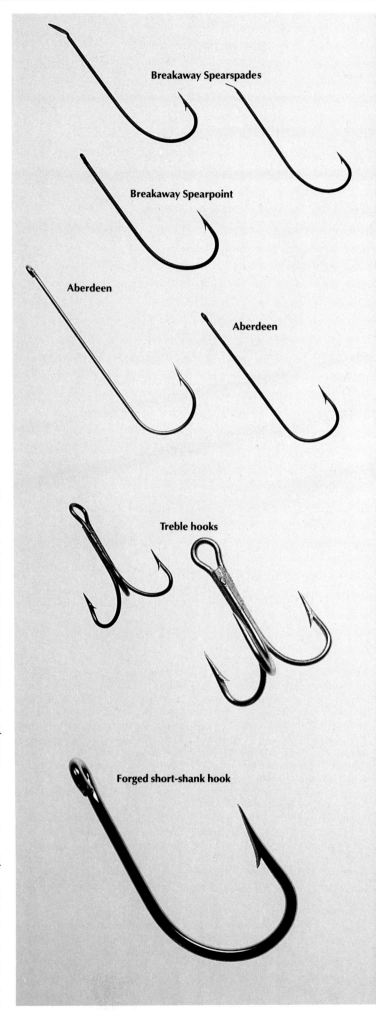

Breakaway Spearspades

Breakaway Spearpoint

Aberdeen

Aberdeen

Treble hooks

Forged short-shank hook

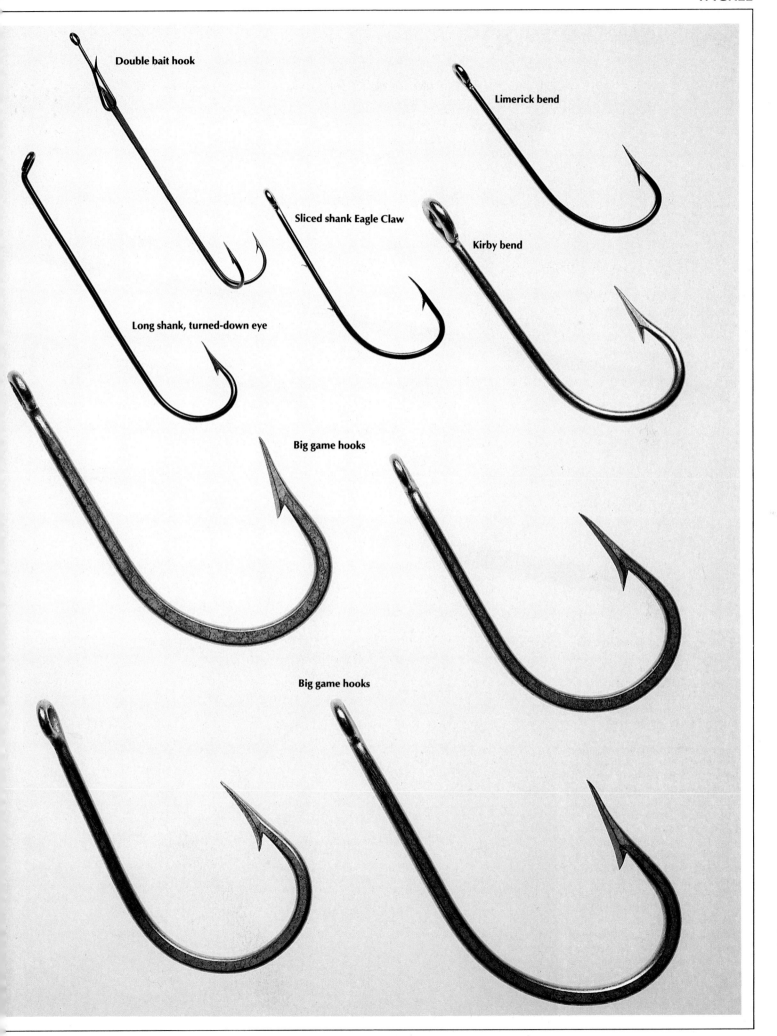

Double bait hook

Limerick bend

Sliced shank Eagle Claw

Kirby bend

Long shank, turned-down eye

Big game hooks

Big game hooks

SALTWATER RODS

SHAKESPEARE 1351/285 'O' SERIES UPTIDE ROD
A 9¹/₂-foot, two-section rod designed specifically for uptide casting from an anchored boat.

The majority of saltwater rods are designed for boat fishing. Some are straightforward fishing sticks, some are custom-built, but most are IGFA-rated in the 6, 12, 20 and 30-pound classes and should be used with lines of the same rating.

Boat rods are made of hollow fiberglass or a glass/graphite mixture. Rods made mainly of graphite don't usually perform well as boat rods, and pure graphite rods have a tendency to split or shatter. The glass-graphite mixture, however, combines the best features of both materials and is ideal for this type of fishing.

Important though the rod blank is, the furnishings of a boat rod are equally crucial. Boat fishing can be a rough business which subjects the rod to more than its fair share of abuse. To ensure that your rod gives you years of good service, choose only the best guides and reel fittings; but bear in mind the need to

DAIWA CB 30FT BOAT ROD
The Daiwa CB 30FT is a two-piece, 7-foot boat rod with an IGFA rating of 30 pounds.

match the type of fittings to the sort of fishing you're going to do. A full set of AFTCO roller guides may make a rod look highly professional, but they won't automatically improve the rod's performance.

If you're going to use wire line, though, you need a tip roller and a double butt roller, in conjunction with a set of lined or hardened steel intermediate guides. The single tip roller won't spoil the action of the rod, but heavy double tip rollers tend to drag the tip down. For nylon or Dacron lines you don't need any roller guides, but all the guides should be good-quality lined or hardened steel.

Reel seatings come under a great deal of pressure when the rod is flexed, so they should be

Left Playing a wreck cod on wire line. The rod is fitted with a tip roller and a double butt roller, which are essential if wire line is used but not needed for nylon.

well made and have enough thickness of metal to avoid splitting. Rod handles are now only rarely made of cork, Hyperlon being preferred because it's lighter and more comfortable to hold.

A new, but highly effective, style of boat fishing is the method known as uptide casting, which is intended to overcome the problem of fish such as bass, flatfish and rays being scared away from the area of the anchored boat by its shadow and vibrations.

This technique, which consists of casting the bait and wired grip sinker uptide and away from the boat, calls for very specialized rods. Uptide casting is similar in many ways to beachcasting, and calls for a 9 to 9½-foot casting rod with a long tip section and a shorter, spigoted butt.

Most uptide rods are designed to cast 4 to 6-ounce lead weights, and the tip section of the rod is fine and sensitive to aid bite

detection. Bites are registered by the tip springing back rather than pulling down in the normal way. This reversed bite indication occurs when the biting fish actually pulls the wired grip sinker out of the sea bed. The rod tip, which has been tensioned against the anchoring effect of the lead, then springs back to show the bite. The technique is essentially a light line method, and the uptide casting rod should be used with a small multiplying reel such as one of the Abu 6500.

If you want to float fish for mullet from rocks or harbours, sea tackle of any description should be avoided. Mullet are wary creatures, easily frightened by thick lines and hefty floats. For this sort of fishing, a 12-foot freshwater float rod with all-through action is best, used with a fixed spool reel loaded with 3 to 5-pound test monofilament. The through action will cast a light float accurately, and pick up a long length of line on the strike.

A heavier rod is essential for rock fishing for fish such as wrasses or pollack. You can use a surfcasting rod, but these are a bit heavy for this type of fish. The best rod to use is an 11 or 12-foot pike or carp rod with a test curve of 2 pounds, which can handle line of between 7 and 15 pounds test. Such a rod will cast sinkers of up to 2½ ounces, yet have the tip sensitivity to register the shyest of bites.

Saltwater fly fishing calls for long, accurate casting. Reservoir trout rods are well suited to this sort of work, one of the best being a 10-foot graphite rod capable of throwing a number 9 weight-forward line. You can use shorter rods, but these generally lack the casting ability and stopping power of a 10-footer. The reel should be a corrosion-resistant graphite or anodized aluminum model such as a Bob Church Lineshooter or a System Two, large enough to take the line plus ample backing.

SALTWATER WEIGHTS AND BOOMS

The great variety of weights is necessary because every fishing area requires a sinker which will suit its particular run of tide and sea bed formation. In some areas, though, where the sea bed is composed of jagged rock or jumbled boulders, using a conventional sinker is pointless.

Weights are not cheap, so to lose one on each cast can be a costly business. In such circumstances it's much better to use an expendable weight: old spark plugs are ideal, and a visit to your local service station should get you enough old plugs for many days of hard fishing.

In less hostile waters, the shape of the weight you use is more important than many anglers realize. To them, a one-pound watch grip sinker is the same as a one-pound bomb-shaped sinker. This is wrong, because most sinkers are designed for a specific form of fishing.

Bomb-shaped sinkers (dipsey sinkers) come in sizes from one ounce upwards. The smaller sizes are perfect for casting over sand or into rocky gullies, while the larger ones, from 8 ounces up to 2 pounds or more, are designed for boat fishing. To eliminate line twist, the small versions have built-in swivels and the larger ones an inset wire loop. In hard tide runs this shape of sinker holds down well and doesn't normally roll and tangle the terminal tackle. In slackish tide runs, pyramid-shaped sinkers are a good alternative to the larger dipsey sinkers.

The old-fashioned watch grip sinkers are still produced in a wide range of sizes, despite being particularly worthless. Their only use is for flatfishing from shallow, slack-tide beaches; fished from boats, they twist over and over in the tide until the terminal tackle is hopelessly tangled.

Wire-armed uptide casting sinkers have four wire spikes, 3 to 10 inches long, molded into them. These spikes dig into the sea bed to anchor the bait, but pull out when a fish picks up the bait. A similar sinker, with shorter spikes, is useful for beachcasting on stony or heavily tidal beaches.

Trolling sinkers have a barrel swivel molded into each end, and their banana-like shape is designed to create minimum water disturbance when they're being trolled. Two other common saltwater weights are the small ball sinker used for drift fishing for flatfish, and the plain barrel

sinker used with floats. This long, thin lead slides freely on the reel line, but is stopped from running down to the hook by a split shot or leader swivel.

A sea boom acts as a link between the line and the sinker (sinker boom), or as a standaway link to hold the bait away from the reel line (bait boom). Among the sinker booms, the traditional Kilmore and Clements booms are still widely used. In its simplest form, the Kilmore boom consists of a loop of wire, which fits around the reel line or leader, and a swivel or snap-on link to which the sinker is attached. An improved version has a ceramic eye inserted in the loop to allow the boom to slide more freely on the leader or reel line.

The Clements boom has a crossbar of wire with an eye at one end, and an eye and a swiveled snap fitting at the other. The line is passed through the eyes, and the sinker is attached to the snap fitting. A more modern style of Clements boom is shaped like a right-angled triangle, made of wire or plastic. The line eyes are at two of the corners, and the snap fitting at the third.

The plastic type of Clements boom, which is a solid piece of plastic, acts as a keel to prevent the terminal tackle from tangling. Longer versions are used in wreck fishing, where the keel stops the tackle tangling when it's on its way down to a deep-lying wreck. Bait booms are very different, their purpose being to prevent the tackle and bait from tangling around the reel line. All bait booms are derived from the old wire paternoster booms once so widely used by boat fishermen.

Modern booms are made of stainless steel wire or clear plastic. Both materials work effectively, and for fish like whiting, codling and sea bream a wire boom makes off-the-bottom bait presentation easy. The best and simplest of the single wire booms is the French boom, which is attached by simply twisting the line around the upright column from which the wire projects, and looping it over a projecting lug. This easy method of attachment means that the boom setting can quickly be changed to raise or lower the fishing level of the bait.

Plastic booms are also useful, but as they slide freely on the line or leader they have to be fixed in place with a swivel. These booms are normally fished in twos or threes on a leader.

Uptide

Cone

Trolling

Spiked torpedo

Pierced ball

Jardine spiral

Breakaway

Wire boom

Clements boom

Clements boom

Clements boom

Torpedo

Grip

Ashpole boom

Kilmore boom

Clements boom

Link

Eddystone boom

Kilmore boom

Lifter

French boom

SPINNING AND BAITCASTING RODS

With some exceptions, spinning and baitcasting rods are principally used for fishing with artificial lures. The spinning ods are used with fixed spool reels, and baitcasters with multipliers or any other reel designed to be used on top of the reel, facing the angler, rather than below it.

Modern rods are made from graphite composites mostly a mix of glass and graphite. In general, the lightness and strength of a rod with a high graphite content is an advantage for most spinning or baitcasting, simply because of the number of times it will be cast during a day's fishing. However, a cheaper glass/graphite mix is worth considering if it's to be used

by youngsters or beginners, and also for the rough usage of creek and estuary fishing over rocky shorelines. Glass/graphite mixes are also a perfectly acceptable alternative to graphite for trolling, where the rod is only held while the fish is being played.

Most graphite rods have the fibers laid at angles around the tube, but 100 per cent linear carbon rods, pioneered by Berkely, have the fibers running in just one direction, along the line of the rod from butt to tip. This produces a significantly lighter tube which is said to provide greater sensitivity.

Some of the most versatile rods, though, are those wrapped in a

mesh of Kevlar fibers which combines good shock resistance with tremendous strength and rigidity, but allows the tube to bend progressively to give an easy action when the fish is being played.

Good rod guides are essential on any rod intended for use with artificial lures because of the amount of wear they have to withstand – a lure fisherman may well make up to 2000 casts in a day. Aluminum oxide-centered guides, such as the Fuji range, are well proven, while those lined with heat-dissipating, diamond-polished silicon carbide offer minimal friction and thus minimal line and guide wear. The

lightweight Dynaflo guides, with either polished stainless steel or titanium centers, also give superbly smooth casting and retrieval with minimal friction.

Whatever type of guides your rod is fitted with, if you can hear the line passing through them then there is excessive friction. Line damage and guide grooving are likely, so the guides should be replaced.

Next to the diminutive ice hole sticks, the smallest baitcasting rods (4½ to 6 feet long) are the shortest of all fishing rods. All baitcasters up to 6 feet long have the short, hand-sized pistol grip with forefinger trigger that's so desirable for a secure grip of both

BAITCASTING RODS
These two baitcasting rods are each 5½ feet long, with short, pistol-grip handles and forefinger triggers. The upper rod is an Eagle Claw Black Eagle from Wright & McGill, a hollow glass rod with a medium tip action, for tossing lures of ¼ to ⅝ ounce on 6 to 12-pound lines. The other rod is home-built of graphite, with a fast tip action and used with 10 to 14-pound lines. Like all baitcasting rods, these rods are used with smaller multiplier reels or closed face fixed spool reels mounted on the top of the handle, which incorporates the reel seat.

reel and rod throughout a day's fishing.

The blank itself is usually inserted into the preformed handle via a ferrule, and glued, but some handles, such as the Fuji range, have ferrule adaptors which enable various different tips to be used with the same handle.

For greater sensitivity, the handle on some modern rods is simply a wider, shaped extension of the blank itself, while on others the blank runs right through the preformed pistol grip to the very end of the rod.

Rod lengths start at around 4½ feet for ultralight, but for serious bass fishing you need one about 5½ feet long and weighing between 5 and 7 ounces. Short baitcasting rods, those less than 6 feet long, are ideal for short, low-trajectory casting beneath overhanging trees when you're working shorelines from a boat. They're also much less tiring than longer rods for continual one-handed casting.

Short rods come in a variety of different actions, from a slow all-through to a super-stiff fast taper. Slow action rods are more forgiving when casting and playing, but they lack the power of the stiffer, fast-taper rods for slinging heavy lures and setting hooks.

For general fishing, a medium tip or compromise action is recommended – a rod which bends enough through the tip and middle section for effortless casting, but has a reserve of power just above the handle for subduing large fish.

For working surface lures, however, there is no compromise. Action cannot be imparted with anything other than a stiffish, fast-tapered rod. Plastic worms are also worked more effectively with such a rod.

Rods in the more versatile 6½ to 7½-foot range differ considerably from the short rods in both power and handle construction. To counteract the greater leverage which comes with a longer rod, the handle length below the trigger is increased so that the handle can be braced against the forearm. There is also a hand grip above the reel fitting for two-handed fishing.

Rods of over 7 feet are either of two-piece construction, or telescopic with several sections which collapse into the handle. Only use a telescopic rod if a two-piece is inconvenient for you to transport, because every joint in the telescopic rod is a potential weak spot.

Choose the action which suits your requirements best, remembering that for general lure work with species such as bass, walleye and pike, a medium-fast tip will handle most situations. For cranking big-lipped diving plugs, though, a rod with a faster, more powerful action and a reserve of power in the butt is the one to choose, while for working very light lures the rod should have a soft middle and tip section.

Within the range of 8 to 11-foot baitcasters, there are rods for just about every form of lure fishing. Some have trigger grips at the reel fitting, although on rods of 9 feet or more this feature isn't really necessary.

An 8 to 9-foot rod with a medium tip action is ideal for bass, walleye and pike, while salmon anglers often use a 10 or

even 11-foot rod with a similar action for systematically covering wide, deep, fast-flowing rivers. These rods can easily handle lines of 10 to 14 pounds test.

For much heavier work, such as trolling on large lakes or on salt water, and for plopping large swimming plugs or surface poppers around mangrove swamps for battlers such as tarpon, the action needs to be stepped up considerably. More power is needed through the middle to the butt section, so use a fast-taper, tip-action rod that can handle lines of 15 to 20 pounds test.

Rods for trolling should also have enough good-quality rod

guides to support the line and keep it away from the blank whatever the curvature, and long handles which fit snugly into the rod holders.

For estuary and heavy shore lure work, the rod needs a powerful but more progressive action, with lightweight fittings so that it can be worked comfortably all day. The handle should be no longer than is necessary; even for two-handed casting, a distance of 22 inches between reel and butt cap is quite sufficient. Anything longer can make it difficult to swap hands after casting.

In many categories, the spinning rod only differs from the

baitcaster in the choice of reel fitting (spinning rods don't need triggers) and the fact that the reel is positioned slightly nearer the butt end on the spinning rod, as well as being used beneath the rod instead of on top.

Spinning rods also usually have guides two sizes larger than those on baitcasters, because of the way the line pulls off in coils from the fixed spool reel. Many rod makers use the same blanks, with different fittings, for each type of reel.

To start a youngster on the road to becoming a lure fishing enthusiast, there's no better outfit than a short spinning rod/fixed

SPINNING RODS
The Hardy Favourite spinning rod is a 7-foot, two-piece, single handed
rod which weighs only 2 ¼ ounces and has a casting weight of 1 ounce on
2/6 pound line, using either a fixed spool or a multiplier reel. The Abu Conolon
870-2M is 7 feet long with a medium action, and the Admiral 590-3P
is a 9-foot rod with a parabolic action. The Daiwa C96-10S
10-foot rod is designed for trout and salmon spinning.

spool combination, whether in hollow glass, a glass/graphite mix or top quality graphite. In the shorter lengths (5½ to 7 feet), the differences in weight between the various materials are not significant, and the simple cork or synthetic handles weigh far less than the preformed pistol grip of a baitcaster. As a result, these short spinning rods weigh little more than short fly rods.

As with baitcasters, there is a range of actions available to suit all techniques, from jigging for crappies and other panfish on 4-pound lines, to cranking large, double-jointed surface plugs for big bass, pike and muskies.

The longer spinning rods, from about 8 to 11 feet long, are perhaps even more versatile than the long baitcasters. A 9-foot, medium-action spinning rod, fitted with a fixed spool reel loaded with 15-pound line, is one of the most useful fishing outfits in the world.

With such an outfit you could plug and spin for steelheads and salmon in fast rivers, fish for pike and muskie in reservoirs and lakes, toss plugs to big estuary jumpers like snook and tarpon, or go bait fishing for huge stillwater carp. You could use it for downrigger trolling for giant lake trout, deadbaiting at night for

catfish and eels, casting into the surf with bait or lures for bass and mackerel, and even for tackling the legendary masheer in the fast flowing rivers of India, with plugs, bait or large spoons. If you had to choose just one outfit for a round-the-world fishing trip, you couldn't choose better than this one.

An 8-foot spinning rod is also a versatile tool, and one which always feels comfortable to fish with. A light, middle-to-tip action is ideal for trout, walleye, bass, and even general pike and muskie fishing. For big fish in snaggy conditions, where heavy lines of over 15 pounds test are needed, a

stiffer, fast tip action is advisable.

The 10 to 11-foot spinning rods usually have a more progressive taper. For playing salmon in deep, fast rivers, they need to bend well or else the hooks will be ripped out.

However, even an 11-footer can be used for pike and steelheads, and is especially useful for presenting livebaits (shiners) to bass where 40 to 60 yards of line needs to be picked up on the strike. Long, easy-action spinning rods are also great for presenting soft crab and fish baits to sea bass over rocky ground.

SURFCASTING RODS

The **Daiwa PK 7461-12** is a 12-foot rod for use with a fixed spool reel.

The **Daiwa 7300D-12** is designed to cast sinkers of 4 to 8 ounces. This model uses a multiplier reel, but a fixed spool reel version (the 7301D-12) is also available.

Years ago, before inshore waters were depleted of their fish stocks by longliners, trawlers, factory ships and other commercial fishing, the need for long casting from the shore was nowhere near as important as it is today.

As a result, the early thick and heavy cane rods, with their brass ferrules and huge, porcelain-centred guides, were perfectly adequate. These beautiful rods would be of little use today, but the development of new rod-building materials and methods has kept pace with the shore angler's need for greater casting distances.

The fiberglass fibre rods were solid, and even heavier than the cane which they were intended to replace, but the arrival of hollow glass revolutionized the design of surfcasting rods.

The revolution began with the 'reverse taper' rod designed by Leslie Moncrieff. This rod, like all surf rods of its day, had two joints connected by brass ferrules, but from the reel fitting downwards the butt became progressively thinner instead of widening. The inherent spring of the reverse taper butt enabled surf fishermen to consistently cast distances of over 100 yards with bait, something quite unknown before.

The reverse taper reigned supreme for over a decade, but by the 1970s it was being steadily supplanted by the fast-tip rods which had been pioneered by Abu of Sweden with their Atlantic 484 beach rods. These rods had a rigid, Duralumin-cored butt and a fast-action hollow-glass tip.

The same high-tensile Duralumin is still used to produce butt rigidity in most contemporary surfcasters, well-covered in a plastic shrink tube to protect it from corrosion. The rigidity allows the full power of the blank to be used in casting, instead of being partly absorbed by the butt. Butts made of graphite are also produced today, and are

The **Ryobi Mastercaster MC110** is an 11-foot surfcasting rod with an optimum casting weight of 6 ounces. The butt section is 68 inches long, and the rod weighs 21 ounces and uses a multiplier reel.

DAIWA PK 7461-12

DAIWA 7300D-12

RYOBI MASTERCASTER MC110

especially popular for tournament casting.

Modern surf rod blanks are of hollow glass, a glass/graphite mix (considered by many to be the ideal) or a material containing a very high proportion of graphite. Some are lighter than others, and some are rather faster in the tip, but all are designed to work best with a particular range of weights, such as 1 to 3 ounces, 4 to 6 ounces, or 6 to 8 ounces, and they all have the power to subdue most species, provided there's enough line on the reel.

Most surf rods have very similar diameters, the most obvious differences between one model and another being in the number of rod guides, the type of reel fitting and the overall length. The most popular lengths,

Left *Surfcasting rods are strong, two-piece outfits designed either for use with fixed spool reels or, like the one shown here, with multiplying reels.*

whether the rods are designed for fixed spool or for multiplier reels, are from 11½ to 11¾ feet, made up of two joints of equal length with individually-rolled internal spigots. Others have a shorter, 4-foot butt and a tip of 7½ feet or so; these are usually more efficient for casting.

Rods for multipliers usually have a finger trigger at the reel fitting, and eight smallish, graduated guides, including the tip guide. For use with fixed spool reels, rods have just four large guides including the tip guide, starting with a 50 mm butt guide set high up the rod to reduce the coils of line as they peel from the large diameter of the fixed spool.

Guides with hard-wearing, non-grooving, heat-dissipating centers are imperative. Well-proven makes include Fuji, which have centers of aluminum oxide or silicon carbide, and the polished stainless steel Dynaflo guides.

Most production surfcasters

are now fitted with the robust yet lightweight tubular (Fuji-type) screw reel fitting, but the positioning of the reel fitting varies tremendously from manufacturer to manufacturer.

Ideally, the distance between the butt grip and the reel should be enough to give good leverage on the cast, but not so long that you can't follow through with the rod tip, pointing it at the lure or sinker until it hits the water. A distance of around 28 to 30 inches from the butt cap to the middle of the reel fitting will suit most anglers. Some rods are fitted with adjustable reel fittings, so that you can position the reel where it suits you best.

When it comes to choosing a surfcasting rod, look for one that's suited to the type of fishing you intend to do. Selecting a powerful rod that can cast heavy sinkers and subdue large fish in fast tides is rather pointless if you're going after little flatfish in a placid estuary or a quiet bay.

BAIT

The purpose of any bait – lure, fly or hookbait – is to fool the fish into taking the hook. Lures and flies are, in general, designed to imitate the natural food of the fish they're intended to catch, while hookbaits are either whole or cut natural fish foods or other edible items such as sweetcorn or pieces of bread.

Many fly fishermen tie their own flies, while others prefer to buy them ready-tied. The range of fly patterns is almost endless, as is the variety of lures on sale, but very often the difference between one lure or fly and another is in its appeal to the angler rather than to the fish.

Some hookbaits can be bought from tackle dealers (or, in the case of baits like bread or canned meats, from supermarkets), which is convenient, but there are many effective baits which can be gathered from the shore or from the water you're going to fish. The angler adept at seeking out natural baits on location will usually be guaranteed a good catch.

In addition to gathering worms from the lawn at night, after heavy rain, in the warmer months the freshwater angler can find a host of good baits, such as caterpillars, snails (crush the shells to remove the flesh), slugs and grasshoppers at the waterside. The freshwater predator hunter can collect a supply of baitfish by using a small net in the shallows. Bullheads, loach and small lampreys make great baits, and in clean streams and rivers you can find crayfish, the freshwater bait *par excellence* for numerous species.

In both running and still waters the caddis grub – the larva of the sedge fly – can be found in its mobile home, clinging to rocks and sunken branches where it feeds on algae. The size of the caddis varies according to its species, but most are roughly the size of a maggot, and they are a first-class natural bait. To remove the caddis from its case, gently squeeze the closed (tail) end until the grub's legs and head appear at the other. Then carefully pull it out, using just the nails of your thumb and index finger.

Freshwater mussels are another great natural bait,

and in just a few minutes you can dig up enough for a day's fishing from the mud and silt in the shallows. There is enough diversity in natural baits to make them effective for almost every freshwater fish, and all they cost is the time it takes to collect them. As a bonus, while gathering them you get to know a lot about the ecology of the water and its banks.

The saltwater angler also has plenty of natural baits to choose from, whether bought or collected from the sea or the shore. Shellfish can be gathered from the beach at low tide, along with small fish, prawns, shrimps and crabs from the rock pools, and baitfish such as sandeels and mackerel abound in the sea.

If you want to use crabs as bait, it's well worth searching specifically for 'peelers'. These are crabs which have shed their shells in order to grow, and whose new shells have yet to harden. During the few days between shells, the crabs are soft and rubbery and are a favorite food of many species which feed in the shallows along the beaches and up the estuaries.

Some of the natural baits found in the sea are as effective for many freshwater species as they are for marine fish. The oily-fleshed mackerel, for instance, is an excellent bait for many marine species such as shark, swordfish and marlin, but presented either whole or halved it is also one of the best deadbaits for catching large pike.

Another such bait is the humble prawn. It's an unbeatable bait for the smaller saltwater and brackish-water species, while in fresh water the mounted prawn is the most deadly bait for salmon. Peeled prawns are also worth using when you're after other large freshwater species, including catfish and carp. Trouble is, if you take a pot of fresh, peeled prawns with you for bait, you tend to eat most of them yourself.

In this chapter, we look at various types of natural and artificial baits, (including flies) which are of merit in freshwater and saltwater angling, and tell you how they're used and the sort of fish you can expect to catch on them.

ARTIFICIAL FLIES

FLY TYING EQUIPMENT

A ostrich herl	G wood duck	M varnish	S dubbing needle	Y peacock herl	5 seal's fur
B goose feather	H brown mallard	N lever action vice	T spigot bobbin holder	Z hen and cock capes	6 tinsel
C lure flash	I squirrel tail	O Veniard hackle pliers	U spring hackle pliers	1 tying thread	7 rayon floss
D cock pheasant tail	J marabou	P scissors	V deer hair	2 polypropylene floss	8 wool
E guinea fowl (dyed blue)	K hen pheasant tail	Q small hackle pliers	W barred teal	3 Superla dubbing	9 Mylar tubing
F teal wings	L golden pheasant tippets	R whip finish tool	X dyed squirrel tail	4 chenille	

Early anglers, with foreheads villanous low, nevertheless noticed those lengthy periods in spring and summer when trout feed greedily on abundant hatches of aquatic insects, and they soon began trying to catch fish on artificial imitations of the natural bugs.

Thus began the primeval fly fishing of the Stone Age. Tackle then was more a limiting factor than the artificial flies themselves. These used hooks carved from antler and bone, or made of soft-boiled thorns bent to shape and then dried. Fleshed out with underfur from an animal and legged with a neck feather plucked from a bird, these flies were delicate, subtle and devious. But before the reel, and before

oiled silk lines made fly casting possible, presentation was limited to dangling a fly over fish, using a long pole with plaited line of horse mane and tail lashed to the tip. This type of pole and line outfit was still in use in the nineteenth century.

It wasn't until the mid 1800s that fly fishing, as we know it now, swiftly bloomed into one of the more challenging sport pursuits. Frederic M Halford did much to create the cult of dry fly fishing in Britain, while his contemporary in North America, Theodore Gordon, was doing much the same thing there. Then around the turn of the century, G E M Skues broadened the horizons of fly fishing with his strong support of fishing for trout

with a sunken imitation nymph.

For many anglers, those years at the turn of the century represented the golden age of fly fishing. Halford had already started the 'exact imitation' tradition, whereby it was almost a mortal sin to cast a fly to a fish unless it was an identical replica of the fly on which the fish were seen to be feeding at that time. Frankly, the whole scene became a little farcical by present-day standards. But between them, Halford, Skues and Gordon brought some semblance of order to fly dressing in that some firm commitment was at least made to 'match the hatch'.

Salmon flies evolved from the trout patterns, long before it was discovered that salmon don't

actually feed during their journey upriver to their spawning grounds. In the early part of this century, salmon fly fishers paid more attention to color and shape than to size and presentation, but their flies were nonetheless very successful, perhaps because salmon were more plentiful then.

Of the natural materials which emerged as essential for fly tying, there is little doubt that silk thread and chicken or bantam neck feathers ranked high. The silk was used for tying and as a body material, while the hackle from a chicken's neck could be wound round the hook shank to form a hackle or wing and so give a rough resemblance to a natural fly.

Feathers from the wings of

BASIC FLY TYING

The art of decorating a hook with feathers, tinsel and fur to imitate a natural insect is one which any angler can acquire. Artificial flies consist mainly of a tail, a body, and where appropriate, a wing. All you need is a few simple tools and neat, precise fingers.

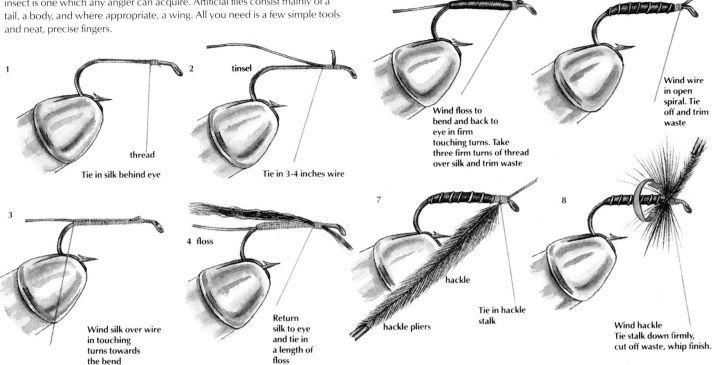

1 Tie in silk behind eye — thread

2 Tie in 3-4 inches wire — tinsel

3 Wind silk over wire in touching turns towards the bend

4 Return silk to eye and tie in a length of floss — floss

5 Wind floss to bend and back to eye in firm touching turns. Take three firm turns of thread over silk and trim waste

6 Wind wire in open spiral. Tie off and trim waste

7 Tie in hackle stalk — hackle — hackle pliers

8 Wind hackle. Tie stalk down firmly, cut off waste, whip finish.

other species of bird, such as teal or mallard, were used for dry flies and salmon flies, while the construction of nymphs relied heavily on copper wire to get the necessary weight. By the time of those golden years between the wars, the sport of fly fishing was flourishing; silken lines could be greased to float, and the fragile horsehair casts were being replaced by silkworm gut.

Silk thread and chicken feathers are still used, but they're now supplemented by an abundance of natural and synthetic materials. As a result, fly dressers can now create so many different fly patterns that things have tended to get a bit out of hand.

While the exact-imitation school of fly dressing is still with us to some extent, hatches of only one specific species of fly at a time are not so common as they once were, and the need for exact imitation has diminished. In addition to all the insect and non-imitative patterns, there are now also many flies which represent the freshwater shrimp, small fry and fish upon which trout feed.

The popularity of fly dressing as a hobby has grown steadily over the years, even among non-anglers. There are many good books on the subject, and there aren't many communities these days, even small ones, where fly tying tuition isn't available.

If you're going to tie your own flies, a vise for holding the hook is essential. This leaves both hands free to manipulate the silk thread and all the other materials which are to be spun on. Frequently, a silk body will be overlaid with tinsel, peacock herl or fur before the final hackle or wings are added and the fly completed.

Dry flies are often winged or hackled with stiff cockerel neck feathers, while wet flies tend to be made with softer hen hackles so that they sink readily. Fancy flies such as lures and streamers may be made from synthetic fibres, while hooks may be singles of a suitable size, or mounted in tandem with single, double or treble hooks.

There are times and conditions when the use of one type of fly or lure is likely to bring more success than another. The early season, for example, when trout are just recovering from spawning and hatching insects are not so frequent, may be a time when a deeply fished lure will attract the fish. Most times, though, lures are more generally used in still waters, either in cold weather when the fish are laid low, or in the very warm weather when they again go down deep to keep cool.

The smaller wet fly patterns may be best used on rivers and streams as spring warms into early summer and there is a portion of the day when flies are hatching. Searching all the likely water will often get a fish or two until a good hatch of fly comes along.

THE WHIP FINISH

1

2

3 A ... B

4 A ... B

Before tying a fly you must learn to whip finish. Practice on a bare hook; the steps for a right-handed tier are as follows. Wind a few turns of thread onto the shank, trapping loose end. Swing bobbin up towards you. Pass the backs of first and second fingers (of right hand) behind, then over, thread, forming a loop in an inverted figure 4. Lay thread A along near side of shank trapping it with thread B. Maintain tension between fingers and lay the bobbin over the rear out of the way. Transfer thread B to left hand. Pass thread B around shank five times, trapping thread A. Insert a needle into loop, using it to maintain tension while drawing thread A towards rear of hook. As loop tightens, slip it out. Finally, trim thread A and varnish.

ARTIFICIAL FLIES — DRY

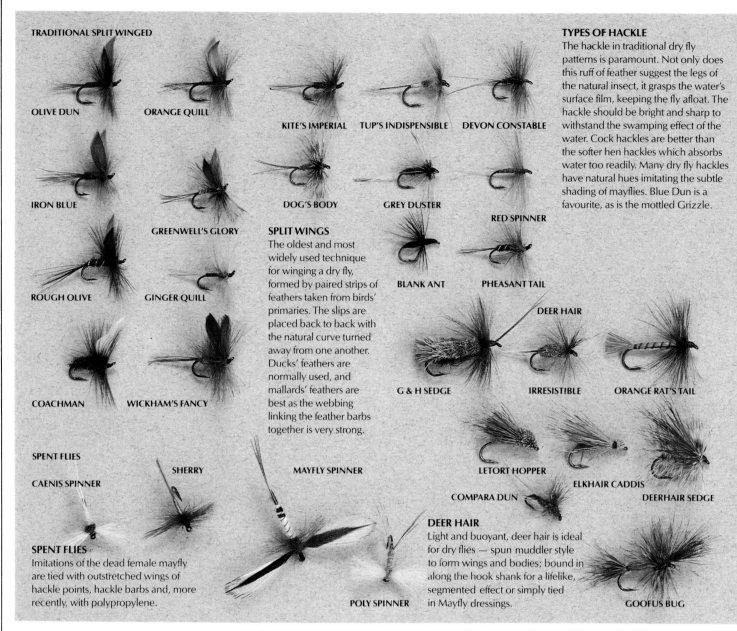

TRADITIONAL SPLIT WINGED

OLIVE DUN

ORANGE QUILL

IRON BLUE

GREENWELL'S GLORY

ROUGH OLIVE

GINGER QUILL

COACHMAN

WICKHAM'S FANCY

KITE'S IMPERIAL

TUP'S INDISPENSIBLE

DEVON CONSTABLE

DOG'S BODY

GREY DUSTER

RED SPINNER

BLANK ANT

PHEASANT TAIL

DEER HAIR

G & H SEDGE

IRRESISTIBLE

ORANGE RAT'S TAIL

LETORT HOPPER

ELKHAIR CADDIS

COMPARA DUN

DEERHAIR SEDGE

SPENT FLIES

CAENIS SPINNER

SHERRY

MAYFLY SPINNER

POLY SPINNER

GOOFUS BUG

TYPES OF HACKLE

The hackle in traditional dry fly patterns is paramount. Not only does this ruff of feather suggest the legs of the natural insect, it grasps the water's surface film, keeping the fly afloat. The hackle should be bright and sharp to withstand the swamping effect of the water. Cock hackles are better than the softer hen hackles which absorbs water too readily. Many dry fly hackles have natural hues imitating the subtle shading of mayflies. Blue Dun is a favourite, as is the mottled Grizzle.

SPLIT WINGS
The oldest and most widely used technique for winging a dry fly, formed by paired strips of feathers taken from birds' primaries. The slips are placed back to back with the natural curve turned away from one another. Ducks' feathers are normally used, and mallards' feathers are best as the webbing linking the feather barbs together is very strong.

SPENT FLIES
Imitations of the dead female mayfly are tied with outstretched wings of hackle points, hackle barbs and, more recently, with polypropylene.

DEER HAIR
Light and buoyant, deer hair is ideal for dry flies — spun muddler style to form wings and bodies; bound in along the hook shank for a lifelike, segmented effect or simply tied in Mayfly dressings.

Dry fly fishing is primarily used for taking the various species of trout and salmon. In North America, especially on Canadian rivers of the eastern seaboard, the dry fly is frequently employed on Atlantic salmon during June, July and August. In Europe, particularly in the United Kingdom, there is rarely an opportunity to attempt serious fly fishing for salmon. Many fly patterns favored by Canadian salmon anglers, are big, bushy creations which represent insects known only to God.

Dry fly fishing for trout needs a representation of the winged stage of ephemerids (mayflies), trichopterans (caddis flies) or of various terrestrials.

Fly dressers keen to imitate all the various stages of a mayfly life cycle start with representations of the nymph, but the dry fly angler is more interested in the second phase, when the 'duns' or subimago flies shed teir nymphal cases and take wing.

Upon leaving the water, the hatched insects get in among trees and bushes. Here they shelter from rain and wind, often on the undersurface of leaves, and undergo a molt or ecdysis, when their outer skin is shed and the final insect emerges as a complete imago or 'spinner'. It is only as a spinner that it can breed.

Shortly after the spinners emerge the lovely mayfly dance begins. Swarms of males fly with a rise-and-fall motion to spot with their top-of-the-head eyes the high-flying females. Mating takes place in flight, and soon the females uncouple and depart to lay their fertilized eggs on or in the water. Having done so, the females drift downstream reposing in a final death stupor, wings and tails drooping flat to the surface. This is called the 'spent spinner', a third object of artificial representation.

By the time the mayfly have laid their eggs most trout are already gorged on the mayfly and they will become more difficult to catch. While looking very realistic to our eyes, many patterns of the spent spinner fail miserably when it comes to deceiving the fish. Because of this, the dun and early spinner stages are of more interest to the fly fisherman.

In Britain, the large spring olive dun and the large dark olive dun play a very important role for the fly fisher during the early part of the season. There are many artificial patterns based on these, the better known ones being the Blue Dun, Blue Upright, Hare's Ear, Dark Olive Quill and the Rough Olive.

The March Brown is another popular fly, dressed to imitate a natural fly of the same name. It's a popular fly with anglers even on waters where the natural fly is unknown or comparatively rare, and it will take trout anywhere in the world. It's an exceedingly 'buggy'-looking pattern.

The iron blue dun is an extremely common fly, particularly during the colder days of spring. Representations of this fly include the Dark Watchet and the Blue Bloa; the spinners of the iron blue, depending on their sex, may be known as the Jenny Spinner or Claret Spinner.

It is doubtful if there are many ephemerids more plentiful than the blue winged olive. This fly is one of the easiest to recognize because close examination will reveal that it is the only olive to

WULFF PATTERNS

WHITE WULFF

GREY WULFF

WULFF PATTERNS
Available in a wide range of shades and sizes. With wings and tails of hair, they are robust and float well even in the roughest water. Dressed on a variety of hook sizes, they can suggest all but the smallest Mayfly, and are often used to tempt salmon.

ROYAL WULFF

PALMERS

SKATER

WHITE MOTH

With a dense hackle along the body, Palmers float well. Though many imitate adult caddis, the hackles allow the fly to be skated across the surface, copying the emerging natural.

BROWN BIVISIBLE

SHADOW MAYFLY

SPECIALS

BLACK SEDGE

SPECIALS
Both hawthorn and crane flies are land-born. Their long legs are imitated by feather or hair tied to suggest joints.

HAWTHORN FLY

CRANE FLY

Left A natural olive dun, the inspiration for many popular and successful dry fly patterns such as the Rough Olive Dun.

Above Mayflies are an important part of the diet of trout, both in their larval stage and after they have hatched.

Left The caddis or sedge fly, like the mayflies, is a widely-imitated natural as well as an important food of the trout.

NATURALS

have three tails. Several imitations are offered, with the Orange Quill being one of the most popular. The Sherry Spinner is a popular choice when the spinner is on the water, and there are many anglers who rely on local patterns of olives in the hope that they will prove successful.

The pale water dun is yet another ephemerid worthy of note. The Blue Quill and the Little Marryat imitations of the dun are well known, as is the Amber Spinner for the imago stage.

Of the many other flies popular with the angler, the most important are the caddis or sedge flies and the stone flies. Caddis flies in flight resemble moths, and may be sought by the fish during a late spring or summer evening just on dusk.

Stone flies, on the other hand, often appear during the late spring, and there are times when trout become so preoccupied feeding on these flies that they refuse to look at the hordes of ephemerids which might be hatching at the same time. The large stone fly, also known as the creeper, may be prolific on many rivers in late April and May.

For trout fishing, the North American fly fisherman has countless patterns to choose from, most of which are variations of only about eight basic types which between them provide flies suitable for most conditions.

When the trout are feeding on mayfly in good light and smooth water, it's best to use a fly which is a good representation of the natural, because the fish are likely to be wary of taking anything that looks very different. In these

conditions try a divided-wing type, such as a Light Cahill.

In poor light or broken water the fly needn't be such a close imitation of the natural mayfly, but it should be a robust pattern which can easily be seen. A hairwing type, such as a Grey Wulff or a Hairwing Royal Coachman, will often raise fish when visibility is poor.

When, as often happens, the trout are feeding on other insects, a mayfly imitation might have little success and other types of fly will get better results. The bivisibles, such as the Brown Bivisible, are good when the fish are taking a variety of different insects, but when the larger naturals such as dragonflies are being taken, a downwing type – a dry Muddler Minnow, for example – is well worth trying. On the other hand, if the trout are

feeding on tiny insects, and ignoring larger food, including mayflies, a midge type fly such as the little Black Midge is called for.

For making a really delicate presentation to trout in smooth, quiet waters the spider type, the Blue Dun Spider, for instance, hits the water gently and floats with minimum drag. Fast, turbulent waters demand a far tougher type of fly, a hair-bodied pattern with hair wings that floats well and isn't easily damaged, such as an Irresistible.

The last of the basic types of trout fly is the fanwing. Fanwings will take trout on most waters, but their wings are delicate, and repeated casting with them will twist and weaken the leader because they spin in flight.

ARTIFICIAL FLIES — WET

The term 'wet fly' covers all those representations of insects which spend all or some of their lives underwater, including larval and nymph stages of the ephemerids whose winged stages are the inspiration for so many dry fly patterns. It also includes imitations of drowned terrestrial insects, not to mention the representation of the fry of various fish – even trout. Trout are usually the major predators in trout streams, and cannibalism is a large part of the diet of trout longer than 12 inches.

Many of the flies devised for fishing beneath the surface are fairly recognizable imitations of non-winged insects and small fish. Others, used especially on still waters, are simply attractor flies based on the fact that highly predatory fish are likely to attack anything that moves or remotely resembles food. As a result, stillwater fly patterns offer a myriad of choices.

It is principally on rivers that fly fishermen seek to imitate the larval and nymphal stages of ephemerids, relying heavily on tried and tested patterns which are known to be best for a specific area. It's not always obvious what some of these patterns are meant to represent. The Partridge and Orange is among these; it's actually based on one of the olive dun family, as is the Waterhen Bloa. But it's not difficult to see that the Snipe and Purple bears some resemblance to the iron blue dun, or that the Alexandra is designed to represent the fry of some fish species, or maybe a minnow.

Fish feeding on nymphs and larval flies will often accept a wide range of artificial patterns, so there's something to be said for getting the size and hue of the fly about right, and for knowing those times when sub-surface activity is likely to be at its highest. During the early season, you might rely heavily on the fact that fish are very hungry, and that their natural food supply is still very scarce. On that basis, it could be assumed that fish will take almost anything you might offer them, but it's not quite as simple as that.

Being cold-blooded creatures, all fish have a metabolic rate which is directly related to water temperature. Trout, for instance, show little inclination to feed in cold water, nor can they very easily or quickly digest any food they may take. In the cold water conditions of early spring, their protein demand is well below what it might be in May or June, or when the water temperature gets to 19°C (66°F), the temperature at which trout are said to feed most voraciously.

Most times in cold water, they're content to rest in the deeper pools, and will only bother to feed avidly when some warming sun breaks through and a few nymphs begin to fidget on the bed of the river. Because of this, it's a good idea to confine early season attempts to short periods between, say, 11 am and 3 pm, although you'll often find that the fish seem to wait until you break for lunch before they start feeding actively. Never make the mistake of offering extra-large flies to early season trout, and do be careful to make your flies move as slowly and as deep as you can.

There are no hard and fast rules about which wet fly patterns to use and when to use them. For instance, Snipe and Purple, Partridge and Orange and Waterhen Bloa can be used throughout the season, but there are scores of alternatives from the whole range of non-specific patterns like the Claret and Mallard, Teal and Green, Grouse and Claret, Peter Ross, Royal Coachman and Bloody Butcher. All will take fish on their day, but they're probably better on still waters than those rivers with good stocks of natural ephemerids. Even then, it would be a clever fish that could tell the difference between, say, a Waterhen Bloa and a Dark Watchet, and a hungry fish wouldn't care to know anyway.

As for nymphs, good all-rounders include the Early Olive Nymph or the Hatching Olive Nymph, the March Brown, the stonefly nymph, the sedge pupa and, specifically for the chalk streams, a few imitations of the freshwater shrimp.

Much the same tactics are used when seeking fish on wet fly anywhere in the world. The trout of Montana, Chile or New Zealand, for instance, are little different in their basic habits. Even the natural subaquatic insects or fry upon which they feed don't vary much from one location to another, but it pays to make a study of the natural life on the bed of any stream you are going to fish. Turn over the stones or stir up the silt or gravel, and use a small butterfly net to see what you can collect.

WINGED WET FLIES

WOODCOCK & RED DUNKELD INVICTA

PROFESSOR MALLARD & CLARET BLUE & BLACK

A combination of different materials is used to produce different effects. The Mallard and Claret series uses mallard wing, golden pheasant tippets for the tail, claret, red, blue or green wool or seal's fur for the body and silver or gold tinsel or wire for the ribbing. Teal, woodcock, partridge or other wings may be used instead of mallard — the range is enormous. Some, such as the Dunkeld, are not so much imitations of flies but spinners, used to trigger off a fish's predatory instincts.

OLIVE QUILL

TEAL BLUE & SILVER

WICKHAM'S FANCY

MARABOU

APPETIZER

VIVA

Marabous stork feathers made flies of good movement even when retrieved slowly. Today, the same results are achieved using feathers from turkey legs.

BABY DOLLS

Lures, imitating small fish, are popular with stillwater fly fishermen. The original Baby Doll was made from baby lamb's wool.

ETHAFOAM DOLL

GREEN BACK DOLL

STANDARD BABY DOLL

SALMON FLIES

FULLY DRESSED FLIES

THUNDER & LIGHTNING

DURHAM RANGER

BLUE CHARM

ORANGE PARSON

Dating back to the last century, these rich, bright flies used feathers from rare, exotic birds. Today, fully-dressed flies like the Blue Charm are simpler, using modern materials.

HACKLED FLIES

ZULU

SOLDIER PALMER

GRENADIER

WELSH PALMER

SPIDERS

WATERHEN BLOA

PARTRIDGE & ORANGE

PHEASANT TAIL

GROUSE SPIDER

SNIPER PURPLE

KE-HE

COCH-Y-BONDHU

BLACK PENNELL

RED TAG

NYMPHS

Nymphs simulate the larval, or sometimes pupal, stage of caddis, dragonfly, midges, buzzers and other forms of aquatic flies which form the trout's basic diet. Nymphs follow simple patterns, made up of small throat or beard hackles with ribbing to imitate the segmented effect of the natural body.

BLOODWORM

TUP'S NYMPH

CLARET BUZZER

HARE'S EAR

EMERGENT SEDGE

COVE PHEASANT TAIL

ORANGE NYMPH

SPRING FAVOURITE

SHARPE'S SEDGE PUPA

PHEASANT TAIL & NYMPH

HATCHING MIDGE

MAYFLY NYMPH

TYPES OF HACKLE

The object of the wet fly hackle is to sink as quickly as possible and imitate the actions of a fly, below the surface.

Soft hen hackles are ideal, though low grade 'soft' cock hackles may also be used. Hackles are tied in a variety of styles. The simplest is the spider or collar hackle, where two or three turns are wound just behind the eye of the hook. Used in both modern and traditional dressings, this type of hackle employs either hen hackles or soft grouse or woodcock feathers, both of which work well in water.

A second type is the beard or 'false' hackle, where a bunch of barbs is stripped from an oversized hackle and trimmed to length before being tied in. This is used on many wet flies and streamers, though providing less action than a wound hackle.

The third type of wet fly hackle is the Palmer where the hackle is wound the length of the hook shank. With its multitude of barbs, each working in the water, Palmer patterns are very effective, particularly for loch-style fishing, where they make ideal top dropper flies.

HAIRWING LURES

ZONKER

TANDEM SWEENY TODD

GOLDIE

CHURCH FRY

WHISKY FLY

Also known as Bucktails, hairwing lures are made from bucktail, calftail, squirrel tail or goat hair.

MUDDLER MINNOWS

So-called because they resemble small minnow-type fish such as the bullhead. Used originally for fishing the Nipigon River in Ontario, the series includes Dick Walker's and Texas Rose, apart from those shown below.

STANDARD MUDDLER

BLACK MUDDLER

WHITE MUDDLER

ORANGE MUDDLER

LOW WATER FLIES

SILVER BLUE

LOGIE

THUNDER & LIGHTNING

HAIRWINGS

HAIRY MARY

JOCK SCOTT

STINCHAR STOAT'S TAIL

BLUE CHARM

TUBE FLIES

WILLIE GUNN

GARRY DOG

In mid-summer when the water level is low and salmon are attracted to small flies, the low-water fly comes into its own. Though small and dressed short, the hook is large.

Easier and quicker to dress than many traditional patterns, hairwings have become one of the most popular, and effective salmon flies in recent years.

A large early season fly. The advantage of the tube fly is that it enables an angler to use a treble hook, offering better hooking. Line is less likely to tangle and though weighty, they are streamlined.

ARTIFICIAL LURES — FRESHWATER

SPINNERS
A spinner is an artificial lure that has a spoon or blade which rotates around a central stem.

The Abu Reflex 7g (**lure A**) and the larger Reflex 18g (**B**) are designed to catch a variety of species including perch, pike, trout and salmon. The Abu Drop Fish 8g (**C**), one of Abu's Droppen range, has a realistic, plastic imitation fish attached to tempt predators.

Lures D and E are two more Abu Droppen spinners. The Drop Flex 6g (**D**) has a patch of reflective plastic on the blade to make it more visible in murky waters. The Droppen 2g (**E**), like the rest of the Droppen lures, has most of its weight concentrated at the rear of its body for good casting.

Lure (**F**) is a half-ounce Mepps Aglia Long. The weighted body casts well, and as with all spinners the rotating blade creates strong vibrations as it spins. The Abu Droppen Sono 18g (**G**) has perforated flanges on its blade to increase the sound produced by its rotation when it's retrieved.

The Taylor & Johnson 2½-inch Colorado spoon (**H**) and the Rapier 2½-inch kidney spoon (**I**) are both spinners despite being known as 'spoons'. The blade of the Colorado rotates around a central bar, to which it's attached at both ends. The kidney spoon is attached to a swivel so that it (and its treble hook) spins as it's pulled through the water.

A lure is any artificial device which, when pulled through the water, incites a predatory fish to grab it, either through territorial aggression, cussedness or hunger. A lure can be made of wood, plastic, rubber, metal, or other materials such as feathers or hair, and rigged with single or multiple treble hooks.

It can be buoyant, heavily weighted so that it sinks, or made to dive on the retrieve by means of a lipped vane built into its head. Its action, an important part of its attractiveness to fish, can be imparted by the angler or result from its body shape or from angled vanes attached to it, with extra vibratory attraction coming from steel balls which rattle inside it. External spinning or vibrating blades also create sound waves, as do hinged arms which flap as floating plugs are wound across the surface.

One of the most straightforward types of lure is the spoon, made from chrome-plated steel, brass, aluminum or hammered copper, with a single treble at one end and a swivel at the other, both joined to the body by split rings.

The spoon has two great assets: its weight gives it good casting ability (particularly into the wind), and it can be counted down, in seconds, to the desired depth before retrieving. It doesn't spin, but simply wiggles or wobbles from side to side and so it can be retrieved at almost any speed. As a general rule, a slow retrieve is best for colored water, and a medium to fast pace for really clear water.

The spoon's shape is usually oval, some being more elongated than others, and the choice of both weight and size depends on the species you're fishing for. Spoons of from four to six inches long (even longer for trolling) are ideal for larger fish such as pike, while those of three inches or less will catch anything from crappies and trout upwards.

Large, 8 to 12-inch spoon blades (without hooks) called dodgers or flashers are often used as an attractor when trolling, rigged 3 feet ahead of the lure. They also help to give a natural movement to the lure, and to natural fishbaits when 'mooching' for salmon. The salmon homes in on the vibration and flash of the dodger, but grabs the fish bait.

There are also many excellent weedless spoons (a fine, sprung wire hook guard protects the point) from which to choose, which have a single hook joined to the body and a rubbery skirt to help mask the point. Unlike the

SPOONS
Spoons are lures that wobble, rather than spin.

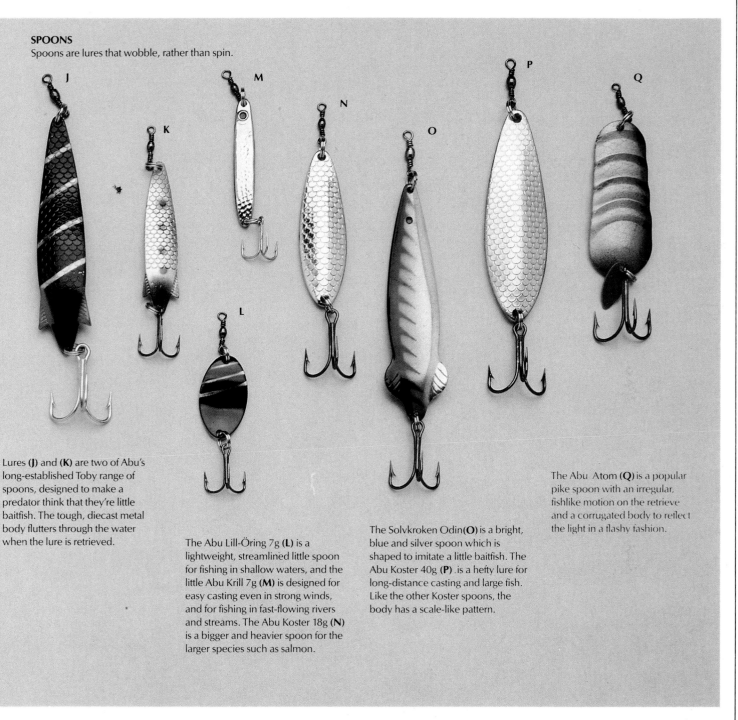

Lures (J) and (K) are two of Abu's long-established Toby range of spoons, designed to make a predator think that they're little baitfish. The tough, diecast metal body flutters through the water when the lure is retrieved.

The Abu Lill-Öring 7g (L) is a lightweight, streamlined little spoon for fishing in shallow waters, and the little Abu Krill 7g (M) is designed for easy casting even in strong winds, and for fishing in fast-flowing rivers and streams. The Abu Koster 18g (N) is a bigger and heavier spoon for the larger species such as salmon.

The Solvkroken Odin(O) is a bright, blue and silver spoon which is shaped to imitate a little baitfish. The Abu Koster 40g (P) .is a hefty lure for long-distance casting and large fish. Like the other Koster spoons, the body has a scale-like pattern.

The Abu Atom (Q) is a popular pike spoon with an irregular, fishlike motion on the retrieve and a corrugated body to reflect the light in a flashy fashion.

trailing trebles on basic spoons, these hooks won't snag, even in thick vegetation.

Many large spoons (and other lures) often come with treble hooks that are far too thick in the wire for general freshwater use. Simply replace them with a more suitable type, and always keep the points sharp. Gently flattening the barbs with pliers also aids hook penetration, particularly into the hard, bony jaws of species like pike and muskies.

A natural progression from spoon baits is the spinner, where the spoon or blade actually revolves around a weighted center bar or stem. These come in a variety of blade colors and hook trimmings, from squirrel tail to red wool tassels or plastic worms and fish.

Colorado spoons and kidney spoons, which are actually spinners because they have revolving blades, have been popular for many years. Both have a red-painted, lead center bar, and red wool tags around the treble which are reputed to be very good at inciting pike.

Devon minnows are a popular type of spinner, used mainly for trout but particularly for salmon. They either have metal bodies of various weights and colors, for fast, deep river work, or wooden bodies for shallow rivers or for fishing the lure above rocks.

With all types of lures that spin, you should guard against line twist and kinking by fitting a plastic anti-kink vane or a vaned swivel guard at the head of the leader.

Evolving from both spoons and spinners come the spinning baits, buzz baits and other lures which rely on a spinning or vibrating blade to create sound to attract the fish, but which also have a soft, tempting body for the fish to grab at. The body incorporates a large, single hook, the idea being that a fish will take the lower, body section or even attempt the entire lure, as do pike, for instance, although fish do sometimes hit the blade in preference to the body.

Some spinner baits have a single blade, others a pair of blades mounted tandem-style on a V-shaped, stainless steel shaft. The lure is leaded so that it always fishes with the blade or blades uppermost, and the body material usually consists of a rubber, squid-like skirt that folds back over the hook to mask it from weed on the retrieve.

Spinner baits can be retrieved either fast or slow, and at all depths, but are particularly effective (perhaps more than any

The Rapala Shad Rap 9CW – a shallow-diving plug.

The Rapala 9P is a little minnow-shaped floating diver.

The Abu Hi-Lo 18g RH plug has an adjustable, six-position diving vane, and its two treble hooks are fixed to the body by screwed-in mounts rather than by split rings.

Another **Rapala Shad Rap**, a silver and black version of the 9CW shallow diver.

The Heddon Wood Vamp is a jointed, two-piece plug with three treble hooks. This enormously successful plug, introduced in the 1920s, is a floating diver which can be worked down to about 3 feet, and it's a big plug designed to catch big fish – pike, bass, muskies, walleye, striped bass and snook.

The Rapala 9CFR is another floating diver, a gold and fluorescent orange version of the 9P plug.

other freshwater lure) in colored water where visibility is low.

Buzz baits are similar in format, but are used as surface attractor lures, with the blade churning through the surface film to create vibrations.

In complete contrast to these noisy lures, lead-headed jigs work on the principle of the weighted head dropping downwards when winding stops or the rod tip is lowered, and quickly 'jigging' upwards on the retrieve or when the rod tip is raised.

The jig has a ball or wedge-shaped head made of painted lead molded onto the hook shank. The shank is bent at right angles some

quarter of an inch from the eye, so that the eye always faces upwards in line with the hook point. This helps to make the jig relatively snag and weed free. Jigs will catch almost any freshwater fish, from crappies to salmon, and are best used on very light tackle.

Many jigs have bodies and tails, made from materials such as rubber, bucktail and marabou feathers, while others incorporate plastic worms, shrimps or various grub-like tails. Some tiny jigs may not even have a body or tail, simply a brightly painted head used bare or with a small livebait such as a maggot, worm, fish fry or grub on the hook.

Another type have tiny heads weighing only a fiftieth or even a hundredth of an ounce, and fluttering bodies of marabou. These are outstanding lures for trout and panfish, and can be used on a fly rod outfit, jigged gently beneath a float when ice fishing, or on ultralight tackle in the normal way.

Plastic worms come in a range of thicknesses and in lengths of from three to ten or more inches. As well as the plain, earthworm type, there are worms with twister tails, crawfish tails, fish tails and other patterns. Often, they're impregnated with special salts and pungent natural oils to make

them smell just like the real thing, or worse.

The color range is astound-ing, but all the reds, purples, yellows and blacks work well, as do some of the fluorescent colors, pink and dark green in particular.

In addition to the basic synthetic worm, there are also soft, jelly-like imitations of creatures such as lizards, frogs and toads. These are all fished in the same way as the worms, either floating on the surface or taken down to the bottom by a bullet-headed worm weight, threaded on the line just in front of the lure. These weights vary from an eighth of an ounce, to over half an ounce, and

The Mitchell Rublex Flopy floating diver is a little imitation prawn for salmon fishing.

The Heddon Meadow Mouse is a surface-disturber type of floating plug which is retrieved slowly to mimic a swimming mouse.

The Heddon Rattle Sonic, a little fish-like plug with a ball within its body cavity that creates a rattling noise on the retrieve.

These little **'delta eel'** lures are made of soft plastic and mounted on single hooks. They will take salmon, but their use is not allowed on some waters.

The Crankbait Hi-Catch, an elegant little plug patterned like a fingerling trout.

The Heddon Crazy Crawler is a rounded, bug-like floating lure with a pair of hinged metal vanes to create plenty of splashy surface disturbance.

A Gordon Griffiths 3-inch floating minnow. The curved vanes on the head of a minnow lure make it rotate as it's pulled through the water. The swivel at the head is connected to the hook by a length of braided wire around which the body rotates.

allow the lure to be fished in all waters, still or running.

The plastic worm is retrieved in a similar way to a jig, but in much longer pulls, and with longer pauses between them. During the pause, the worm can be left on the bottom for dead, or twitched on the surface.

Lastly, there's the large and very popular range of wooden or plastic lures known as plugs — floating plugs, floating divers and sinking plugs.

The floating plugs are surface attractor lures, and some have skirts, tassels, revolving blades or vibrating arms to help them create maximum disturbance on the surface. For casting into dense cover, weedless surface poppers will provide just what's needed: a splashy, floppy, non-hangup retrieve to bring the fish out of their cover and after the lure. Surface plugs are among the most exciting to use, because you not only anticipate the surface take, you also see it.

Floating divers, which float on the surface after being cast, begin to dive when they're retrieved; the faster the retrieve, the deeper they dive. If you pause during the retrieve, they'll pop back up to the surface again. By using a combination of fast and slow retrieve rates, with the occasional pause, you can create strikingly lifelike action in the lure.

Floating divers are the most versatile and probably the most widely used of all plugs. The diving action is created by an aluminum or plastic diving vane (or lip) set into the head of the plug. A good-sized vane will take the plug down to ten or fifteen feet on a fast retrieve.

The bodies of floating divers are often brightly colored in fluorescent enamel or have an extremely effective, light-reflecting prism pattern. Some have a steel ball sealed within the body cavity, which rattles around inside the plug to make it vibrate, while others have jointed bodies to give them a good action.

Floating divers can be used for trolling as well as for casting, as can the sinking plugs. Designed for fishing deep waters where the lure has to sink some distance before it can be fished effectively, these plugs are heavy, strongly built and come in a variety of weights and colors. Most are up to about 4 or 5 inches long, but a few, intended for trolling rather than casting, are up to 10 inches in length. Sinking plugs often have rattles inside them, but few are fitted with a diving vane because their weight is enough to take them down to fishing depth.

ARTIFICIAL LURES — SALTWATER

Lure A is the Tony Accetta PET 23, a large chromed steel spoon with a 7-ounce, 10-inch blade and a single hook, for trolling for big game fish such as wahoo and barracuda. **Lure B** is a plastic sandeel, a deadly lure for predators such as cod, ling and pollack. **Lures C** and **D** are also plastic — Shakespeare Wondershine imitation squid, 3 inches long, and one of the most successful types of lure for cod, ling and other predators.

Lure E is a 7-ounce Abu Sextett pirk, which has reflective sides to make it more visible.

The little Nils Master Invincible floating diver plug, **lure F**, is 3 inches long and weighs just over ¼ ounce. The body is made of balsa, and the hooks are attached to a stainless steel wire inside the plug. **Lure G**, at the top of this picture, is a large, soft plastic squid with a big single hook, a good lure for big game trolling for species such as bluefin tuna and broadbill swordfish.

Lure H is a Kona Head lure. The Kona Head, first developed in Hawaii, is one of the standard big game fishing lures, and it will take a large number of species including bonito, marlin, tuna and dorado.

The Ilander, from Tournament Tackle Inc, **lure I**, is a 9-inch, 2-ounce trolling lure designed to be used at speeds of between 4 and 10 knots, mounted on a wire or mono leader with an 8/0 to 10/0 hook.

The lures used in saltwater fishing range from tiny trout and salmon flies adapted to saltwater fly casting up to the huge Kona Head lures designed for fast big-game trolling.

Many standard freshwater fly patterns can be used to good effect for the smaller saltwater fish, one of the most successful patterns being the Dog Nobbler, a weighted fly which incorporates a long, flowing marabou tail. When this fly is retrieved, the tail undulates enticingly through the water to give the fly a natural-looking, swimming motion.

Streamer flies, which are also extremely good, range in size from little, inch-long patterns up to huge, six-inch creations designed to take small tuna, tarpon and sailfish. For bottom feeding fish such as bonefish or permit, a shrimp imitation fished with a slow retrieve can be a deadly bait.

Japanese feathers were originally designed as lures for commercial bonito and tuna fishing, but rod-and-reel anglers soon discovered their potential and they have now become a standard trolling lure. Japanese feathers have a chromed lead head, which gives them weight, red glass eyes, and a bunch of mixed hackle feathers which form the tail, the most popular tail colors being red/white, green/yellow, all black and all dark blue.

These lures are available in weights of one to ten ounces, and they attract and catch many kinds of predatory fish. For example, the smaller lures are perfect for bonito, while the larger patterns will take big tuna.

Another good trolling lure is the wobbling spoon. As its name suggests, this is a one-piece, concave lure designed to wobble rather than spin through the water. Many of these lures originated in Sweden and Canada, where they were designed for deepwater trolling for giant lake trout, pike and muskellunge.

Their success in freshwater eventually led to their adoption by saltwater fishermen, and they are particularly useful as attractor spoons for cod or as barracuda lures. Wobbling spoons are now made in many sizes, colors and scale patterns, and some are designed specifically for casting; these are made from thicker metal to give them casting weight.

Spinners used in saltwater are also based on freshwater patterns, especially the Colorado and kidney spinners devised in the last century for pike fishing. Modern engineering and design have improved on these basic patterns to produce a wide range of revolving lures. Most of the available patterns are designed for ultralight spin fishing techniques for bass, mackerel, needlefish, medium-weight barracuda and a host of small sporting fish such as flounders.

Lures **L** and **Q** are both mackerel spinners, excellent lures for most of the smaller predatory species. The triangular blade is brazed to a small tube which rotates around the axial wire. **Lure M** is a lead-headed fly similar to a Dog Nobbler, which is a useful pattern for saltwater fly fishing.

The Rapier Glo Spoon, **Lure N**, is a tough 2-inch plastic spoon for flounder fishing, used with a bait such as ragworm on the hook.

Lure O is another plastic sandeel, a larger, green and purple, version of lure B.

Lures R, **S** and **T** are size 4/0 Solvkroken plastic eels. These are simple lengths of plastic tubing into which the hook and swivel are inserted. The shanks of the hooks are bent to varying degrees to give the eels a variety of actions.

Lure J is a mackerel feather with a weighted head and a single hook. Feathers are probably the best artificial bait for mackerel, but they'll take other species as well.

The Cisco Kid 1812, **lure K**, is a large plug with three treble hooks, and it can be trolled for the larger species such as king mackerel, tarpon and groupers.

Lure P is a Tony Accetta trolling feather, similar to the mackerel feather (lure J) but larger, and unrigged which allows the angler to use it with a wide variety of hook sizes and patterns.

The saltwater plug bait is another lure which has its origins in freshwater fishing. Some of the deadliest patterns come from Finland, where they were once hand carved for pike and trout fishing. Other extremely good patterns started life in America, again being hand carved by anglers for their own personal use.

A few modern plugs are still made of wood, but most are made from molded plastic. Floating plugs are designed to work in the surface layers, slow sinkers mainly in midwater, and fast sinkers for searching the bottom.

Plug baits range from inch-long midgets up to the 19-inch giants designed for trolling for many species of open-ocean game fish.

Plugs are often hand finished, which makes them expensive, but very cheap plugs seldom have the good, inbuilt action of a top quality lure and are best avoided.

Some models have a diving vane, or lip, which can be altered to several different positions, allowing the plug to be changed in seconds from deep diving to shallow running. Such lures can be very useful when fish come up or go down after bait fish shoals.

Like the early plugs, the original Kona Head lures were hand carved from hardwood, but they were then fitted with improvised skirts. These baits were found to be very effective for a host of game fish including blue and white marlin and tuna. So great was their popularity, a whole industry has grown up around this style of big game lure, producing hundreds of variations on the original patterns.

The modern lure has a plastic head and a brightly colored plastic skirt or skirts. Head styles include singles, double-jointed knuckled heads and triple action heads. Some are molded in a single colored plastic such as nylon, while others have translucent acrylic heads containing molded plastic eyes that move and roll as the bait trolls through the water. The heads are either dished, scooped out, drilled or fluted to add movement, vibration and overall attraction to the lure.

Most big game anglers use two skirts of different colors on each lure, and the color combinations are often intended to mimic a particular fish, for instance blue/white for bonito, silver/white for mackerel and green/yellow for dorado.

Other combinations are intended just to create a flashy bait that will trigger off the attack reaction of predatory fish. An interesting variant of this is the 'bird', a modern version of an old Japanese fish attractor called a *shiva-shava*. The bird, which has short, stiff 'wings', splashes crazily over the surface like a crippled flyingfish trying to get airborne. This is a good lure for dorado.

FRESHWATER BAIT — NATURALS

Although they're less conven-ient to use than artificial lures, natural baits have their advantages; they're usually part of the fish's natural diet, there's a wide choice, and you can get most of them for free.

The common earthworm, for instance (also called the lobworm or nightcrawler), will catch any freshwater fish from greedy little perch up to bass, barbel or salmon. You can dig them up, or simply collect them from the lawn at night, especially after prolonged rain.

Brandling worms, which are much thinner and shorter than earthworms, are usually found in manure heaps. These worms, dis-tinctly ringed with white or yellow bands, emit a smelly, yellow fluid when they're hooked which is most attractive to bottom feeding fish. Another type of worm that appeals to most fish is the redworm, a dark red, slow-moving little worm found in compost heaps.

The humble maggot, which is seldom seen in the USA except for ice fishing, is by far the most widely used freshwater bait in Britain. The larva of the bluebottle fly, it's effective for all fish both large and small, except for the pike family. Some anglers prefer maggots dyed bronze, yellow or red to the natural white ones, because in certain water conditions the fish seem to show a liking for a particular color.

Smaller maggots such as squats (housefly larvae) and pinkies (greenbottle fly larvae) are generally used as loose-feed groundbait, or chum but they can be used on the hook for smaller fish. They are particularly effective when the water's very clear and the temperature low.

To hook a maggot without breaking the skin, squeeze it gently until a little 'tab' protrudes from the blunt end, then simply nick the hook point through. Always use a hook size to match that of the maggot, and loose feed sparingly for the smaller shoaling species. Little and often is the rule to follow.

The same goes for fishing with casters, which are pupated maggots. Initially, the caster is heavy and juicy and will sink, but as the grub changes slowly into a fly it becomes ligher and so it floats. Floating casters are great for surface feeding fish such as dace, rudd, chub and even carp, while the sinkers catch good roach, bream and chub.

Slugs are excellent chub bait, as are large, juicy caterpillars and grubs, which are also very good for catching trout.

You can find many subsurface naturals in shallow water during the summer months. One of the best of these is the caddis grub, the larva of the sedge fly, which builds its protective case with tiny stones and twigs. To get it out of its case, squeeze gently at the tail end and pull it out by its head. Also very effective, especially for trout, grayling and chub, are large mayfly and stonefly nymphs and small crustaceans such as freshwater shrimp and crayfish.

Predatory species, including trout, pike and perch, all love crayfish, the freshwater answer to lobster. It can only grow by periodically shedding its shell and then growing a new one, and during its soft or 'peeler' stage it hides under large stones while its shell hardens. Use a size 4 or 6 hook, put once through the last tail segment. Crayfish are equally effective on the retrieve or drifted downstream, and although the peeler stage is preferable, small hard-shelled ones will also work.

Freshwater mussels, particu-larly the large swan mussel, are another fine natural bait. Gather them from the muddy shallows, and open the shell by cutting through the strong hinges with a thin-bladed knife. Use the orange flesh on a number 4 hook, freelined on the bottom, for catfish, carp and eels, or cut into half-inch cubes for smaller species.

Seafood naturals, like shellfish, shrimps and prawns, work superbly for freshwater species. Unpeeled shrimps and prawns, raw or boiled, will take bass, crappies, barbel, carp, tench and chub, and if peeled just about everything loves them. Large prawns are, of course, one of the deadliest of salmon baits, float fished down with the flow or worked across the current on a weighted cast.

Any small, live freshwater fish, as long as it's presented properly, will catch predators. The size of the bait fish you use should be related to the size of fish you're after: up to three inches long for trout, walleye, perch and chub, and four to six inches for larger fish such as bass, pike and catfish.

Any drifted, wobbled or static freshwater deadbait will catch predators effectively, but so too will many small sea fish. Smelt, herring, mackerel and sprat all make good deadbaits, and almost any readily-available small sea fish will catch pike. Pilchard, sardines and mullet in the five to seven inch range are all great pike baits; larger fish can be cut in half, and half baits catch just as many pike as whole baits do. What is important is that the bait lies static on the bottom, where the big old lazy pike prefer to spend much of their time.

Baby squid is another good pike bait, and the freshwater eel is even better – cut a twelve inch eel in half and use either end. Small eels, or just the tail ends, are also good for trolling and wobbling because they are tough and move in an enticing way.

Many soft-fleshed sea fish break up easily when continually cast, so for spinning or wobbling stick to small freshwater fish. Little trout are particularly tough, and can usually be bought quite cheaply from a trout farm.

Right: Some of the many natural baits used in freshwater fishing. Freelined slugs are one of the most deadly chub baits, and will also take barbel and tench, but they're nowhere near as versatile as worms, which will catch almost any freshwater species. Another bait which will take most species is the maggot, fished singly or in bunches. The caster, the pupated form of the maggot, is a useful bait for many of the smaller species of fish such as bream and roach. Shellfish, such as mussels, together with prawns and shrimps, make excellent bait, especially for the larger species, while whole or cut seafish such as mackerel and mullet are ideal baits for predators

HOOKING NATURAL BAITS

Short shank hook

Caster

MAGGOTS AND CASTERS
To hook a caster, pierce the thick end with the hook point, then push the bend and most of the shank in. A maggot should be hooked through the little tab at the blunt end, which avoids breaking the skin of the body and lets the hooked maggot wriggle.

WORMS

With a large worm the hook should pierce the body at least twice, to prevent it wriggling off. A small worm should be pushed round onto the bend and shank.

MUSSELS

To open a mussel, slide a sharp knife between the shell halves to sever the hinge. Thread the yellow flesh onto the hook shank, leaving the barb exposed.

Earthworm

Brandling worm

Crayfish

Mussel

CRAYFISH

Crayfish should be hooked through the tail, with the point pushed in from below through the second or third segment. Remove the shell if it's hard.

EELS

To hook a freshwater eel tail, pass the leader through it leaving the point and barb exposed at the cut end.

Eel tail

FRESHWATER BAIT — PROCESSED

As well as all the natural freshwater baits, there's an almost endless choice of raw or cooked baits which, although very effective, are rarely part of the fish's natural food. Bread, cheese, sweetcorn, vegetables, nuts, seeds and canned meats are just a few of the possibilities.

Bread, in one form or another, is a bait much loved by most non-predatory species, especially the cyprinids. Cubes of crust can be trotted or ledgered on the bottom for roach and bream, or floated on the surface for carp and chub, while the soft inner crumb can be squeezed onto the hook shank as 'breadflake'. Always use a fresh, doughy loaf for breadflake, or it won't stay on the hook for more than a few seconds.

Stale bread is best used in the form of a paste. Soak the crumb, then squeeze it in a piece of cloth to remove excess water and form the paste. Use it on its own, or mix it with an equal amount of grated cheese or sausage meat. Mashed sardines or fish-based cat food also make great paste ingredients, especially for catfish bait.

For convenience, a chunk of canned tuna is a bait few catfish can resist, and luncheon meat cut into half-inch cubes is one of the finest instant carp and chub baits yet discovered. Equal to canned meat in convenience, as far as carp are concerned, are small dog or cat biscuits used as a floating bait. Some of the richer, spicier biscuits can be crushed, mixed with a binder such as beaten egg, and stiffened with maize meal to form a paste.

Many grains and seeds make excellent freshwater baits. Sweetcorn is one of the most deadly of all the grain baits, especially for carp and tench. Hard maize, its elder brother, is equally good but it has to be softened before use. You can do this by soaking it in water for a few hours, then giving it about twenty minutes in a pressure cooker. It will swell to about twice its size during cooking, so leave plenty of room in the pan for expansion.

Wheat and barley are useful baits if you prepare them properly. Tip the grain into a large, lidded bucket, then pour in enough boiling water to cover it by at least three or four inches. Stir it thoroughly with a stick, put the lid on, and leave it overnight to stew and absorb the water.

In the morning, strain off any excess water, and if you're not going to use it that day, pack it in freezer bags and freeze it. Preparing enough for several fishing sessions at a time and then freezing it will save you a lot of time. You can use the same method to prepare other normally-hard baits such as seedbaits, dried peas and beans.

Stewed hempseed is the most productive of the seedbaits, because it's highly attractive to all cyprinids. Use it on the hook, or as a loose feed with a maggot, caster, elderberry or tare seed on the hook. Tare seeds are almost as good, but they lack that special aroma of stewed hempseed so they should only be used as hookbait.

Peanuts, dried peas, chickpeas and haricot beans, when softened, can be used in rivers or still water, but you usually need to prebait the swim with them for a few successive nights before fishing so that the fish can acquire a taste for them.

Other vegetable baits worth trying are potatoes and carrots. The potatoes should be part-boiled to soften them slightly, and used sliced, cubed or, if they're small enough, whole. Prebait the water with small balls of mashed potato, or make the hookbait even more attractive by dipping it in honey or molasses. Small, thin baby carrots can be used as a spinning bait instead of an artificial lure.

Macaroni and pasta shells, cooked until soft but not sloppy, will also take fish if the swim has been prebaited. They work better in rivers than in still waters, because then they twist and turn in the current and the movement attracts the attention of the fish.

A more convenient bait, which needs no preparation or prebaiting, is cheese. Cheddar cheese, or similar, works well in summer but cold winter waters can turn it rock-hard, so processed cheese spread should be used then. Cheese will take most non-predators, and even perch and pike on occasions, and in running water the scent will drift downstream and attract fish from some distance away. For this reason, strong cheeses will often be more effective than mild ones.

High protein (HP) bait mixes are now a big part of the British and European carp fishing scene. These baits are derived from refined milk products, wheatgerm, animal proteins and eggs, and sold as ready-prepared pastes or balls, or as powders to which water is added to make a paste.

Colorings and flavorings can also be added, and the bait is used either as a paste or in balls called 'boilies'. These are made by dropping small (¼ to ¾ inch) balls of the paste into boiling water for a couple of minutes. This gives them a thin, tough skin which makes it difficult for fish other than carp or tench to take them.

Sweetcorn

Cheese

High Protein (HP) baits

Peas, beans and pasta

Sweetcorn: the most convenient form is the canned, ready-cooked corn. An excellent bait for most non-predatory fish.
Cheese: like sweetcorn, cheese will take most non-predatory species, but it will also, on occasion, take pike and perch.

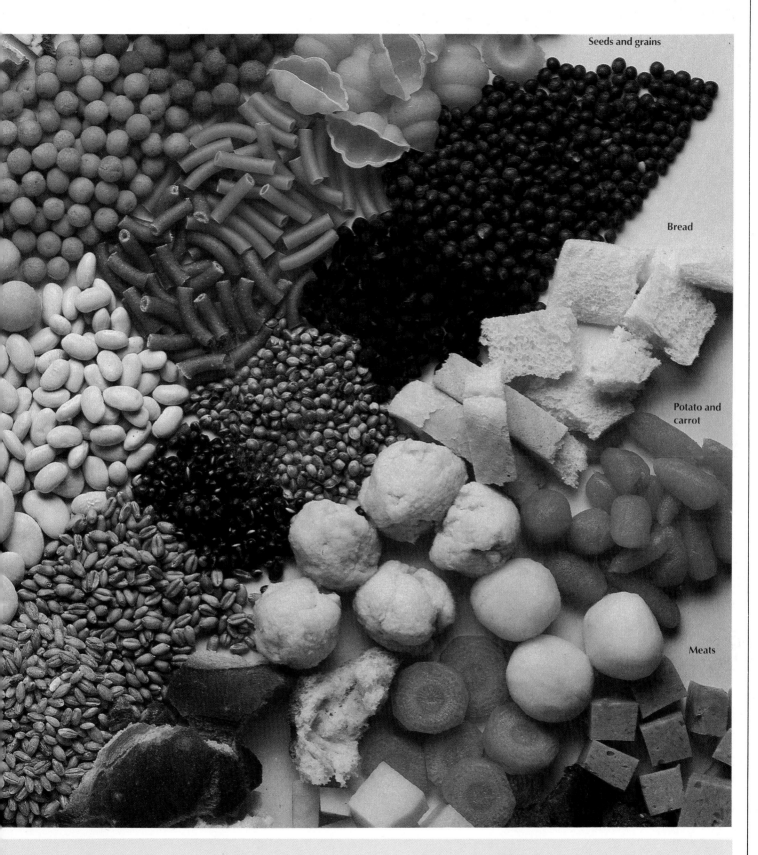

Seeds and grains

Bread

Potato and carrot

Meats

High protein (HP) baits: these baits were formulated originally for carp fishing, but by varying the ingredients they can be made attractive to most species. On waters where the fish have never seen high protein bait, it may be necessary to prebait the swim to give them a taste for it.

Peas, beans and pasta: clean and convenient, these baits will take a good variety of non-predatory fish, but prebaiting may be needed.
Seeds and grains: these must be softened before use, but not allowed to get so mushy as to be unusable. Good for most non-predators.

Bread: a cheap and versatile bait which can be prepared in a number of ways. Excellent for species such as carp, catfish, grayling, bream, chub, roach, rudd, tench and barbel. Bread paste can be made even more effective by mixing it with cheese, meat, fish or cat food.

Potato and carrot: these should be part-boiled to soften them before use. As with other vegetable baits, prebaiting is usually needed.
Meats: canned meats are effective and convenient baits for species such as carp, catfish, eels and chub and sometimes predators.

FRESHWATER GROUNDBAIT

When you're fishing for coarse fish, one way to increase your success is by the careful use of groundbait. Unlike prebaiting – where you put bait into the swim hours, or even days, before you fish, so that the fish get used to the bait or to feeding at that spot – groundbait is done while you're actually fishing.

What confuses most anglers about groundbait is whether they should use it to feed the fish or to attract them – or, indeed, whether they should use it at all. Ultimately, the decision depends on the kind of fish you're after, how numerous they are, and the type of water they're living in.

Always remember the two basic functions of groundbaiting. The first is to attract fish into the area of your hookbait (if they're not already there). The second is to keep them feeding in the area long enough to notice and take the baited hook, without feeding them so much that they ignore it.

For instance, there's no way you will keep a large shoal of bream around with just three balls of groundbait, but the same amount thrown to a small group of wily old roach in a clear little stream would ruin any chance of a bite. So think carefully before using any groundbait other than a few loose feed fragments. Whether the water is running or still, groundbait scores best where fish have to compete strongly for food.

A good basis for groundbait mixtures is stale bread. You might be able to get stale, unsold bread from a local store, but if not, save all the household bread scraps and soak them for a few hours in a bucket of water. Then drain off the water and squeeze the bread between your hands to make a mushy pulp. Mix in bran, maize meal or any other cereal meal to give it bulk and weight, plus fragments of the hookbait you're going to use (such as sweetcorn, maggots or chopped worm), and you'll have a good, heavy groundbait which will sink to the bottom of the swim before it breaks up.

If you need to throw or catapult it a long way, add two cupfuls of flaked maize or cornflakes to each half-bucket of groundbait and work it in until the mixture's stiff (add more if necessary). Then you can squeeze it into balls for throwing or catapulting. If you leave these to harden for a few hours before you use them, you'll be able to throw them much further than when they're fresh.

This basic mixture can be made even more attractive by adding flavorings and colorings. Trial and error is probably the only reliable way to find the best mixture for a particular swim or type of fish, but some additives worth considering are honey, molasses, maple syrup, fish oil and aromatic oils such as aniseed to flavor it, and food dyes to color it.

Another type of groundbait – cloudbait – can be made from breadcrumbs. This is used to attract fish in still or slow-moving waters by creating a cloud of fine particles which fish will explore, looking for something that's big enough to eat.

Cut stale bread into slices (or use stale sliced bread) and leave them to dry out, or heat them in an oven, until they're crisp. Then crush them down into fine crumbs and sieve them to remove any lumps. When you get to the water, dampen the crumbs and squeeze them into small balls. When you throw these into the swim, they'll break up as they sink and create a cloud of crumbs. You'll get an even better cloud if you mix dried milk powder in with the crumbs: a large spoonful for every two pounds of dry crumbs should be enough.

When you're ledgering, you can concentrate groundbait close to the hook by using a swimfeeder. This is a perforated plastic tube about two to three inches long and an inch in diameter, usually attached to the line about 15 inches from the hook.

The open-ended version is packed with hookbait particles and the ends are plugged with groundbait. When it hits bottom, the groundbait disintegrates and releases the hookbait particles.

The blockend feeder is closed at each end by plastic caps, one or both of which can be removed so that it can be filled with maggots. When it's on the bottom, the maggots escape through the holes in the side and attract fish to the area of the maggot hookbait.

When swimfeeders are packed with bait, they are comparatively heavy and so they can be accurately cast a considerable distance, usually much further than you could throw or catapult a ball of groundbait.

Above right *You can get good results by using a catapult to put groundbait into distant swims.*

CATAPULTS
A catapult is useful for putting groundbait, especially stiff mixes, into distant swims. When you're using one, hold it at arm's length and chest height, never near your face – then if the elastic breaks, you're less likely to get it in your eye.

SWIM FEEDERS
Open-ended swimfeeders are packed with hookbait particles and plugged with groundbait to keep them in. These three are fitted with swivels and weighted with strips of lead.

Blockend feeders are closed at each end by plastic caps, one or both of which can be removed so that the feeder can be filled. The type shown above has a removable upper cap, a nylon link to attach it to the line and a bronze weight riveted to the side of the perforated plastic tube.

This type of blockend also has a removable top cap, but the weight is fixed below it. The weights on these four are $\frac{1}{8}$, $\frac{1}{4}$, $\frac{1}{2}$ and $\frac{2}{3}$ of an ounce respectively.

SALTWATER BAIT

The choice of baits for saltwater fishing is enormous, ranging from worms up to cut or whole fish and octopus.

One of the most popular sea fishing baits is king ragworm, which is big, easy to get, and has instant fish appeal. A large king ragworm can be 15 to 20 inches long, and when broken will provide at least three good baits. King ragworm live in U-shaped tunnels and become increasingly common the closer you get to the low spring tide mark. Smaller ragworm can also be found in harbors. There are various other sorts of ragworm which can be used as bait, including one species which burrows into soft rock, and the white ragworm which is normally found sheltered away where the beach is of soft, yellow sand.

Lugworms are another common and very popular worm bait, the variety known as black lug being the best, and they can be used fresh or as a preserved and salted bait. Earthworms can make a good substitute for marine worm baits, and they're particularly good for rock fish and flounder.

Many kinds of fish eat crab, and while some will happily eat hardbacked shore crab, others prefer to take the crab when it's in the process of molting its shell. In the various stages of molting, crabs are called softbacks and peelers.

When molting, crabs are extremely vulnerable to attack from passing fish, so to avoid this danger they hide up beneath weed-fringed rocks, sea walls or other solid structures which give them shelter. Crabs that are hidden away like this are often easy to catch in quantity, and they can be kept alive in a bucket half full of seaweed, or deep-frozen for later use.

Many bottom-living fish feed on shellfish of one sort or another, one of the most popular bait types being the slipper limpet; two or three limpet bodies make one good bait. For rock fishing, the conical limpet can provide a good standby, and because of its extremely tough flesh it will stay on the hook almost indefinitely.

Edible mussels also make excellent bait, especially for flatfish and cod, but one of the finest of all shellfish baits is the razorshell. It lives in a little tunnel which it digs for itself and it's never easy to gather in quantity, but it makes a bait which few fish can resist.

Another deadly bait for most predatory sea fish is the sandeel or lance. These eels can be caught either by hand or, better still, by a specially constructed sandeel seine net. The greater lance, which may measure 12 to 15 inches long, can also be taken on feathers.

Sandeel are best used as live-bait, but unfortunately they are very difficult to keep alive, needing constant water aeration to keep them in perfect condition. Once dead, they lose much of their attraction, but they can still be useful as bottom fishing bait. Sandeel can be frozen, although when they're thawed out their flesh tends to be rather soft.

Fish such as mackerel, herring and pompano can be cut into strips or fillets for bait. The oilier the fish, the better the bait it makes. Balls of fish scraped clear of the skin can also be used for soft-mouthed fish like mullet. Any fish used as bait should be as fresh as possible, because fresh fish stays on the hook far better than stale fish.

Whole fish make an excellent bait for the larger predatory fish, and again a fresh bait will always outfish a stale one. Choice of bait is wide, but most fish have a natural preference for certain types of bait fish. Giant common skate and halibut, for example, will fall readily to a whole pollack, while conger prefer mackerel. Shark show a distinct preference for oily-fleshed fish, and bonito, Spanish mackerel and horse mackerel are the three best shark baits. Tuna take herring, mackerel and flyingfish, while billfish will take just about any food-sized fish they come across.

Livebaits seem to work better than deadbaits, except when the bait is being trolled, when a deadbait correctly mounted will catch as well as a live fish. A good trick when using dead fish for shark bait is to tip the point of the hook with a pair of pilchard or sardine, because the truly oily flesh of these fish will encourage the shark to take the whole bait.

All predatory fish will eat squid, octopus or cuttlefish. For the smaller fish these large baits can be cut into sections or strips. Californian squid is now exported to many parts of the world, and although it's intended for human consumption much of it ends up as bait. Large cod are particularly fond of it.

Large squid can be used for drift fishing for shark, or as a

Above *For both shore fishing and boat fishing, popular saltwater baits are razorshells, sandeels, marine worms such as ragworms, and squid, cuttlefish and mussels.*

deepwater bait for mighty broadbill swordfish. Cuttlefish, a near relative of the true squid, is normally used as a cut bait. Both squid and cuttlefish should be skinned before use. This skinning only takes a matter of seconds, but it definitely improves the attractiveness of the bait.

Octopus is another bait which works well in any part of the world. Most octopus are too large to be used whole, so each tentacle should be cut from the main body and chopped into bait-sized sections. You can usually get frozen octopus from Chinese supermarkets.

HOOKING SALTWATER BAITS

RAGWORMS
Ragworms and other marine worms can be used whole or cut. They should be threaded onto the bend and shank of the hook, leaving the point exposed.

MACKEREL
A piece of mackerel cut from the tail end is a good bait for smaller species. The bait is threaded onto the hook and tied to the shank near the eye.

OCTOPUS
Small pieces of octopus tentacle should be threaded onto the hook and bound to the shank near the eye to hold them firmly in position.

RAZORSHELL
Open the shell by cutting through the hinge, then remove the flesh and thread it onto the hook with the foot at the bottom, supporting the softer flesh.

SANDEEL
Sandeel can be rigged for livebait by passing the hook through the lower lip and then hooking it into the belly.

SALTWATER GROUNDBAIT

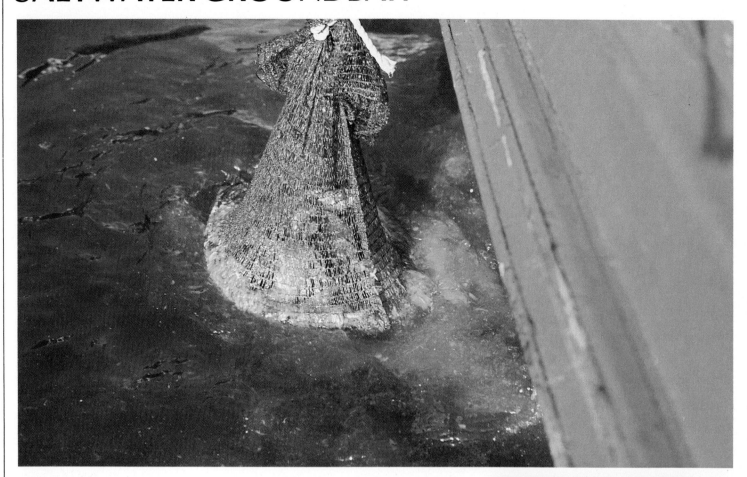

Many kinds of sea fish respond to the use of groundbait or chum, but groundbaiting methods can vary considerably from one locality to another, as much because of different local traditions as because of differences in the fish.

On rocky coastlines with deep tidal gullies, a low-tide prebaiting session can often attract a number of good fish into the gully area. The type of groundbait to use depends on the type of fish you hope to attract and catch. For instance, fish makes the best groundbait for bass or conger, but crushed crab is better for wrasses.

Place the groundbait in position when the tide is at its very lowest, stuffing mashed fish or crushed crab into every likely crevice between the low water and high water marks. If you do this correctly, the rising tide will wash out a continuous stream of bait particles that will attract the fish to the gully.

When you're bottom fishing from an anchored boat, a simple but useful method of groundbaiting is to tie a large mesh bag full of mashed fish to the anchor rope several feet above the anchor. It's important to make sure the bag isn't actually on the bottom, or it will quickly be

ripped open aand emptied by crabs. Some fish can also destroy a bait bag, small shark being particularly good at chewing through a mesh to get at the fish inside.

The beauty of this style of groundbaiting is that all the smell and the bait particles pass under the boat to wash across the area covered by the baited lines. This method is good for conger, cod, tope and many kinds of rock fish.

Another way of groundbaiting the bottom is to use a custom-built bait dropper. This consists of a square box with its front loosely hinged at the bottom. A heavy wire runs through holes in the top and bottom of the box, near the front, with its top end shaped into a hook and a lead weight fixed to the end beneath the box.

You fill the box with mashed fish, crab, and/or worm, then close the hinged front and fasten it with the hooked end of the wire. Using a rope attached to the top of the box, lower it to the bottom. As the lead touches down, the wire is pushed up through the box so that its hooked top releases the front panel, which drops open allowing the bait to spill out onto the bottom.

A very effective way of attract-

Above *Lowering a bag of chum (or 'rubby dubby') over the side of a boat to create a trail of groundbait particles that can drift miles with the tide flow. This trail attracts cruising sharks and other fish, which follow it back to the boat.*
Right *Rubby dubby is a mixture of mashed fish, bran and fish blood or fish oil.*

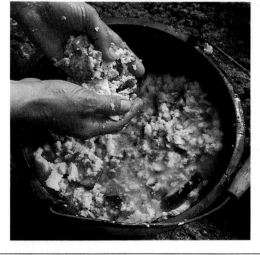

Left *Groundbait for mullet can be made from meat, meat fat, fish blood and bran, or (as shown here), from a mixture of bread and pilchard oil. As with rubby dubby, these groundbaits are usually mixed in a bucket before use.*
Right *The mixture of bread and pilchard oil is put into a mesh bag and lowered into the sea.*

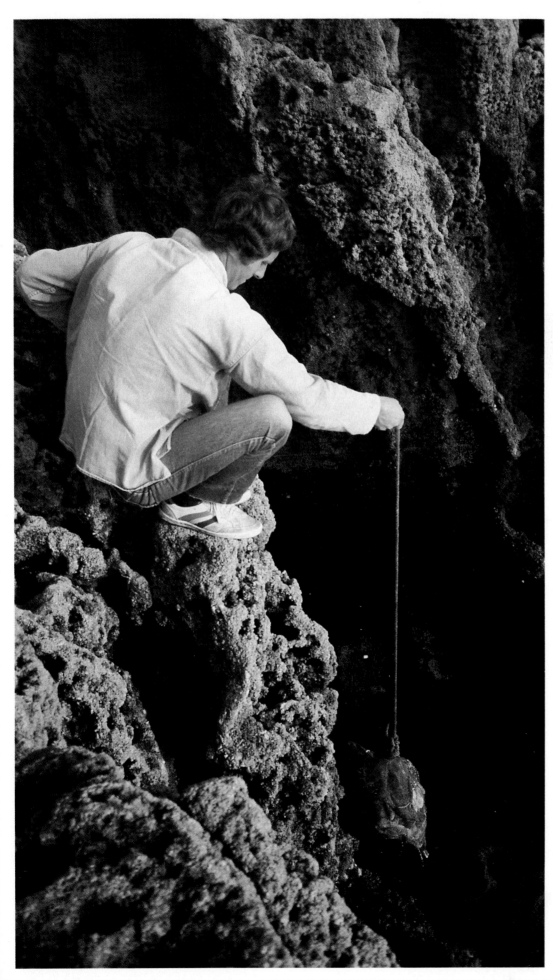

ing shark is to use rubby dubby, a noxious mixture of mashed stale fish, bran (or sawdust) and fish blood or fish oil. This mess is mixed in a bucket until it forms a thick paste, then it's put into a mesh bag or a perforated zinc container which is hung over the side of the boat so that it just touches the surface.

The natural rise and fall of the boat will continually slam the bag or container down on the surface. Each time this happens, particles of bait are released to drift away with the tide flow. Some boatmen prefer to use frozen blocks of rubby dubby, which are used in the same way but are easier to handle.

To be effective, the bag or container must be constantly replenished, but during a single day's drifting it's possible to lay a bait trail eight or ten miles long. This technique is primarily used to attract cruising shark, but it also incidentally attracts mackerel shoals and packs of surface-running bluefish.

Chumming is another method used mainly for shark fishing, although it can also be used for tuna. It can be used either as the sole method of groundbaiting or in conjunction with the rubby dubby bag. Cut fish and squid are the ingredients used in chumming, and to be effective it needs one man constantly chopping bait and dropping it into the water.

Stale mackerel, herring and horse mackerel are the main fish used for this type of groundbaiting. Each fish should be chopped into a number of small pieces so that each piece entering the water creates its own tiny scent lane.

If you're shore fishing for mullet, you can groundbait with a mixture called shirvy. This is very similar to rubby dubby in content, except that finely minced meat and meat fat is used as a substitute for the fish, and fish blood (but not fish oil) is used to blend the meat and fat with the bran.

Mullet are shoaling fish which, once attracted, will remain in an area for long periods. Experienced mullet fishermen distribute their shirvy with an old serving spoon on a little-but-often basis. Being a comparatively small fish, mullet will actually eat the meat and fat particles instead of just being attracted by the scent. If you throw in too much groundbait they will overeat and refuse the hookbait.

FISH
SPECIES

In this chapter, which gives brief descriptions of the major sporting fish of European and North American waters, the species (or groups of species) appear in alphabetical order under their most widely-used common names.

A species is an individual type or breed of fish, and in biological terms two or more closely-related species can be grouped together as a *genus*, and two or more related genuses (or genera) make up a family. The size of fish families and genera varies considerably. The wrasse family (the Labridae), for example, has some 450 members, while the bowfin, on the other hand, is the only living member of its genus, and its genus is the only one in its once-large family.

One of the most important of fish families, from an angling point of view, is the Salmonidae, which includes the salmons, trouts, chars, graylings, whitefishes and others. Within this family, the genus *Salmo*, for instance, includes the Atlantic salmon *(Salmo salar)* and the brown trout *(Salmo trutta)*, while the members of the genus *Oncorhynchus* include the chinook salmon *(Oncorhynchus tshawytscha)* and the chum salmon *(Oncorhynchus keta)*. There are also subspecies, such as the brown trout subspecies the Caspian trout *(Salmo trutta caspius)* and the Black Sea trout *(Salmo trutta labrax)*.

In freshwater, the species of interest to anglers range in size from tiny dace and bullheads to the huge catfish which, apart from the rarely-hooked sturgeon which enters rivers to breed, are the largest freshwater fish an angler is likely to encounter. In North America, the biggest catfish are the blue and the flathead, both of which attain weights of over 100 pounds. The only catfish living in British waters is the wels or Danubian catfish, an introduced species which in its native Eastern European waters can grow to several hundred pounds.

All catfish are voracious predators, but even more voracious are the members of the pike family – the pike, the muskellunge and the pickerels. Few fish, either freshwater or saltwater, have as many teeth or can move as fast over short distances as these can. Pike are, in fact, one of the few species held in high esteem by anglers on both sides of the Atlantic; the brown trout is another.

In complete contrast, members of the carp family (the Cyprinidae) are not. While cyprinids form the mainstay of British freshwater fishing, they are mostly regarded as nuisance fish in North America. For the American freshwater angler, the most highly-prized species are probably the largemouth and smallmouth basses. These are members of the freshwater sunfish family (the Centrarchidae), a group of 30 species which collectively provide the bulk of American freshwater sports fishing. In addition to the basses, the sunfishes include popular panfish species such as the pumpkinseed and the bluegill.

Although most species spend all their lives in either fresh water or salt water, some migrate from one to the other to spawn. The *anadromous* fish, such as the sea trout and most of the salmons, are born in rivers but spend most of their lives in the sea, returning to their native rivers only to spawn. *Catadromous* fish – eels, for instance – do the opposite. The young fish travel from their saltwater birthplaces to mature in fresh water, and go back to the sea to spawn.

Some other species are nominally saltwater fish, but live in inshore waters and are often found quite far up estuaries into brackish waters. Mullet and flounder are typical of the sea fish that enter brackish waters, while the tarpon and snook are more truly *euryhaline*, that is, they can tolerate waters of greatly differing salinities. Such fish are often found well inland as well as along the coast.

Among the saltwater species are fish which offer some of the best sport an angler could wish for; even small species such as the saltwater basses and breams will put up a good fight. For sheer speed, power and stamina, though, the warm water pelagic species (fish which live near the surface, as opposed to the demersal species which stay near the bottom) like swordfish, sailfish, marlin and tuna are in a league of their own. Smaller warm water species such as barracuda, wahoo, amberjack, permit, bonefish and tarpon are also amazing fighters, and there is simply no comparison with freshwater fish of similar size.

Each of the entries in this chapter on fish species includes a brief guide to the tackle, techniques and bait that you can use when fishing for that particular species. The methods given are by no means the only ones you can use, but they are well worth trying; those for saltwater fish are tinted in blue, and those for freshwater species in green.

ANATOMY

Although there are almost twenty-five thousand species of fish, they are biomorphically divided into two groups. The vast majority belong to the group known as the *bony* fish, that is, fish whose skeletons are made of bone. The others, including the sharks, rays and skates, are the *cartilaginous* fishes. These have skeletons of cartilage rather than bone.

Cartilaginous fishes also differ from most, though not all, bony fishes in that their eggs are fertilized within the bodies of the females, the eggs of most bony fishes being expressed into the water and then fertilized by milt from the males. After fertilization, the eggs of many cartilaginous species hatch within the mother and the young are born alive. Others, such as the skates, lay their fertilized eggs (each covered in a hard protective casing) to hatch in the sea.

Unlike the bony fishes, the cartilaginous fishes don't possess a gas or air bladder. This bladder allows a bony fish to control its buoyancy by regulating the amount of gas (usually oxygen, but sometimes nitrogen) in the bladder. This enables the fish to hover in the water at any depth it chooses, whereas the shark, for instance, must keep swimming or sink to the bottom.

The respiratory systems of both bony and cartilaginous fishes are similar, despite the fact that the former are equipped with gill *plates,* as opposed to the 4 to 7 gill *slits* of sharks. A fish breathes by taking water into its mouth and passing it out through its gills, extracting oxygen from the water as it moves through the gill filaments. The oxygen is absorbed into the blood vessels of the gill filaments, and carbon dioxide from the blood is released from the blood vessels into the water.

Being constantly immersed in water, fish have to be able to cope with the effects of osmosis. Osmosis is a process that occurs when a concentrated solution of salts (or sugars) is separated from a weak one (or plain water) by a thin membrane. The two solutions try to equalize their concentrations of salts; water from the weaker solution will pass through the membrane into the stronger one, which will lose salts through the membrane into the weaker one.

As a result, freshwater fish, whose bodies contain a greater concentration of salts than does the water in which they swim, have to be able to conserve their body salts and to get rid of the water which they absorb through the linings of their mouths, gills and intestines. Any body salts picked up by the absorbed water are removed by the fish's kidneys before it is excreted, and there are various glands whose function is to prevent salts being lost to the surrounding water.

Because of the absorbed water, freshwater fish don't need to drink as such, but saltwater fish do. Being surrounded by water that is saltier than they are, saltwater fish are continually losing water from their bodies – which they have to replace by drinking – and absorbing excess salt, which they have to excrete. Fish which migrate from fresh to salt water, or vice versa, are able to adapt to the changes in salinity.

The sensory systems of fish are more complex than most people realize. They are less aware of pain than are the higher vertebrates, but their senses of touch, sight, taste, smell and hearing are well developed, and in addition they have a line of sensory organs – the lateral line – along each side of the head and body. These sensory organs detect low-frequency sounds and vibrations, enabling the fish to sense movements or obstacles close to it, and they also sense changes in pressure and temperature and help the fish to maintain its balance.

Most fish swim by flexing their bodies from side to side in a wave-like motion, using their pectoral and pelvic fins as stabilizers, for braking, and for making small changes in position. Some fishes can produce enormous thrust from seemingly little actual body movement, relying instead on their powerful tails and the muscles around the tail root. Members of the tuna and marlin families, for example, have tails made of rigid bones and rays which propel their large, heavy bodies through the water at high speeds over enormous distances.

The bodies of most fish are covered with protective scales, but not all species have them. Many catfish, for instance, are completely scaleless, as is the leather carp. Usually, fish keep the same scales for life, and close examination of a scale reveals growth rings, like the annual growth rings of a tree. Should a scale be lost, a new one will grow in its place.

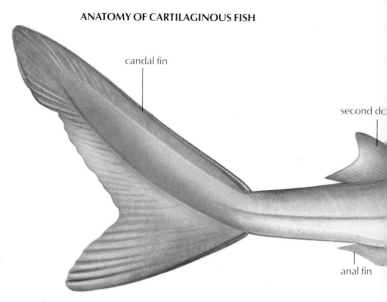

ANATOMY OF CARTILAGINOUS FISH

caudal fin

second dorsal

anal fin

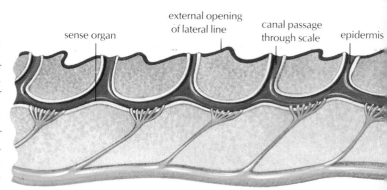

sense organ

external opening of lateral line

canal passage through scale

epidermis

CROSS-SECTION OF THE LATERAL LINE

The lateral line of a fish is a row of sensory organs on the mid side of the body and running from the gill cover to the caudal fin. These organs detect sound, vibrations and changes in temperature and pressure, and help the fish to keep its balance. This cross-section shows the sense organs and the nerves which connect them to the fish's central nervous system.

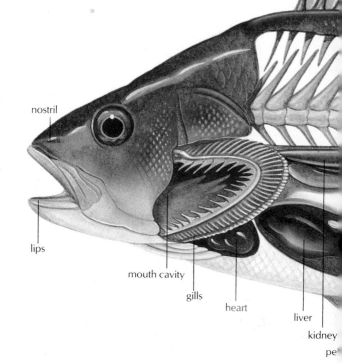

nostril

lips

mouth cavity

gills

heart

liver

kidney

pe

first dorsal fin

muscle segments

spleen

sperm duct

oesophagus

nerve cord

cartilaginous backbone

gills

kidney

testis

spiracle

nostril

pelvic fin

rectal gland

pharynx

er (male only)

anus

spiral valve

liver

heart

pancreas

intestine

stomach

pectoral fin

**SKULL OF A
BONY FISH**

supracleithrum

preoperculum

maxilary

premaxilary

dentary

articular

quadrate

interoperculum

operculum

suboperculum

nerve endings

al line nerves

first dorsal fin
with spiny rays

second dorsal fin
with soft branched rays

spine

scales

lateral line

candal fin

anus

swim bladder

gonad

vertelorae
containing nerve cord

anal fin

intestine

stomach

spleen

caeca

ANATOMY OF BONY FISH

AMBERJACKS

The amberjacks are a widely-distributed group of marine gamefish, the largest and most important of which are the greater amberjack *(Seriola dumerili)*, which is found in the Atlantic, and the similar but smaller Pacific amberjack *(S. colburni)*.

A big, powerful fish much sought after by sports fishermen, the greater amberjack can be caught in a variety of ways: trolling, freelining with live or dead fish or squid, and even on occasion by bottom fishing. Most amberjacks are hooked close to the surface, however, and only bottom-feed in really bad weather.

The greater amberjack commonly reaches weights of over 100 pounds, and it ranges from the western to the eastern Atlantic and into the Mediterranean. The lesser amberjack *(S. fasciata)* is a small and rare inhabitant of the western Atlantic.

The Pacific amberjack is found in the eastern Pacific from Ecuador up to the south of California, where its range overlaps the territory of the related California yellowtail *(S. dorsalis)*. As well as its yellow tail, this fish has yellow fins and a broad yellow band separating the bright blue/green upper body from the silvery white lower.

CALIFORNIA YELLOWTAIL *Seriola dorsalis*
The California yellowtail occurs from Baja California north to Oregon, but is commonest south of Los Angeles. It can reach 80 pounds.

PACIFIC AMBERJACK *Seriola colburni*
The range of the Pacific amberjack extends from southern California south to Ecuador.

BARBEL *Barbus barbus*

The barbel, a large European member of the carp family, is a long, wiry fish, with a body almost heart-shaped in cross-section and a decidedly flat belly which enables it to keep close to the bottom in fast water. Although occasionally found in sluggish rivers, the barbel prefers fast, clean, well-oxygenated water.

It breeds in the late spring among the weeds on gravelly shallows, and the translucent, yellowy eggs hatch in 12 to 15 days. The fry hide between the stones and in the weed, feeding at first on algae and then, as they mature, on nymphs, shrimps, snails and even tiny fish.

The adults are a greeny bronze on the back, fading downwards and along the flanks into a pale, yellowy bronze with a dull white belly and throat. The scales are small and set very close to the skin, which produces very little protective mucus.

The snout is long, with an underslung, protrusible mouth and thick, rubbery lips. Four long barbules on the upper lip are used for probing for food in the silt and gravel. The enormous mouth contains powerful pharyngeal teeth, set far back in the throat.

Barbel average 3 to 6 pounds in weight and a length of 30 inches or more, even in sluggish rivers. The maximum weight, in fast, clear rivers, is about 17 pounds.

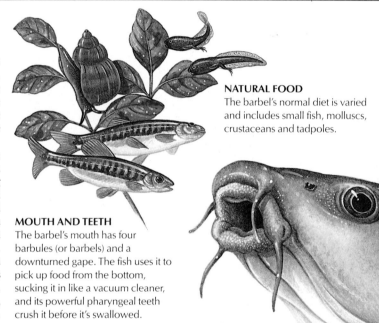

NATURAL FOOD
The barbel's normal diet is varied and includes small fish, molluscs, crustaceans and tadpoles.

MOUTH AND TEETH
The barbel's mouth has four barbules (or barbels) and a downturned gape. The fish uses it to pick up food from the bottom, sucking it in like a vacuum cleaner, and its powerful pharyngeal teeth crush it before it's swallowed.

TEETH
The barracuda's mouth is equipped with an awesome set of teeth. The large ones are used to seize and grip the prey, then the smaller, dagger-edged teeth cut it to ribbons. They will attack humans, even in shallows.

GREAT BARRACUDA *Sphyraena barracuda*
The great barracuda can weigh over 100 pounds, but most are less than 50 pounds. Small fish are found in shallow water, but larger ones prefer the depths.

TECHNIQUE	ROD	REEL	LINE	TERMINAL TACKLE	HOOK	WEIGHT	BAIT
Greater barracuda: trolling or spinning	30-pound class boat rod or heavy spinning rod	Multiplier or large fixed spool	30-pound nylon	Wire	6/0 or 8/0	Banana-shaped for trolling	Spinner, plug, dead/live fish
Pacific barracuda: trolling or spinning	12-pound class boat rod or light spinning rod	4/0 multiplier or fixed spool reel	12-pound nylon	Wire	4/0 or 6/0		Spinner, plug, dead/live fish

NATURAL FOOD
Amberjacks feed on squid and most species of small fish.

GREATER AMBERJACK *Seriola dumerili*
The largest of the amberjacks, the greater amberjack can grow to about 5 feet in length.

TECHNIQUE	ROD	REEL	LINE	TERMINAL TACKLE	HOOK	WEIGHT	BAIT
Trolling, Livebait drifting	30-pound class	4/0	30-pound nylon	Wire on nylon	Single 6/0 or 8/0		Lures, squid, live fish

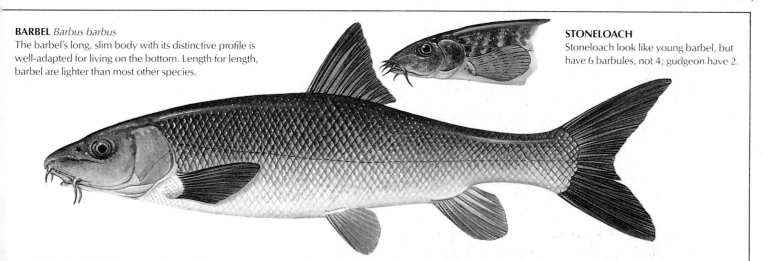

BARBEL *Barbus barbus*
The barbel's long, slim body with its distinctive profile is well-adapted for living on the bottom. Length for length, barbel are lighter than most other species.

STONELOACH
Stoneloach look like young barbel, but have 6 barbules, not 4; gudgeon have 2.

TECHNIQUE	ROD	REEL	LINE	TERMINAL TACKLE	HOOK	WEIGHT	BAIT
Ledgering downstream or across the flow, with heavy blockend swimfeeder	10-12-foot Avon action, 1¼-pound test curve with built-in quivertip	Fixed spool	5-6 pounds test, or 7-8-pounds for swims	Fixed paternoster 8-inch feeder link 12-inch hook link	Sizes 12 to 8, eyed, tied direct		Maggots, canned meat, tares

NATURAL FOOD
Barracuda feed voraciously on almost any shoaling fish, especially silvery, flashy species.

BARRACUDAS

The barracudas are fierce, sharply-toothed predators found in both Atlantic and Pacific waters. The largest member of the family is the great barracuda (*Sphyraena barracuda*), an Atlantic species whose range extends from Africa, through the Azores to the West Indies and Florida, and down to Brazil.

The guaguanche (*Sphyraena guachancho*) and the northern sennet (*Sphyraena borealis*) are two other members of the barracuda family found in the Atlantic, the guaguanche from Florida south to Brazil and the northern sennet from New England to Florida; south of Florida, the variety known as the southern sennet (*Sphyraena picudilla*) replaces the northern sennet.

The guaguanche, a little barracuda with an olive-gray back and a silver belly, averages about 20 inches in length when fully grown. Guaguanche normally form small schools and can be caught on lures, and livebait.

The northern sennet is closely related to the four barracudas found in the Pacific. The largest of these, the Pacific barracuda (*Sphyraena argentea*), occurs from Alaska down to Mexico. Of the others, the Gulf barracuda (*S. lucasana*) is found in the Gulf of California, *S. ensis* from Mexico to Panama, and *S. idiastes* from there south to Peru.

BASSES

The term 'bass' covers a number of different species of freshwater and saltwater fish. The freshwater basses include the six species and various subspecies of black bass, which are members of the sunfish family, plus the white bass and the related yellow bass. These last two are also related to the saltwater basses – the striped bass, which is also found in freshwater, the black sea bass and the European sea bass. Of the black basses, the most important are the largemouth bass *(Micropterus salmoides)* and the smallmouth bass *(M. dolomieui)*.

The largemouth bass is happiest in waters with plenty of vegetation, where it finds shelter and a good supply of the insects, crustaceans, fish, crayfish, waterdogs and even small waterfowl on which it feeds.

The largemouth differs from the other black basses in several respects, but the most reliable way of identifying it is to look for three key points. Firstly, the line of the upper jaw extends beyond the rear of the eye; secondly, the spiny part of the dorsal fin is almost separate from the soft rays; and thirdly, there are no scales on the base of the soft dorsal rays. These features are absent from the other black basses.

Largemouth bass, because of introduced stocks, are found all over the USA. The Northern largemouth, whose original range was the Great Lakes Basin and most states east of the Rockies, averages about 3 pounds and seldom tops 10 pounds, but a subspecies, the Florida largemouth *(Micropterus salmoides floridanus)*, grows to over twice these weights.

The smallmouth bass has also benefited from nationwide introduction from its original range in the Ohio River and Lake Ontario systems. Its average and maximum sizes are a pound or two higher than those of the Northern largemouth, although it's a somewhat slimmer fish.

This acrobatic bass, one of the most exciting of North American freshwater sports fish, feeds on much the same prey as the largemouth, but prefers a very different habitat. Clear waters, still or flowing, with rocky, uneven bottoms and little vegetation are where you're likely to find it. There is one subspecies, the now-rare Neosho smallmouth *(Micropterus dolomieui velox)* found in the Neosho River and other waters in Oklahoma, Missouri and Arkansas.

The other black bass species are the spotted, redeye, Suwanee and Guadalupe basses. The spotted bass *(Micropterus punctulatus)* is greenish in color, with a white belly and a row of diamond-shaped dark patches along each flank. Found mainly in the Ohio and Mississippi drainage systems, has two subspecies – the Alabama and Wichita spotted basses.

The redeye bass *(M. coosae)* is similar in coloring to the smallmouth, except for its red eyes and fins. It can reach weights of over 6 pounds but the average is less than a pound. Found in Tennessee, Alabama and Georgia, the redeye occurs in two slightly different forms, the Apalachiola River form and the Alabama River form.

The Suwanee bass *(M. notius)* of Florida also resembles the smallmouth, but has bright blue-green underparts. The Guadalupe bass *(M. treculi)* is found in Texas. This fish is similar in appearance to the spotted bass, but is smaller and has more distinct markings.

Although it has a wide distribution in North America, the white bass *(Morone chrysops)* is most popular with anglers in the southern and southwestern states of the USA. A silvery-colored fish with 8 to 10 thin, dark horizontal stripes, the white bass does attain weights of over 5 pounds, but most of those caught are only about 1½ pounds.

The smaller yellow bass *(Morone mississippiensis)*, a close relative of the white bass, has a dark olive-green back, bright yellow sides and a white belly, plus 6 or 7 dark horizontal stripes.

The striped bass *(Morone saxatilis)* is much bigger than its white and yellow cousins, often reaching a length of over 4 feet and weights of 60 pounds or more.

Unlike the striped bass, the black sea bass *(Centropristis striata)* of the northwest Atlantic never enters fresh water. Though small – averaging 14 to 18 inches and 1½ to 3 pounds – the bottom-feeding black sea bass is very popular with anglers and has tasty flesh.

The black sea bass is found inshore during the warmer months, but it moves offshore when winter comes. This pattern of behavior is shared by the European sea bass *(Dicentrarchus (Morone) labrax)*, which is found from the coasts of southern England and northern France down to the Iberian Peninsula and into the Mediterranean.

LARGEMOUTH BASS *Micropterus salmoides*
The largemouth has been introduced into waters all over the USA, and to some lakes in Britain. It can grow to over 10 pounds.

NATURAL FOODS – FRESHWATER BASSES
Freshwater basses have a varied diet which includes insect larvae, tadpoles and fish, plus crustaceans, crayfish and waterdogs, and the larger species will even take small waterfowl.

NATURAL FOOD – SEA BASSES
The sea basses and the striped bass feed on fish, crabs, shellfish, shrimps, prawns, worms and squid.

SMALLMOUTH BASS *Micropterus dolomieui*
The smallmouth bass has a bronze tint, in contrast to the green of the largemouth, and dark vertical markings.

STRIPED BASS *Morone saxatilis*
The striped bass is found in inshore waters on both coasts of North America. It also lives in brackish and fresh waters, migrating into rivers to spawn, and has been stocked in many landlocked lakes.

BLACK SEA BASS *Centropristis striata*
Black sea bass prefer habitats of reefs or rocks, and are also found around wrecks and pier supports. The sharp spines of the dorsal fin can cause painful injuries if the fish is handled carelessly.

EUROPEAN SEA BASS *Dicentrarchus labrax*
This bass reaches a maximum weight of over 20 pounds, but most of those caught are under 10 pounds.

TECHNIQUE	ROD	REEL	LINE	TERMINAL TACKLE	HOOK	WEIGHT	BAIT
Black bass: lure fishing	5½ to 7-foot snappy action bass spinning or baitcasting rod	Fixed spool or multiplier	6 to 10-pound nylon				Artificial lures
Black bass: fly rodding	7 to 9-foot fast taper bass fly rod	Single action fly reel	Floating bass bug taper, sizes 7 to 9	6 to 8-foot leader, 6 to 10 pounds			bugs, jigs, bucktails
Black bass: trolling/drifting livebaits under float rig	9 to 10-foot, stiff action 2¼-pounds test curve	Muliplier	10 to 20-pound nylon	3-foot swiveled nylon or Dacron	2/0 to 5/0	Keel weight or split shot	Minnows, shiners
European sea bass: surfcasting	11 to 12-foot light surfcaster, 1 to 3-ounce range	Fixed spool or multiplier	12 to 15-pound nylon	Running ledger or paternoster	1/0 to 4/0	1 to 3-ounce	Peeler crab, worm, squid
European sea bass: anchored	7 to 9-foot uptide rod, 12 to 20-pound class	Multiplier	12 to 15-pound nylon	Running ledger	1/0 to 3/0	24-ounce	Sandeel, worm, squid, sprats
Striped bass: surfcasting	11 to 12-foot tip-action surfcaster	Multiplier or fixed spool	20 to 25-pound nylon	3-foot nylon, running sinker above swivel	2/0 to 5/0	1 to 4-ounce	Menhaden, worm, squid
Striped bass: spinning	8 to 9-foot powerful, medium to fast action spinning rod	Fixed spool or multiplier	12 to 15-pound nylon				Plugs or spinners

BLUEFISH *Pomatomus saltatrix*

Much sought after as a sport fish, the bluefish is a hard-hitting, savage predator capable of putting up a tremendous battle when hooked on lightish tackle.

The body of the bluefish is broad but streamlined. The mouth is large with extremely sharp, triangular teeth, the lower jaw projecting pugnaciously to give the fish a hard, aggressive appearance. The fish has two dorsal fins.

The lateral line angles smoothly above the pectoral fins, and the scales are smooth and small, covering both the head and the body. The body is blue/green above, fading to silvery white on the belly, and there's a dark patch at the base of each pectoral fin.

A voracious feeder, the bluefish swims in huge schools, destroying just about anything edible in its path. Once mad on the feed, bluefish have been known to invade bathing beaches, and numerous attacks on swimmers have been recorded.

Highly migratory, bluefish have a worldwide distribution. Anglers often locate bluefish shoals by literally sniffing them out: bluefish have a distinctive, cucumberish odour which is easy to detect. Bluefish can be caught on live or deadbaits, spinners or plugs, using mashed or minced fish to induce them to feed.

NATURAL FOOD

The bluefish is a voracious predator which will take young fish of its own species but is usually found following shoals of menhaden, herring or anchovy. Bluefish eat whatever you put in front of them, including the fingers trying to unhook them. Old bluefishermen talk about their scars rather than their bait.

YOUNG FISH

Non-breeding and younger bluegill have heavier vertical bars on their flanks than do the breeding adults.

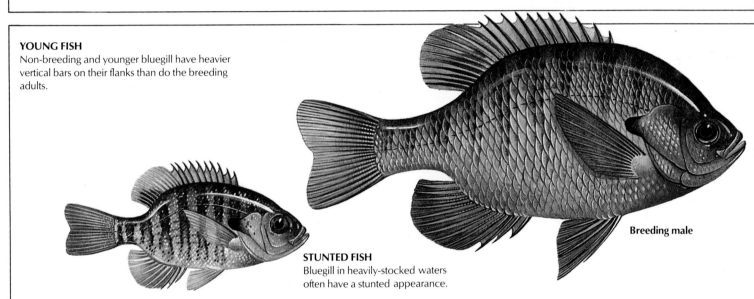

STUNTED FISH
Bluegill in heavily-stocked waters often have a stunted appearance.

Breeding male

TECHNIQUE	ROD	REEL	LINE	TERMINAL TACKLE	HOOK	WEIGHT	BAIT
Jigging or float fishing	6 to 7-foot ultralight Spinning rod	Fixed spool	3-pound nylon	With or without small float	Sizes 10 to 14		Worms, tiny baited jigs

NATURAL FOOD

The food of the bonefish consists mainly of shrimps and small crabs, plus shellfish, worms, squid, sea urchins and small fish. It often feeds tail-up, digging in the bottom with its snout.

TECHNIQUE	ROD	REEL	LINE	TERMINAL TACKLE	HOOK	WEIGHT	BAIT
Fly fishing	Fly rod	Fly reel	8-pound fly line	Nylon leader	1/0 or 2/0		Shrimp imitator
Bait fishing	Spinning rod	Fixed reel	8-pound nylon	Nylon leader	1/0 or 2/0		Shrimp

BLUEFISH *Pomatomus saltatrix*
Bluefish weighing over 50 pounds have been caught by commercial fishermen, but most rod-caught specimens are less than half that weight.

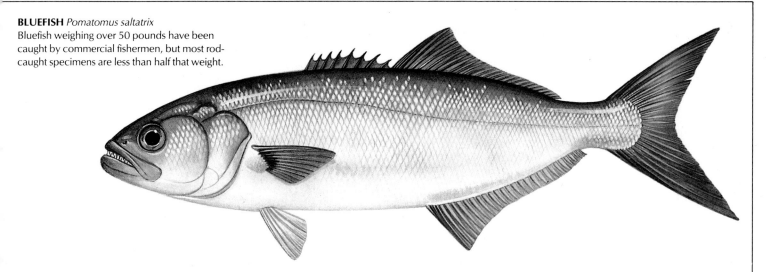

TECHNIQUE	ROD	REEL	LINE	TERMINAL TACKLE	HOOK	WEIGHT	BAIT
Trolling	20-pound class boat rod	4/0 multiplier	20-pound nylon or Dacron	Wire	4/0 to 6/0	Trolling weight	Plugs or live fish

BLUEGILL *Lepomis macrochirus*
The bluegill is an attractive little panfish which prefers waters with plenty of weed in which it can hide and feed.

NATURAL FOOD
Bluegills eat the larvae, nymphs and adult forms of aquatic insects, plus snails, crustaceans, fish fry, fish eggs and water weed.

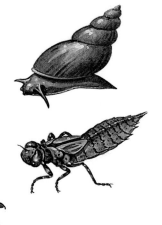

BLUEGILL *Lepomis macrochirus*

The bluegill, sometimes called the bream or brim, is one of the largest of the thirty members of the sunfish family native to North America. Highly popular with anglers, the bluegill makes excellent eating.

In coloration, the bluegill is a dusky fish with a pronounced dark flap on the tip of each gill cover, which is normally (though not always) the blueish that gives the fish its name. There's another dark spot on the rear section of the soft dorsal fin, and there are also normally seven or eight dark, vertical bars on its sides. Large specimens have a dark orange/red tint to the breast and a purplish overall cast.

These beautiful fish can reach lengths of around 14 inches and weights of 3 to 4 pounds. Mostly, though, they are between 6 and 9 inches long, and 8 to 10 ounces in weight.

The bluegill is a common and widespread fish in the USA, its distribution having been widened by its introduction into waters across the country as a food for black bass. It can also be found in southern Ontario, Canada, and along with several other sunfishes is a popular aquarium fish in Britain and Europe.

In still waters it is normally found in the deeper parts, and in streams it prefers to keep strictly to the deep pools.

BONEFISH *Albula vulpes*
The eight or nine dark bars across the back of the bonefish are prominent when the fish is young but fade as it grows older, and when it's taken out of the water. Most bonefish caught weigh between 2 and 10 pounds.

BONEFISH *Albula vulpes*

The bonefish, which is found in most tropical and subtropical seas, is essentially a shallow-water, inshore species that feeds on shrimps, prawns, crabs, clams and sea urchins.

Early in its life, the bonefish looks more like an eel than a true fish, undergoing a larval stage during which it grows to a length of about 2½ inches. Once this point is reached, the eel-like larva undergoes a reversal of growth, shrinking to half its former size. Then it begins to grow fins, and after 10 to 12 days, a tiny, true bonefish appears, a little over an inch long, which then grows and matures in the normal way.

As the name suggests, bonefish have an abundance of bones, but despite this they make excellent eating. Sometimes referred to as 'ocean dynamite', the bonefish is one of the fastest fish in the sea. This fish has a long, slender body and a prominent, overhung snout; the lower jaw is small and unobtrusive and the teeth are tiny.

Often found in small schools, bonefish can be located by looking for projecting tails or for areas of stirred-up mud. They can be caught on natural prawn or conch flesh, or on small lead-headed jigs, and they also present a great challenge to the fly fisherman. Most are caught in depths of 6 inches to 6 feet.

BONITOS

The bonitos are members of the mackerel family, the most important being the Atlantic bonito (Sarda sarda), the Pacific bonito (S. chiliensis) and the striped bonito (S. orientalis).

The Atlantic bonito has a distinctive steel blue or occasionally blue-green back, with silvery lower flanks and belly and prominent stripes running from just below the wavy lateral line back towards the dorsal fin. The body is covered in minute scales, and there are 20 to 26 large, conical teeth on each side of the lower jaw plus a few scattered teeth in the upper jaw and on the tongue.

The Atlantic bonito is found in the Mediterranean and the Black Sea, as well as in the Atlantic, and reaches weights of 12 pounds or more. The Pacific and striped bonitos are very similar in appearance to the Atlantic bonito, the main differences between the three being in the number of spines in the first dorsal fin, the number of gillrakers, and the size and weight.

The Pacific bonito, which grows to over 20 pounds, occurs from British Columbia south to Mexico, and from Peru down to Chile. The much smaller striped bonito (around 7 to 10 pounds) is found in between, from Mexico to Peru. Bonito are pelagic-feeding fish, feeding on squid and small fish taken just beneath the surface. They can be caught on live or deadbaits, or on trolled natural or artificial baits.

FEEDING COLORATION
A feeding Atlantic bonito has dark vertical bars and a yellow stripe on its back. These fade when the fish is landed or stops feeding.

NATURAL FOOD
Bonitos feed mainly on schooling fish, such as mackerel and herring, and on squid.

BOWFIN *Amia calva*

The bowfin, a voracious predator found in shallow lakes and slow-flowing rivers, is the last surviving member of a once-large family whose fossil remains have been found in Europe and North America. Today, the bowfin occurs in eastern and southern states of the USA, feeding on small fish and crayfish and growing to about 3 feet in length and 20 pounds in weight.

The overall color is a drab, mottled olive, with a noticeable dark spot high on the base of the powerful tail. In the males, this spot is ringed with orange, but in females it is either un-ringed or else absent altogether. The body is thick-set and elongated, and the head is rather squat. The mouth is large and the jaws are equipped with strong, sharp teeth, and beyond the throat is an air bladder which acts as a lung. This lung enables the bowfin to breathe air, which means that it can survive in poorly-oxygenated water.

The bowfin breeds in the spring, when one or more females spawn in a nest that a male has made by clearing a small patch from an area of thick weed. The eggs hatch in 8 to 10 days, guarded during incubation by the male. The newly-hatched larvae stay on the bottom of the nest for about 9 days, watched over by the male, until they start to swim.

TAIL SPOT
The spot on the tail of the male bowfin is clearly marked in bright orange, but that of the female is dull and indistinct.

Male   **Female**

BRONZE BREAM/ROACH HYBRID
Bronze bream/roach hybrids are usually infertile, but can grow to a good size because they don't use up protein by spawning.

YOUNG BREAM
The younger bronze bream are paler than the adults, being silvery with a pinkish hue.

NATURAL FOOD
The bronze bream feeds mainly on worms, plus other small creatures.

TECHNIQUE	ROD	REEL	LINE	TERMINAL TACKLE	HOOK	WEIGHT	BAIT
Float fishing close in or laying bait on bottom	13 to 14-foot light action match or float rod	Fixed spool		Waggler float fixed bottom end	16 to 18 or 10 to 14	Bulk BB or AA	Maggots, breadflake
Quivertip ledgering	11 to 12-foot ledger with built-in quivertip	Fixed spool		Blockend feeder	16 to 20		Maggots, casters

ATLANTIC BONITO *Sarda sarda*
The first dorsal fin of the Atlantic bonito has 20 to 23 spines, while those of the other bonitos have only 17 to 19 spines.

TECHNIQUE	ROD	REEL	LINE	TERMINAL TACKLE	HOOK	WEIGHT	BAIT
Trolling	12-pound class boat rod	2/0 multiplier	12-pound nylon		2/0		Plugs or spoons
Spinning	Light spinning rod	Fixed spool	12-pound nylon		2/0		Plugs or spoons

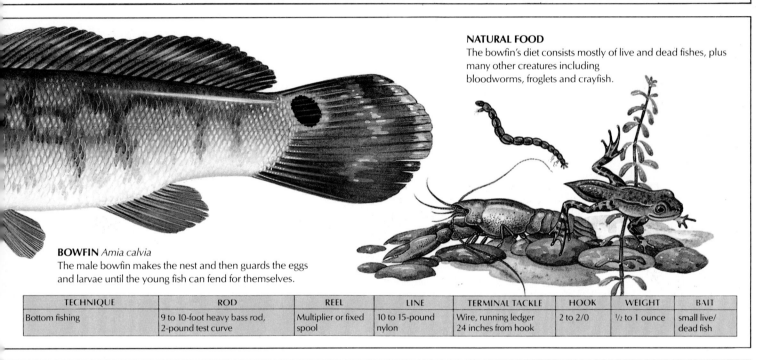

NATURAL FOOD
The bowfin's diet consists mostly of live and dead fishes, plus many other creatures including bloodworms, froglets and crayfish.

BOWFIN *Amia calvia*
The male bowfin makes the nest and then guards the eggs and larvae until the young fish can fend for themselves.

TECHNIQUE	ROD	REEL	LINE	TERMINAL TACKLE	HOOK	WEIGHT	BAIT
Bottom fishing	9 to 10-foot heavy bass rod, 2-pound test curve	Multiplier or fixed spool	10 to 15-pound nylon	Wire, running ledger 24 inches from hook	2 to 2/0	½ to 1 ounce	small live/dead fish

BREAMS

BRONZE BREAM *Abramis brama*
In crowded waters the average bream weighs about 4 pounds, but in better conditions they average 7 pounds and can reach 16 pounds.

Among the many species of bream, those of most interest to anglers are the freshwater bronze bream, the black sea bream and the red sea bream.

The bronze bream *(Abramis brama)* has the deepest and most laterally compressed body of all British and European freshwater species.

The body color varies according to the environment. In clear waters, the back is a deep bronze color, softening into golden bronze sides and a cream belly. In highly colored waters, though, the back is dark gray and the color lightens in shades of pale parchment along the sides to an off-gray belly.

The black sea bream *(Spondyliosoma cantharus)* has a deep, compressed body with long dorsal and anal fins, large eyes, and strong jaws with rows of sharp teeth. The back is dark, and there are 6 or 7 dark vertical bars along the silver-gray flanks. It prefers a rocky habitat where it feeds on fishes, worms and crabs, and it can reach over 7 pounds.

The black sea bream is common in north European waters, the Mediterranean and around the west coast of Africa, as is the red sea bream *(Pagellus bogaraveo)*. This fish is a pinky-red color with silver sides and a dark 'thumbprint' just above the gill cover. It prefers very deep water, feeding on worms, crabs, fish and squid. It can grow to over 10 pounds.

CARP *Cyprinus carpio*

The carp originated in Asia, where it was farmed for food as early as 400 BC. It slowly spread across Europe, both naturally and by introduction, and was brought to Britain in the middle of the fifteenth century. In 1876, the United States Fish Commission introduced the carp to North America. These fish, from Germany, were put into breeding ponds in Baltimore, Maryland, and for several years carp were distributed enthusiastically around the country. However, it was soon realized that the introduced carp were disrupting the natural balance of American waters and often displacing the native species, and the emphasis switched from propagation to eradication. Despite this, the carp remains well-established in the USA.

The original, fully-scaled wild carp is a slow-growing, long, wiry and incredibly strong fish which rarely exceeds a weight of 20 pounds. In general, the average weight is much less, being only 2 to 5 pounds in most environments.

From this wild carp, different strains were produced by selective breeding over the years in European countries such as Hungary, Yugoslavia, Poland and Germany, resulting in a faster-growing, deeper-bodied fish known as the king carp.

These larger, heavier carp now form the basis of carp fishing in Britain and Europe, although plenty of wild carp are still caught.

Like the wild carp, king carp breed in late spring or early summer. Each ripe female is often accompanied by several males, which chase her and sometimes even lift her out of the water in their eagerness to fertilize her eggs. The spawning can be a noisy business, with much splashing and shuddering as each group of fish crashes through weedbeds, reeds and the fibrous underwater roots of bankside trees. The eggs stick to the plants, and those which aren't eaten by small fish, or even by the carp themselves, hatch after 8 to 10 days.

King carp grow quickly, gaining 1 to 3 pounds a year to a maximum of about 10 pounds in poor environments, and 20 to 30 pounds in most rich waters if they're not overstocked. They can grow much larger than this; king carp of 50 to 70 pounds are regularly caught in France, and fish of over 50 pounds have been taken in Britain, Germany and the USA.

Crucian carp

CRUCIAN CARP *Carassius carassius*
The crucian carp is more closely related to the goldfish (*Carassius auratus*) than to the wild and king carps. The Prussian carp (*Carassius carassius gibelo*) is a subspecies of crucian.

Common carp

Wild carp

WILD CARP *Cyprinus carpio*
The wild carp is the species from which the various strains of king carp were produced by selective breeding on fish farms over hundreds of years.

MUTANT CARP
While selective breeding can and does produce good results, it can also result in mutants. In some waters, particularly lakes and canals where the genetic variety is limited, mutant carp may occur. These very deep-bodied, clumsy and somewhat grotesque fish can be almost spherical in shape.

TECHNIQUE	ROD	REEL	LINE	TERMINAL TACKLE	HOOK	WEIGHT	BAIT
Crucian carp: float fishing, lift method	12 to 13-foot light action float match rod	Centrepin, closed-face or fixed spool	1½ to 2½-pounds	Small waggler or antennae float	18 to 12	8 to BB split shot	Sweetcorn, breadflake
Common, mirror carp: float fishing, lift method	11 to 12-foot 1¼-pound test curve	Centrepin/ fixed spool	6 pounds	Waggler float, one shot 3 to 6-inches from hook	Sizes 10-8	AA to swan shot	Breadflake, sweetcorn
Freelining	10 to 12-foot 1½ to 1¾-pound test curve	Fixed spool	8-10 pound	Hook only	Sizes 8-4	None	Worms, pastes
Float fishing for surface feeding carp	11 to 12-foot 1 to 1½-pound. test curve	Fixed spool	6 to 8-pounds well greased	self cocking controller float	Sizes 12-8	None	Breadcrust
Sliding link ledgering	11 to 12-foot 1½ to 2¼-pound test curve	Fixed spool	8 to 11-pounds	12 inch hook link with 1-inch fine Dacron hair tied to hook	Sizes 10-6	½ to 1½-ounce bombs	Boiled baits
Shock or bolt ledger rig	11 to 12-foot 1¾ to 2¼-pounds test curve	Fixed spool	11 to 12-pounds	Fixed or running bomb	Sizes 8-6	1½ to 2½-ounce bombs	Boiled baits

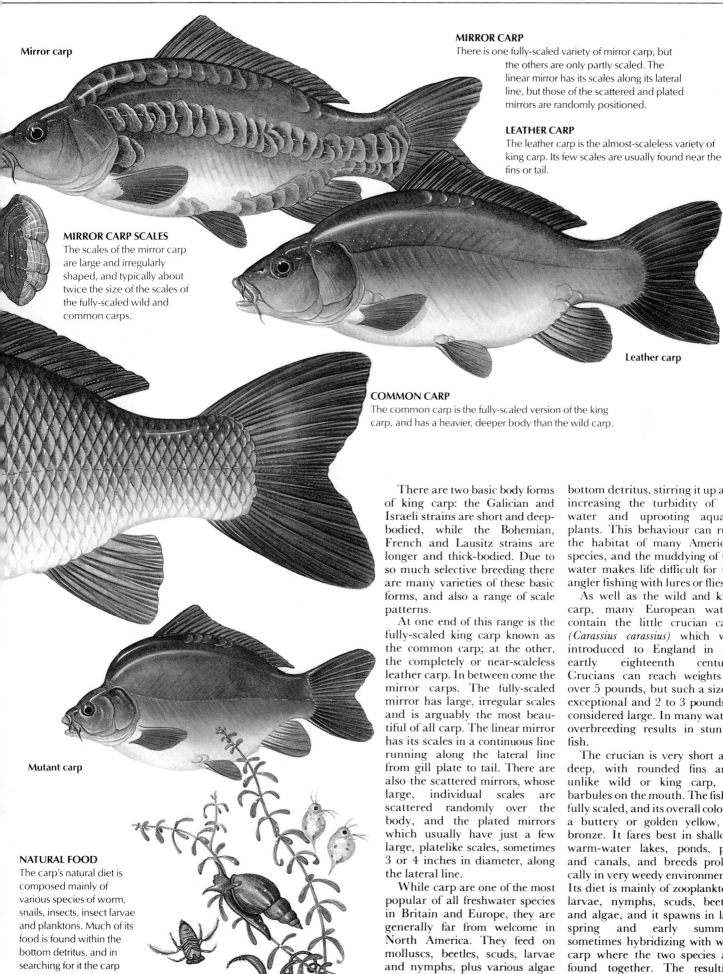

Mirror carp

MIRROR CARP SCALES
The scales of the mirror carp are large and irregularly shaped, and typically about twice the size of the scales of the fully-scaled wild and common carps.

MIRROR CARP
There is one fully-scaled variety of mirror carp, but the others are only partly scaled. The linear mirror has its scales along its lateral line, but those of the scattered and plated mirrors are randomly positioned.

LEATHER CARP
The leather carp is the almost-scaleless variety of king carp. Its few scales are usually found near the fins or tail.

Leather carp

COMMON CARP
The common carp is the fully-scaled version of the king carp, and has a heavier, deeper body than the wild carp.

Mutant carp

NATURAL FOOD
The carp's natural diet is composed mainly of various species of worm, snails, insects, insect larvae and planktons. Much of its food is found within the bottom detritus, and in searching for it the carp can muddy the water and uproot many types of aquatic plants.

There are two basic body forms of king carp: the Galician and Israeli strains are short and deep-bodied, while the Bohemian, French and Lausitz strains are longer and thick-bodied. Due to so much selective breeding there are many varieties of these basic forms, and also a range of scale patterns.

At one end of this range is the fully-scaled king carp known as the common carp; at the other, the completely or near-scaleless leather carp. In between come the mirror carps. The fully-scaled mirror has large, irregular scales and is arguably the most beautiful of all carp. The linear mirror has its scales in a continuous line running along the lateral line from gill plate to tail. There are also the scattered mirrors, whose large, individual scales are scattered randomly over the body, and the plated mirrors which usually have just a few large, platelike scales, sometimes 3 or 4 inches in diameter, along the lateral line.

While carp are one of the most popular of all freshwater species in Britain and Europe, they are generally far from welcome in North America. They feed on molluscs, beetles, scuds, larvae and nymphs, plus various algae found within the bottom silt or mud. When they're feeding, they often rummage through the bottom detritus, stirring it up and increasing the turbidity of the water and uprooting aquatic plants. This behaviour can ruin the habitat of many American species, and the muddying of the water makes life difficult for the angler fishing with lures or flies.

As well as the wild and king carp, many European waters contain the little crucian carp (*Carassius carassius*) which was introduced to England in the early eighteenth century. Crucians can reach weights of over 5 pounds, but such a size is exceptional and 2 to 3 pounds is considered large. In many waters overbreeding results in stunted fish.

The crucian is very short and deep, with rounded fins and, unlike wild or king carp, no barbules on the mouth. The fish is fully scaled, and its overall color is a buttery or golden yellow, or bronze. It fares best in shallow, warm-water lakes, ponds, pits and canals, and breeds prolifically in very weedy environments. Its diet is mainly of zooplankton, larvae, nymphs, scuds, beetles and algae, and it spawns in late spring and early summer, sometimes hybridizing with wild carp where the two species are found together. The resulting hybrids are not so golden in color as the crucian, nor so deep in the body, and have tiny barbules.

CATFISH AND BULLHEADS

There are at least 15 families of catfish around the world, both freshwater and sea, characterized by numerous barbules around the mouth and an absence of scales.

The largest is the wels or Danubian catfish (Siluris glanis), native to the rivers of central and eastern Europe. The wels is the only catfish found in British waters, having been introduced over 100 years ago. It still has limited distribution, confined mainly to lakes and pits in Bedfordshire and Buckinghamshire, although it is spreading slowly to other parts.

The wels has a long, tapered body with a tiny, stunted tail and a huge, flattened head. The large, wide mouth has rubbery lips and many little teeth, with two long barbules on the upper lip and four smaller ones below the chin.

It feeds mainly on fish, but will eat almost anything, including frogs, rats and water birds. It usually feeds at night, but will occasionally go on a daylight feeding binge during hot or thundery weather. The British record is a little over 40 pounds, but in Europe 100 and 200 pound wels are quite common. In the large rivers of the USSR, such as the Dneiper, it can reach over 650 pounds and a length of 16 feet; such fish are probably around a hundred years old.

The largest North American catfish is the blue catfish (Ictalurus furcatus), which can grow to over 100 pounds although 20 to 50 pounds is more typical. The blue catfish is silvery blue on the back, lightening down the sides to a silver or white belly. The tail is forked, and like all North American catfish the blue has two short barbules on the top of the snout, two large ones extending back from the jaw hinges and four more slender ones below the chin.

The fish thrives in large, clear fast-flowing rivers, where it feeds on fish and crayfish, and is widely distributed through the midwest and south of the USA and in Mexico.

The channel catfish (Ictalurus punctatus) is reared commercially for its fine-tasting flesh, and also offers good sport for the angler. Found in large, clean lakes and rivers from the Great Lakes south to the Gulf of Mexico, the channel cat migrates to small streams to spawn. The younger fish have a relatively slender body, with a silvery blue or olive back, paler flanks and a silver-white belly, and varying numbers of black spots. Older fish are thicker in the body and much darker in color. The channel catfish can grow to 60 pounds, but most rod-caught fish are less than 15 pounds.

The flathead catfish (Pylodictis olivaris) is a large, mottled brown fish with a noticeably flattened head, which lives in the larger rivers of the Mississippi Valley. It feeds mainly on fish, and although its maximum weight is about 100 pounds, most of those caught weigh only a few pounds.

The flathead catfish is popular for its tasty flesh, as is the little white catfish (Ictalurus catus) found in the coastal streams of the eastern and southern USA, and in western waters where it has been widely introduced. It grows to about 3 pounds, and its color varies from a pale, silvery blue to a silvery beige or white, with a white belly.

The most important of the American saltwater catfishes are the sea catfish (Arius felis) and the gafftopsail catfish (Bagre marinus). These are found from Cape Cod to the Gulf of Mexico, and there are several closely-related species in Pacific waters. The sea catfish has a maximum weight of about 3 pounds, around half that of the gafftopsail.

The bullheads are a group of small freshwater catfish which grow to weights of 1 to 3 pounds and are often caught for the pan. The brown bullhead (Ictalurus nebulosus) is a sleek, mottled brown fish found from the Great Lakes south to Florida and west to Mexico, living in weedy lakes and slow-flowing streams.

The black bullhead (Ictalurus melas) is green to black on the back, with paler sides and a white or yellow belly. Originally found from North Dakota south to Texas, and from there north east to New York, it has been introduced to many other parts of the country, and to some European waters where it has often multiplied to almost plague proportions, especially in France.

The natural range of the yellow bullhead (Ictalurus natalis) is from North Dakota to New York and Florida. This mottled yellow catfish prefers sluggish streams, ponds and lake shallows with muddy bottoms, and is often confused with the flat bullhead (Ictalurus platycephalus). This fish, which occurs in the south eastern states, is best distinguished from the yellow bullhead by its flattened head, and a dark patch on the lower part of the dorsal fin.

CHANNEL CATFISH Ictalurus punctatus
The channel catfish is the only spotted North American catfish which also has a deeply-forked tail.

BROWN BULLHEAD Ictalurus nebulosus
A very popular panfish, the brown bullhead is a small catfish which grows to about 16 inches long.

NATURAL FOOD
Small freshwater catfish live on insects, larvae, molluscs and small fish, but the larger ones feed on any species of live or dead fish as well as seemingly unlikely prey such as ducklings.

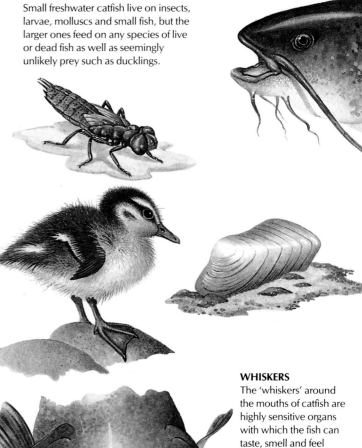

WHISKERS
The 'whiskers' around the mouths of catfish are highly sensitive organs with which the fish can taste, smell and feel when they're searching for food. The wels and the sea catfish have 6 whiskers, the gafftopsail 4, and the North American freshwater catfishes have 8.

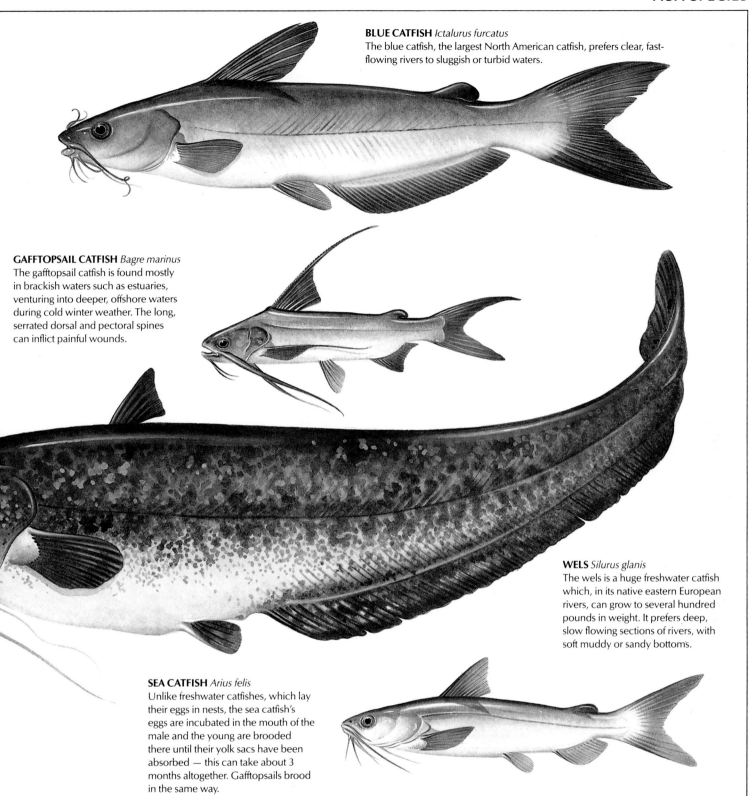

BLUE CATFISH *Ictalurus furcatus*
The blue catfish, the largest North American catfish, prefers clear, fast-flowing rivers to sluggish or turbid waters.

GAFFTOPSAIL CATFISH *Bagre marinus*
The gafftopsail catfish is found mostly in brackish waters such as estuaries, venturing into deeper, offshore waters during cold winter weather. The long, serrated dorsal and pectoral spines can inflict painful wounds.

WELS *Silurus glanis*
The wels is a huge freshwater catfish which, in its native eastern European rivers, can grow to several hundred pounds in weight. It prefers deep, slow flowing sections of rivers, with soft muddy or sandy bottoms.

SEA CATFISH *Arius felis*
Unlike freshwater catfishes, which lay their eggs in nests, the sea catfish's eggs are incubated in the mouth of the male and the young are brooded there until their yolk sacs have been absorbed — this can take about 3 months altogether. Gafftopsails brood in the same way.

TECHNIQUE	ROD	REEL	LINE	TERMINAL TACKLE	HOOK	WEIGHT	BAIT
Wels: freeline short to medium range	10 to 12-foot powerful all through action, 2 to 2½-pounds test curve	Fixed spool	11 to 15-pounds	Hook only on 24-inch 15 to 20-pound Dacron swiveled hook length	Sizes 4 to 2/0	None	Worms mussels
Ledgering, distance casting	11 to 12-foot powerful all-through action, 2 to 2½-pound test curve	Fixed spool	11 to 15-pounds	Dacron hook length, with running bomb, stopped by bead and swivel	Sizes 4-2/0	1-ounce bomb	Live baits, squid
Ledgering, running bomb	9 to 10-foot heavy bass rod 1 pound test curve	Fixed spool	6 to 12-pounds	2-foot hook length with bead and swivel	Sizes 6-1/0	½ to 2-ounce bombs	Worms deadbaits
Float ledgering	9 to 10-foot bass rod or long pole	Fixed spool	6 to 8-pounds	Hook tied direct with shots 12-inches above	Sizes 6-2	Split shot	Worms, grubs

CHAR *Salvelinus alpinus*

The char, or Arctic char, is widely distributed in the cold waters of the high latitudes of the Northern Hemisphere. In its migratory form, it's found in Alaska, northern Canada, Greenland, Iceland, northern Norway and the north of Siberia. The non-migratory, lake-dwelling form occurs further south, in Britain, Ireland, France, Germany, Scandinavia and the USSR.

Migratory char are mostly silver when they're at sea, with a steely blue-green back, pale pink spots on the sides and a pale orange-red tinge to the belly. When the fish enters the rivers to spawn the colors deepen, giving the fish a predominantly orange or red appearance. The non-migratory char are greeny-brown with an orange-red belly and reddish and white spots on the sides.

The non-migratory char spawn in late winter or early spring, just about the time when migratory char are leaving the fresh water for the sea. These fish spend the summer in the sea, returning to spawn in late summer.

A close relative of the Arctic char, the Dolly Varden or bulltrout *(Salvelinus malma)*, is found in the rivers and lakes of lands bordering the northern rim of the Pacific, from northern California round to Korea and Japan.

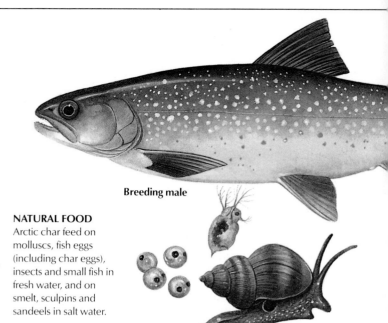

Breeding male

NATURAL FOOD
Arctic char feed on molluscs, fish eggs (including char eggs), insects and small fish in fresh water, and on smelt, sculpins and sandeels in salt water.

CHUB *Leuciscus cephalus*

The European chub is primarily a river fish, although it has been successfully introduced into many still waters. It prefers a secluded river habitat, either between beds of thick weed or close in to the bank where the branches of willows and alder trees provide shelter.

The chub has a thick-set body, rounded yet streamlined, with a wide, blunt head and enormous mouth. The jaws are toothless, but the pharyngeal teeth are strong and sharp. The coloration along the back is slate gray to bronze, quickly lightening to pale gold on the large, even-patterned scales along the sides. The belly is a creamy white, and the pelvic and anal fins are tinted orange-red while the dorsal fin and the forked tail are steel grey.

Chub are found in most English river systems, some of the southern Scottish rivers, and much of Europe. Spawning takes place in late spring, when chub gather on fast, gravelly shallows to lay their eggs on streamer weed and the fibrous underwater roots of bankside trees.

Immature chub form scavenging shoals, often with other species such as dace or roach. The shoals break up when the fish mature, and the older chub lead more solitary lives. However, because of this mixed shoaling, hybridization is quite common.

NATURAL FOOD
Chub are ominvorous, but particularly enjoy caddis larvae and small fishes.

MOUTH
The chub has a very large mouth and will gulp down almost anything that comes its way. Chub often wait under overhanging trees for falling berries and insects.

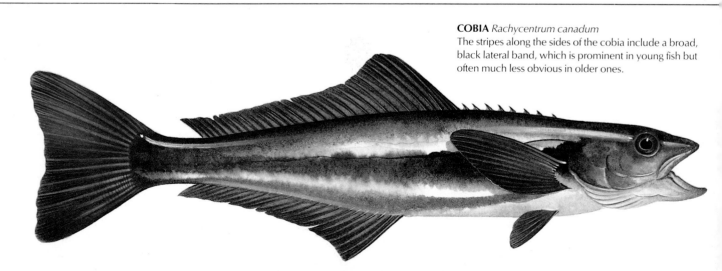

COBIA *Rachycentrum canadum*
The stripes along the sides of the cobia include a broad, black lateral band, which is prominent in young fish but often much less obvious in older ones.

TECHNIQUE	ROD	REEL	LINE	TERMINAL TACKLE	HOOK	WEIGHT	BAIT
Livebaiting Light bottom fishing	Heavy duty spinning rod	Multiplier	20-pound nylon	Fine line light ledger	Sizes 2/0-4/0	Pear or bomb	Live fish, crab/prawn

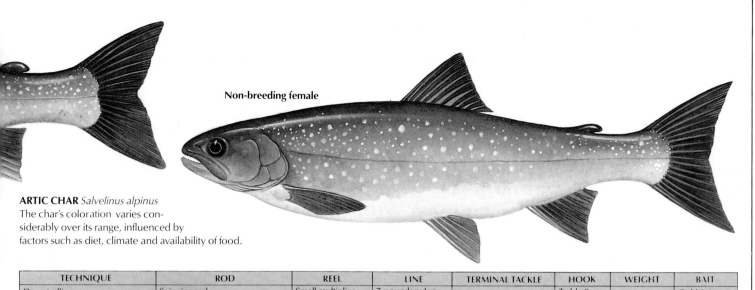

Non-breeding female

ARTIC CHAR *Salvelinus alpinus*
The char's coloration varies considerably over its range, influenced by factors such as diet, climate and availability of food.

TECHNIQUE	ROD	REEL	LINE	TERMINAL TACKLE	HOOK	WEIGHT	BAIT
Deep trolling	Spinning rod	Small multiplier	7-pounds nylon		Treble 8		Gold Spinner
Bait fishing	Spinning rod	Fixed spool	4-pounds		Treble 6	Bomb lead	Worms

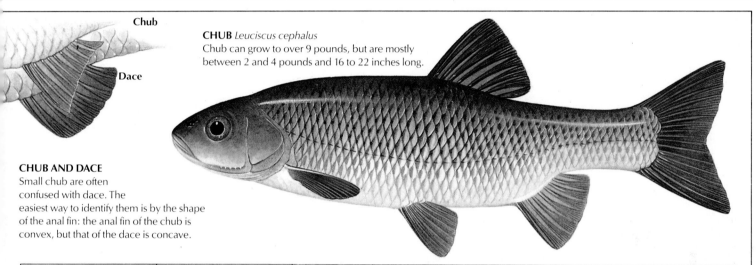

Chub

Dace

CHUB *Leuciscus cephalus*
Chub can grow to over 9 pounds, but are mostly between 2 and 4 pounds and 16 to 22 inches long.

CHUB AND DACE
Small chub are often confused with dace. The easiest way to identify them is by the shape of the anal fin: the anal fin of the chub is convex, but that of the dace is concave.

TECHNIQUE	ROD	REEL	LINE	TERMINAL TACKLE	HOOK	WEIGHT	BAIT
Ledgering	11 to 12-foot ledger rod with built-in quivertip	Fixed spool	4 to 5-pound	Fixed paternoster ledger or blockend feeder rig	Sizes 8-16	¼-¾-ounce bomb or swan shot link	Casters, maggots, cheesepaste
Long trotting in rivers	12 or 13-foot match, float rod	Fixed spool	2 to 2½-pounds	Waggler float rig	Sizes 14-20		Maggots

NATURAL FOOD
The cobia's varied diet includes most kinds of small fish, but it's especially fond of squid and crabs.

COBIA AND SHARKS
The cobia is not closely related to any other species, but its shape is similar to that of the sharksuckers (remoras) and it often swims alongside sharks such as this whale shark.

COBIA *Rachycentrum canadum*

The cobia is a large, strong predatory fish which is found worldwide in warm and tropical waters. The body is elongated, and tapers from the middle to the strong, broad, rather flattened head and to the large, crescent-shaped tail. Along the back, 8 to 10 short dorsal spines precede a dorsal fin with one spine and 28 to 33 soft rays. Both the dorsal fin and the anal fin, which has one spine and 23 to 26 soft rays, are very long and noticeably peaked at the front end.

The cobia is distinctively colored, with a chocolate-brown back and paler sides which carry horizontal stripes of brown and silver or bronze and white. The belly is yellowish-white.

The overall shape is not unlike that of the remora, and like the remora the cobia is often found in the company of cruising sharks. Cobia usually inhabit shallow, continental-shelf waters and are attracted to buoys, floating wreckage and other flotsam.

In really shallow waters, small schools of cobia often follow rays, picking up crabs and other crustaceans stirred out of the mud by the passing ray. In Australia, the cobia is nicknamed 'crabeater' because of its fondness for crab meat. Cobia can reach weights of over 100 pounds, but 30 to 50 pounds is more common. They can be caught by bottom fishing.

CODS

The many species of the large cod family live mainly in the temperate and arctic waters of the Atlantic and Pacific Oceans. Many of them, such as the Atlantic cod (*Gadus morhua*), are of considerable commercial importance as well as being of interest to anglers.

The Atlantic cod is a large, heavy fish with a single chin barbel, receding lower jaw, squared tail and arched lateral line. Like many other members of its family, it has three separate dorsal fins and two separate anal fins, and the tips of all these fins are rounded. The Pacific cod (*Gadus macrocephalus*) is very similar, but smaller and with pointed rather than rounded fins.

Cod are bottom feeders which show a liking for rough ground composed of sand and exposed rocks, and they also frequent wrecks. They feed on fish, squid, crabs, starfish and marine worms. The pollack (*Pollachius pollachius*), haddock (*Melanogrammus aeglefinus*) and pollack or coalfish (*Pollachius virens*) are all Atlantic members of the cod family. The burbot (*Lota lota*) is an unusual codfish in that it lives in fresh water. The cod family also includes the little Atlantic and Pacific tomcods (*Microgadus tomcod* and *M. proximus*), but the hakes are now usually classified as a separate family, the Merlucciidae. These include the Atlantic or silver hake (*Merluccius bilinearis*) and the Pacific hake.

BURBOT *Lota lota*
Thought to be extinct in Britain but fortunately still widespread in northern Europe and North America, the burbot is the only freshwater cod species.

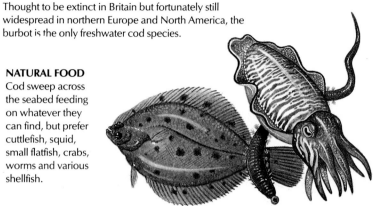

NATURAL FOOD
Cod sweep across the seabed feeding on whatever they can find, but prefer cuttlefish, squid, small flatfish, crabs, worms and various shellfish.

CONGER EEL *Conger oceanicus*
The conger eel has a rounded, cylindrical body which is smooth, scaleless and slimy. The gill slits are large, and the jaws have strong, very sharp teeth.

TECHNIQUE	ROD	REEL	LINE	TERMINAL TACKLE	HOOK	WEIGHT	BAIT
Rock fishing	Heavy-duty surfcaster	4/0 multiplier	30 to 35-pounds	Running ledger wire	Size 6/0	Pear/pyramid	Fish, squid
Boat fishing	50-pound class boat rod	8/0 multiplier	50 to 60-pounds	Heavy nylon	Sizes 8/0	Pear/pyramid	Cuttlefish

NATURAL FOOD
Young crappies eat zooplankton and insect larvae; adults also take crustaceans and fish such as threadfin shad.

BLACK CRAPPIE *Pomoxis nigromaculatus*
Although the black crappie can grow to more than 3 pounds, it averages 12 to 24 ounces.

TECHNIQUE	ROD	REEL	LINE	TERMINAL TACKLE	HOOK	WEIGHT	BAIT
Jigging	6 to 7-foot light tip action spinning rod	Fixed spool	4 to 5-pounds				Lead headed grub tails, marabou jigs
Dabbling from a boat	10 to 14-foot cane pole	None. Line tied to end of pole	6 to 15-pounds	Small float. Make hook knot so jig hangs level			

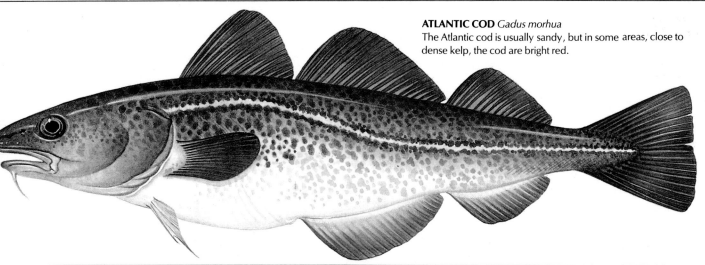

ATLANTIC COD *Gadus morhua*
The Atlantic cod is usually sandy, but in some areas, close to dense kelp, the cod are bright red.

TECHNIQUE	ROD	REEL	LINE	TERMINAL TACKLE	HOOK	WEIGHT	BAIT
Bait fishing (boat), jigging, feathering, surfcasting	30-pound class boat rod or 12-foot surfcaster	4/0-6/0 multiplier, or beach size multiplier	30-pound wire or nylon	Heavy nylon/wire tackle/running ledger	Sizes 2/0-8/0	Bomb-shaped or grip lead	Squid, cuttle fish, feathers

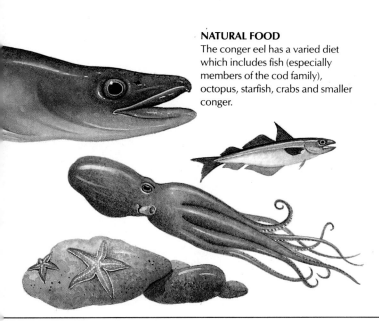

NATURAL FOOD
The conger eel has a varied diet which includes fish (especially members of the cod family), octopus, starfish, crabs and smaller conger.

CONGER EEL *Conger oceanicus*

Eight distinct species of conger are found in the Atlantic, but *Conger oceanicus* is the largest and commonest of the tribe. The biggest on record is a 250-pound monster caught by a commercial fishing boat; numerous other conger up to and over 150 pounds have been recorded.

The color of the conger eel depends on the type of bottom it inhabits; on rocks, the back is charcoal gray and the underparts are pale, but over sand the back is a light gray-brown. The margins of the dorsal and anal fins are black.

The conger is a bottom feeder more than capable of catching live food. Crabs, squid, fish and smaller congers are all eaten avidly. In shallow waters the conger are mostly nocturnal feeders, but in depths of more than 60 feet they feed at any time.

Conger migrate to the sub-tropical Atlantic to breed, spawning at depths of 10,000 to 12,000 feet. The larvae are transparent and flattened, and drift at the surface for up to 2 years before reaching the shoreline. When they do, they change shape to become cylindrical; at this stage they are still transparent, and about 3 inches long. The full coloring doesn't appear until the eel is about 12 inches long.

WHITE CRAPPIE *(Pomoxis annularis)*
The white crappie can grow larger than the black and is paler overall, but it's sometimes difficult to distinguish between the two. The most accurate way is to count the spines on the dorsal fin: the black has 7 or 8, the white only 6.

CRAPPIES

The black crappie *(Pomoxis nigromaculatus)* and the white crappie *(P. annularis)* are two of the most popular North American panfish. Members of the sunfish family, the crappies are widely distributed in ponds, lakes and rivers, and the black crappie is even found in brackish water.

The black crappie has a deep, compressed body with silvery sides marked in dark blotches that form short, irregular horizontal lines. It has 6 spines at the front of the anal fin and 7 or 8 on the dorsal; the white crappie has 6 spines on each of these fins, and counting the spines is the most accurate way of telling the black crappie from the white.

The black crappie prefers rivers, lakes and reservoirs with clear water and rich vegetation, where it feeds on aquatic insects, crustaceans and small fish. It breeds in late spring.

The white crappie is lighter in overall color than the black, with dusky vertical bars along the flanks, and the body is more elongated. It also grows larger than the black, but although weights of over 5 pounds have been recorded the average is about 16 to 24 ounces.

White crappies will tolerate more turbid water than the black will, and are usually grouped in larger concentrations. They are often found in deep water, although not on the bottom, or lurking among brush piles, reedbeds or sunken tree stumps.

DACE *Leuciscus leuciscus*

The European dace is the smallest freshwater species to be taken seriously by British and European anglers. The maximum weight is under 1½ pounds, and a fish of 10 to 12 ounces and 11 inches long is a good specimen. Yet this diminutive shoal fish, which inhabits the well-oxygenated water of streams and rivers, remains popular with anglers because it can be readily caught on light float tackle.

The dace is a slim fish, almost round in cross-section, with a small, neat mouth and head. The color is olive-gray along the back, lightening quickly to bright silver along the flanks and a white belly. The dorsal fin and tail are light grey, while the pectoral, anal and pelvic fins are usually tinted a warm pink. The anal fin is concave, unlike that of the chub (which is often mistaken for dace) which is convex, and the dace has a smaller mouth than the chub.

The dace is found throughout England and Wales, but not in Scotland and in only a few rivers in Ireland. It's also widespread in continental Europe and in Asia. It feeds on all the smaller crustaceans, plus the nymphs of most aquatic flies, caddis in particular. Often in spring and summer, dace can be seen rising freely to emerging flies, and taking the nymphs just below the surface.

DACE/CHUB
Though similar, the chub has a wider head and larger mouth. The dorsal and anal fins of the chub are convex, while those of the dace are concave, and chub has a less deeply forked tail.

DORADO *Coryphaena hippurus*

The dorado or dolphin is without question one of the most beautiful of all marine game fish. In the water, the color of the dorado is iridescent blue-green on the back, with sides of speckled, burnished gold and silver-white underparts. Once out of the water, the color fluctuates between blue, green and yellow, and when the fish dies it fades to gray, or at best golden gray.

The foreheads of large males are almost vertical, whereas those of the females are more rounded. There is just one dorsal fin, which rises steeply from its origin just above the eyes and then tapers down to the root of the tail, and has between 55 and 66 soft rays.

The anal fin, with 25 to 31 soft rays, starts midway along the belly and also tapers away towards the tail.

Dolphin are distributed worldwide in tropical and warm seas, feeding on flyingfish and squid. They reach weights of over 80 pounds, but most of those caught are only 5 to 15 pounds. They are a popular light-tackle fish, and can be taken on trolled naturals and lures or on spinning tackle.

The pompano dolphin (*C. equiselis*) is often confused with the dorado, but it can be identified by its dorsal fin, which starts further back, and its anal fin, which doesn't have an extended anterior lobe or such a concave outline.

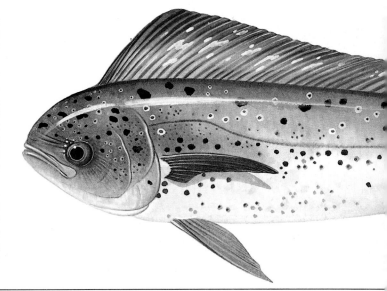

DRUMS

The drums, or croakers, are a large family of American fish which consists of over thirty saltwater species and one freshwater. They get their name from the drumming sound which the males make by rapidly contracting a special muscle connected to the swim bladder.

The red drum (*Sciaenops ocellata*) is a great favorite with shore and small boat anglers along the Atlantic coast. This copper-colored fish, which has a large black spot on the base of its tail, can weigh over 80 pounds, but most are in the 15 to 40-pound range.

The black drum (*Pogonias cromis*) is found in the same waters as the red, but is generally heavier with a deeper body and a dark brassy-brown color. It lacks the black tail spot of the red drum, and unlike the red it has small barbules under the chin. The commonest Atlantic drum, the Atlantic croaker (*Micropogon undulatus*) is a small, silver to bronze fish which averages 2 to 4 pounds in weight.

The Pacific drums are found mainly along the Californian coast. The most important is the white seabass (*Cynoscion nobilis*), which is found as far north as Alaska.

The freshwater drum (*Aplodinotus grunniens*) is found in lakes and large rivers, in Canada from Manitoba to Quebec, and in the USA in most states to the east of the Missouri drainage.

BLACK DRUMS
Heavier than the red drum, with a deeper body and more brassy. Up to 6 feet in length.

DACE

Dace are more slender than roach, and have yellowish eyes with dark spots on the iris. There are 47-54 scales on the lateral line and two rows of pharyngeal teeth.

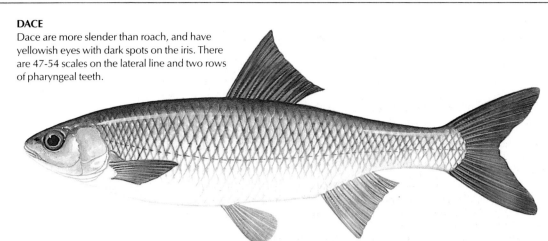

NATURAL FOOD

Dace feed on surface insects, such as damselflies in summer, as well as snails, daphnia and leeches. In cold weather dace are restricted to bottom feeding.

TECHNIQUE	ROD	REEL	LINE	TERMINAL TACKLE	HOOK	WEIGHT	BAIT
Long trotting – rivers, shallow glides, confluences, weir pools	12 to 13-foot match or float, light tip action	Centrepin, closed face or fixed spool	2-pound	Light float waggler or stick	16 to 20	4 to BB	Casters, maggots
Dry fly fishing	8½ to 9-foot light action DT6	Single action fly	DT 6 floating	10-foot tapered cast down to 2-pounds tippet			Black Gnat, Blue Olive Dun

DORADO

The body is elongated with very compressed sides, tapering sharply from the high, blunt forehead to the deeply forked tail.

NATURAL FOOD

Dorado feed in shoals or groups on the surface, eating tiny animals floating on the sea, and squid and flyingfish.

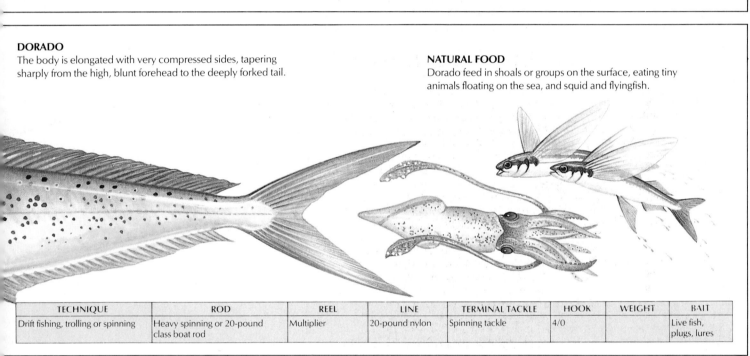

TECHNIQUE	ROD	REEL	LINE	TERMINAL TACKLE	HOOK	WEIGHT	BAIT
Drift fishing, trolling or spinning	Heavy spinning or 20-pound class boat rod	Multiplier	20-pound nylon	Spinning tackle	4/0		Live fish, plugs, lures

RED DRUM

Much smaller than the black drum, the red drum is identified by a red spot on the origin of the caudal fin. At depth it changes from copper to brick red.

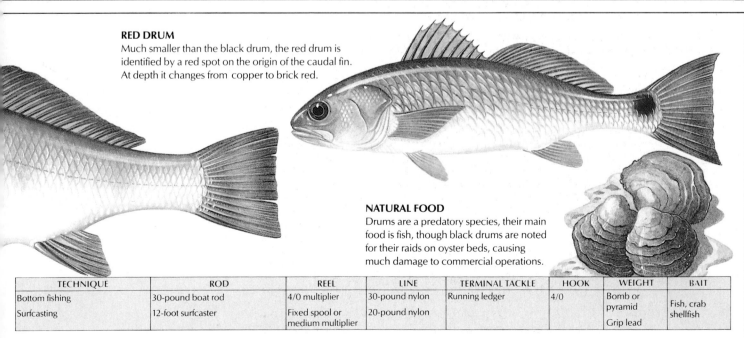

NATURAL FOOD

Drums are a predatory species, their main food is fish, though black drums are noted for their raids on oyster beds, causing much damage to commercial operations.

TECHNIQUE	ROD	REEL	LINE	TERMINAL TACKLE	HOOK	WEIGHT	BAIT
Bottom fishing	30-pound boat rod	4/0 multiplier	30-pound nylon	Running ledger	4/0	Bomb or pyramid	Fish, crab shellfish
Surfcasting	12-foot surfcaster	Fixed spool or medium multiplier	20-pound nylon			Grip lead	

EELS

The European eel *(Anguilla anguilla)* and the closely-related American eel *(A. rostrata)* both spend most of their lives in fresh water, but to breed, they make a long and hazardous journey to the Sargasso Sea, from which they never return. The Sargasso Sea is a relatively calm area of the Atlantic Ocean, north east of the West Indies. After spawning, the adult eels die and the larvae which hatch from the eggs make their way to the rivers from whence their parents came.

The journey to the rivers takes about a year for the American eel larvae, but three years for the Europeans. By the time the larvae reach shore, they have changed into little elvers. Large numbers of these are netted as they run up estuaries. They travel by night, and many leave the water on damp, moonless nights to travel overland to ponds and lakes unconnected with the sea.

The elvers grow into yellow eels, which are yellow to brown in color, darker on the back, and have a pair of small, rounded pectoral fins and long dorsal and anal fins which merge at the tail. Sexually mature eels take on a deep, silvery hue, and these silver eels set off in fall for the sea and their ocean journey to the Sargasso. The females are larger than the males, and can grow to over 4 feet in length.

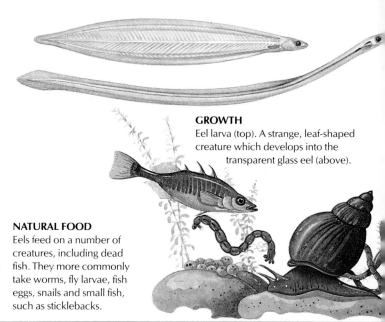

GROWTH
Eel larva (top). A strange, leaf-shaped creature which develops into the transparent glass eel (above).

NATURAL FOOD
Eels feed on a number of creatures, including dead fish. They more commonly take worms, fly larvae, fish eggs, snails and small fish, such as sticklebacks.

PLAICE
A right-eyed (or righthanded) flatfish, that is, with eyes tending towards the right side of the head.

WINTER FLOUNDER
Like the plaice, winter flounder are right-eyed.

SUMMER FLOUNDER
Identified by the eyes being on the left-hand side. Some species are both left and right-eyed.

COLORATION
Flatfish are generally very varied in color, tending to take on the color of the bottom they are lying on.

TURBOT
A European flatfish ranging from northern England and Ireland to north Africa and the Mediterranean. Scaleless, maximum growth 39 inches. An active predator, large turbot eat smaller fish almost exclusively.

TECHNIQUE	ROD	REEL	LINE	TERMINAL TACKLE	HOOK	WEIGHT	BAIT
Bottom fishing	20-pound class	4/0 multiplier		Running ledger	Sizes 2/0-4/0	Bomb pyramid	Fish, sandeel crab, squid, worm
Surfcasting	50 to 80-pounds (halibut)	6/0					
Spinning	Spinning or beach rod	Fixed spool		Flounder spoon rig	Long shank	Barrel lead	

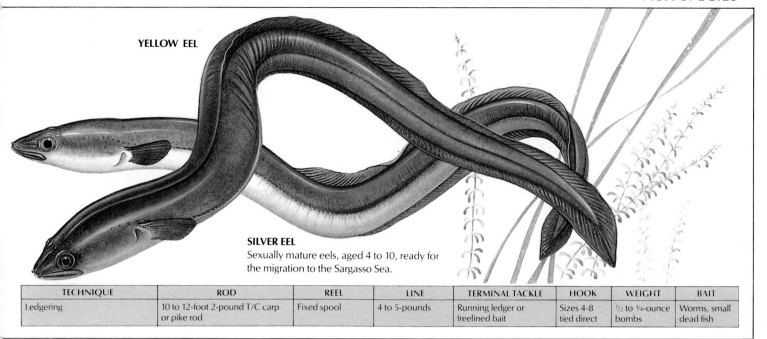

YELLOW EEL

SILVER EEL
Sexually mature eels, aged 4 to 10, ready for the migration to the Sargasso Sea.

TECHNIQUE	ROD	REEL	LINE	TERMINAL TACKLE	HOOK	WEIGHT	BAIT
Ledgering	10 to 12-foot 2-pound T/C carp or pike rod	Fixed spool	4 to 5-pounds	Running ledger or freelined bait	Sizes 4-8 tied direct	½ to ¼-ounce bombs	Worms, small dead fish

EYE MIGRATION
The illustration shows the development of eye migration in the plaice, seen head-on. As a hatchling the plaice, in common with other true flatfish species, begins life as a round fish. Gradually the eyes migrate to one side of the head and the fish lies flat on the bottom as an adult. Plaice swim with their right side uppermost.

Poor cod,
food of
the turbot

NATURAL FOOD
Smaller species of flatfish feed on mussels, razorshells and lugworms, while larger species, such as turbot and halibut, feed mainly on other fish species.

FLATFISH

Of the many species of flatfish (a term which doesn't include rays and skates), the largest is the Atlantic halibut (*Hippoglossus hippoglossus*), which is also one of the largest bony fish in the sea. The largest recorded specimen was caught off the Swedish coast and weighed 720 pounds.

Halibut of such a size are, however, extremely rare, and even fish of 300 pounds or so – which measure about 8 feet long and 4 feet wide – are seldom found.

The Atlantic halibut is a righteye (or righthanded) flatfish, that is, it swims with its right hand side uppermost, and during its larval stage its left eye migrates over its head towards the right eye. The eye migration begins when the larva is about an inch long, and by the time the larva has grown to about 1½ inches the eye migration is complete and the tiny fish begins to live on the seabed, instead of drifting with the current.

The immature fish live in relatively shallow water, feeding on crustaceans, sandeels and small flatfish. As the fish mature, they move into deep water, preferring depths of from 200 to 3000 feet, where they feed on fish such as cod, haddock, coalfish, herring and even shark. They hunt their prey in mid water as well as on the bottom, and supplement their basic diet of fish with squid, octopus, cuttlefish, lobster and crab.

Halibut can be caught on live or dead baits fished on the bottom or on the drift, or on baited pirk-type lures. The Pacific halibut (*Hippoglossus stenolepis*), which can reach a weight of 500 pounds, can be caught in the same way.

Another Pacific flatfish, the California halibut (*Paralichthys californicus*) which grows to over 60 pounds, is a lefteye flatfish. It swims with its left side uppermost, and during its larval stage it is the right eye which migrates. However, both lefteye and righteye flatfish species occasionally produce larvae which show reversed eye migration, and this trait is especially common in the California halibut.

Other lefteye flatfish include the brill (*Scophthalmus rhombus*), turbot (*S. maximus*), summer flounder (*Paralichthys dentatus*), Gulf flounder (*P. albigutta*) and the megrim (*Lepidorhombus whiffiagonis*), and a host of other species.

The major examples of righteye flatfish are the Atlantic and Pacific halibuts, but there are many others, including the plaice (*Pleuronectes platessa*), the dab (*Limanda limanda*), the sole (*Solea solea*) and the winter flounder (*Pseudopleuronectes americanus*).

The plaice is one of the most popular of the flatfish in European waters from the Baltic to Biscay, and is taken both by shore anglers and by boat fishermen. On the American side of the Atlantic, the winter flounder and the summer flounder (or fluke) provide shore and small-boat anglers with much of their sport.

GARS

The freshwater gars are members of an ancient family of predatory fish. Of the nine species found in North American waters, only five are of interest to anglers. The largest is the alligator gar (*Lepisosteus spatula*), which is found from northeast Mexico to the Mississippi Valley, up to Missouri and Kentucky.

The alligator gar can reach a length of 10 feet, and a weight of 302 pounds has been recorded. It feeds on fish, and will also attack and eat ducks and other waterfowl. One 163-pound specimen was found to contain no less than 40 pounds of fish.

The other gars – including the longnose gar (*L. osseus*), shortnose gar (*L. platostomus*), spotted gar (*L. oculatus*) and Florida gar (*L. platyrhincus*) – are all much smaller. The longnose reaches about 50 pounds, the shortnose only 4½ pounds; the spotted grows to over 7 pounds, and the Florida to over 20 pounds.

The longnose is the commonest and most widely distributed of the gars, occurring from Montana east to Quebec and south through the Mississippi River system and into Mexico.

All the gars can survive in very poorly-oxygenated water, because their air bladders are supplied with blood vessels that enable them to be used as lungs. Their scales are so hard that pioneer farmers once used the skin and scales to cover their wooden plowshares.

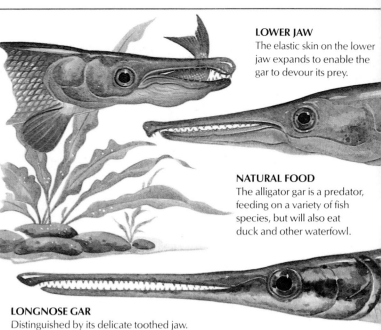

LOWER JAW
The elastic skin on the lower jaw expands to enable the gar to devour its prey.

NATURAL FOOD
The alligator gar is a predator, feeding on a variety of fish species, but will also eat duck and other waterfowl.

LONGNOSE GAR
Distinguished by its delicate toothed jaw.

GRAYLING

The European grayling (*Thymallus thymallus*) and the closely-related American grayling (*Thymallus arcticus*) are beautiful freshwater members of the salmon family, living in swift, clean, gravel-bottomed rivers and pure, well-oxygenated lakes. The European grayling is found in most of Europe except Ireland, Spain, Portugal, southern France and the south of Italy. Most of the American grayling live in northern waters, from Alaska through to Saskatchewan, but small numbers are found in Montana, Wyoming and Utah.

The grayling is distinctive in appearance, with a long, slim body, a pointed snout, bony jaws and gill plates and hard scales. The adipose fin is tiny, but the dorsal is huge and sail-like and spotted and edged with red. The dorsal fin of the male is low at the front and rises towards the rear, whereas that of the female is high at the front and is either level or slopes to the rear; it's also smaller than the male's.

Grayling will not tolerate anything but the purest of waters, and they feed on scuds, snails, nymphs and small fishes. They spawn in the spring, and the European grayling reaches weights of from just over 3 pounds in Britain to more than twice that in Scandinavia; American grayling grow to about 1½ pounds in their more southerly habitats, and reach over 5 pounds further north.

STUNTED GROWTH
Like other commercially bred species, a dwarf form occurs in stocked rivers.

NATURAL FOOD
As well as surface flying insects, grayling will eat aquatic insect larvae, fish fry, freshwater shrimps, snails, nymphs and small fishes.

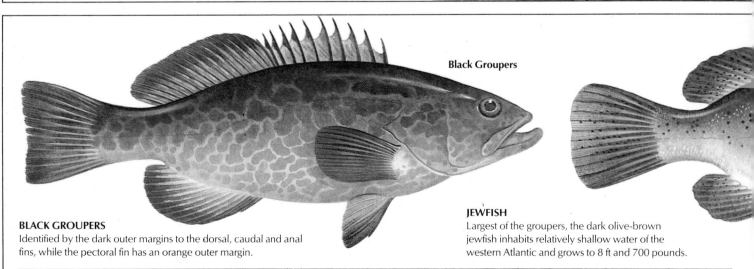

Black Groupers

BLACK GROUPERS
Identified by the dark outer margins to the dorsal, caudal and anal fins, while the pectoral fin has an orange outer margin.

JEWFISH
Largest of the groupers, the dark olive-brown jewfish inhabits relatively shallow water of the western Atlantic and grows to 8 ft and 700 pounds.

TECHNIQUE	ROD	REEL	LINE	TERMINAL TACKLE	HOOK	WEIGHT	BAIT
Bottom fishing	30-50-pound class boat rod	4/0-6/0 multiplier	35-pound nylon	Running ledger	4/0-6/0 eyed	Pyramid egg, bomb	Live fish, cut squid, crab
Trolling	80-pound class	9/0 multiplier	80-pound nylon	Heavy wire	10/0 eyed	egg	Yellow Japanese feathers

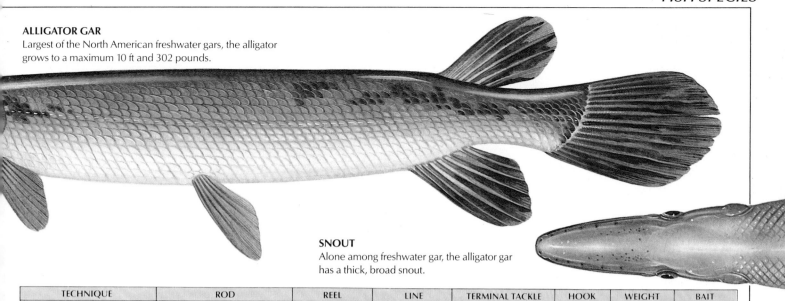

ALLIGATOR GAR
Largest of the North American freshwater gars, the alligator grows to a maximum 10 ft and 302 pounds.

SNOUT
Alone among freshwater gar, the alligator gar has a thick, broad snout.

TECHNIQUE	ROD	REEL	LINE	TERMINAL TACKLE	HOOK	WEIGHT	BAIT
Spinning	Medium 9-foot spinning rod	Fixed spool	8-10-pound nylon		6, 4, 2 eyed	Barrel	Spinners, squid, crab, fish

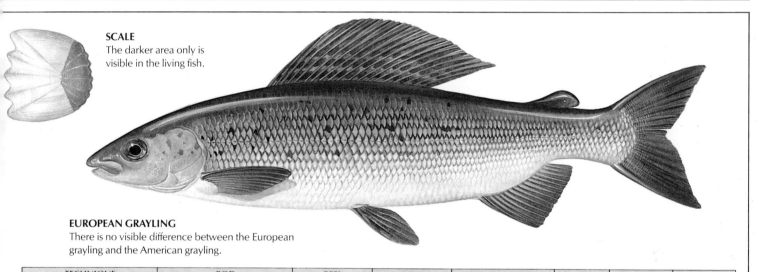

SCALE
The darker area only is visible in the living fish.

EUROPEAN GRAYLING
There is no visible difference between the European grayling and the American grayling.

TECHNIQUE	ROD	REEL	LINE	TERMINAL TACKLE	HOOK	WEIGHT	BAIT
Trotting	11-13-foot float rod	Fixed spool	2-3-pound	Chunky float with 4AA-4 swan shot	10-16	Bulk shot low down	Maggots bloodworms
Fly fishing	8½-9-foot medium action, 6/7	Single action fly reel	Dry line	Long cast			Leaded shrimp

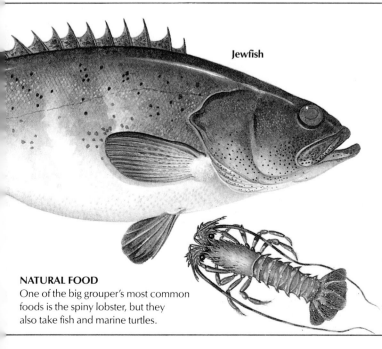

Jewfish

NATURAL FOOD
One of the big grouper's most common foods is the spiny lobster, but they also take fish and marine turtles.

GROUPERS

Groupers, of which there are more than 400 known species, are large, predatory fish distributed worldwide in temperate to tropical freshwaters and seas. Groupers range in size from small to very large, but most are caught in similar ways and, being good table-fish, are commercially valuable.

Some of the commonest groupers are the red grouper (*Epinephalus morio*), the Nassau grouper (*E. striatus*), the black grouper (*Mycteroperca bonaci*), the yellowfin grouper (*M. venenosa*) and the jewfish (*E. itajara*).

The jewfish is the largest of the groupers, and can grow to 8 feet in length and a weight of over 700 pounds. Jewfish are found in the western Atlantic from Florida to Brazil, including the Gulf of Mexico, and the eastern Pacific from Costa Rica down to Peru.

The jewfish is brownish green or brownish yellow, mottled with dark brown spots and blotches and having 5 or more dark vertical bars on each side. Very large specimens tend to be darker, and may be uniformly olive-brown or even black.

Despite its size, the jewfish normally lives in comparatively shallow water close to the shore, rocks, reefs and ledges being its preferred habitat. It lives on fish and crustaceans, and has also been known to catch and eat turtles. There are even reliable reports of huge jewfish trying to swallow divers.

JACKS

The jacks are a large family of marine fishes widely distributed in the warmer waters of the world. One of the jacks most popular with anglers is the crevalle or jack crevalle *(Caranx hippos)*. This is a superb fish to catch on light tackle, a hard-hitting predator that can be taken by spinning, trolling, jigging or surfcasting.

The body is deep and rather fat, with a deeply forked tail and long, elegant pectoral fins. The forehead is blunt and steep, and the metallic blue-green color of the back gives way to silver or silvery yellow on the flanks and belly.

The crevalle is found in the western Atlantic, and an almost identical species *(C. caninus)* occurs in the eastern Pacific. It grows to at least 55 pounds, and although most are taken in coastal waters they also inhabit the deeper offshore areas.

The crevalle differs from other jacks in that its chest area is scaleless apart from a small, circular patch of scales. The other jacks, such as the Atlantic and Pacific horse-eye jacks *(C. latus and C. marginatus)* are fully scaled on the chest.

The jack family also includes the yellow jack *(C. bartholomaei)*, a pale silvery-blue Atlantic species with an overall yellowish tinge that is more prominent when the fish is dead, and the beautiful blue runners of the Atlantic *(C. crysos)* and Pacific *(C. caballus)*.

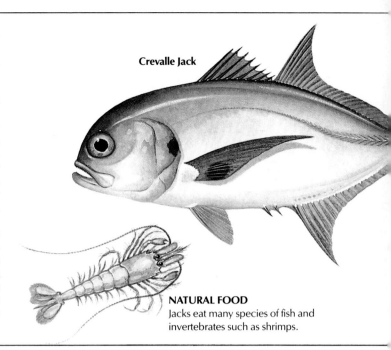

Crevalle Jack

NATURAL FOOD
Jacks eat many species of fish and invertebrates such as shrimps.

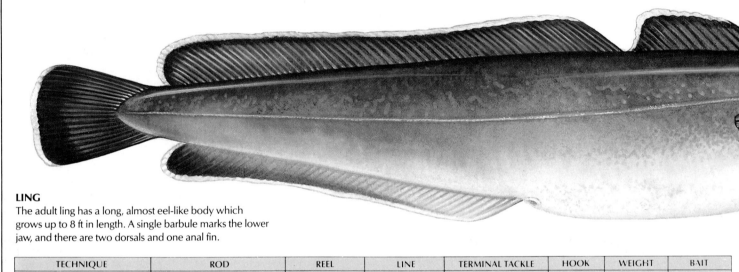

LING
The adult ling has a long, almost eel-like body which grows up to 8 ft in length. A single barbule marks the lower jaw, and there are two dorsals and one anal fin.

TECHNIQUE	ROD	REEL	LINE	TERMINAL TACKLE	HOOK	WEIGHT	BAIT
Baited pirk	50-pound class boat rod	6/0 multiplier	50-pound nylon	Pirk and wire trace	Size 8/0	Pirk acts as weight	Fish, squid, cuttlefish

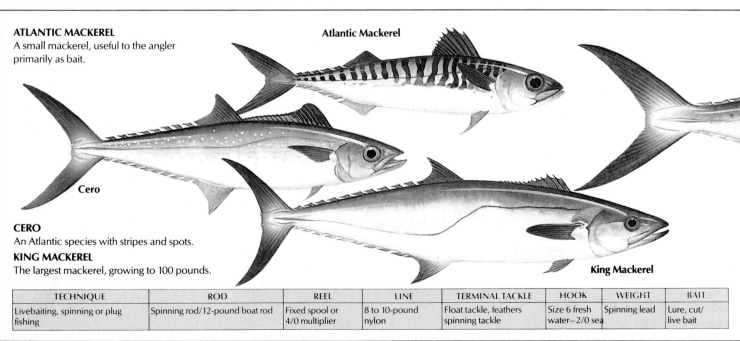

ATLANTIC MACKEREL
A small mackerel, useful to the angler primarily as bait.

Atlantic Mackerel

Cero

CERO
An Atlantic species with stripes and spots.

KING MACKEREL
The largest mackerel, growing to 100 pounds.

King Mackerel

TECHNIQUE	ROD	REEL	LINE	TERMINAL TACKLE	HOOK	WEIGHT	BAIT
Livebaiting, spinning or plug fishing	Spinning rod/12-pound boat rod	Fixed spool or 4/0 multiplier	8 to 10-pound nylon	Float tackle, feathers spinning tackle	Size 6 fresh water—2/0 sea	Spinning lead	Lure, cut/ live bait

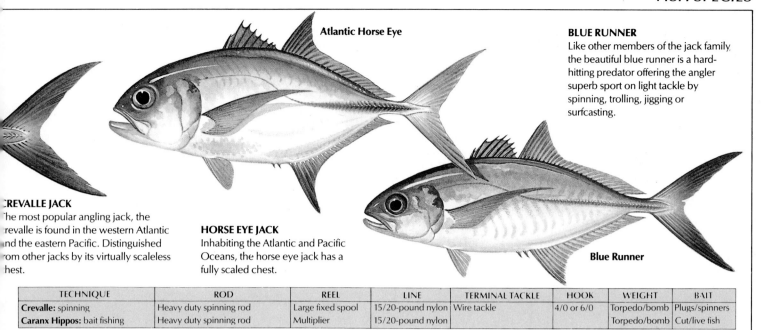

Atlantic Horse Eye

BLUE RUNNER
Like other members of the jack family, the beautiful blue runner is a hard-hitting predator offering the angler superb sport on light tackle by spinning, trolling, jigging or surfcasting.

CREVALLE JACK
The most popular angling jack, the crevalle is found in the western Atlantic and the eastern Pacific. Distinguished from other jacks by its virtually scaleless chest.

HORSE EYE JACK
Inhabiting the Atlantic and Pacific Oceans, the horse eye jack has a fully scaled chest.

Blue Runner

TECHNIQUE	ROD	REEL	LINE	TERMINAL TACKLE	HOOK	WEIGHT	BAIT
Crevalle: spinning	Heavy duty spinning rod	Large fixed spool	15/20-pound nylon	Wire tackle	4/0 or 6/0	Torpedo/bomb	Plugs/spinners
Caranx Hippos: bait fishing	Heavy duty spinning rod	Multiplier	15/20-pound nylon			Torpedo/bomb	Cut/live fish

LING *Molva molva*

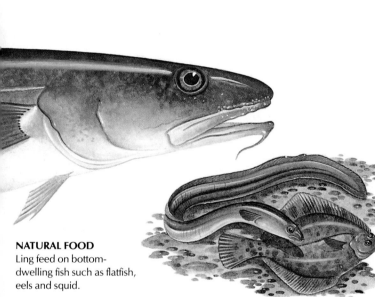

NATURAL FOOD
Ling feed on bottom-dwelling fish such as flatfish, eels and squid.

The ling is a large member of the cod family, widely distributed in the northeast Atlantic from the Arctic south to the Bay of Biscay. It lives mainly in deep waters from about 150 feet down to 1200 feet or more, preferring rocky or rough ground and wrecks.

Ling are active hunters, feeding on all kinds of small fish, crustaceans, squid and cuttlefish. They are normally caught on cut fish or squid baits, fished with heavy bottom tackle, and grow to over 6 feet long and 80 pounds.

Ling are dark brown-green on the back with white underparts, and the body is long and almost eel-like. There is a single barbule on the lower jaw, and there are two dorsal fins, the first short and rounded and the second long and even in height. The single anal fin is also long, although not as long as the second dorsal, and the rounded tail is small for the size of the fish. There is a dark blotch on the rear edge of the first dorsal fin, and the leading edges of the fins are tinged with blue.

Ling spawn between March and July, and a large female can produce up to 60 million eggs. The eggs, each about one millimeter in diameter, float on the surface until they hatch. The young ling live in shallow water for the first two or three years before moving to deeper waters.

MACKERELS

SPANISH MACKEREL
Found off the Florida coast and in the Gulf of Mexico, Spanish mackerel is a popular gamefish, averaging between 6 to 10 pounds, reaching a maximum of 20 pounds.

NATURAL FOOD
Mackerel are predators, feeding on shoaling species such as the easy pickings offered by anchovy.

Mackerels are an abundant and commercially-important group of fishes found in both the Atlantic and the Pacific. The small species are useful to the angler more as bait than sport, but the larger species are popular gamefish. The small Atlantic mackerels include the common or Atlantic mackerel *(Scomber scombrus)* and the chub mackerel *(S. colias)*. The small Pacific mackerel *(S. japonicus)* is very similar to the chub mackerel.

The giant of the mackerel tribe is the king mackerel *(Scomberomorus cavalla)* of the western Atlantic, which can grow to 100 pounds. A long, lean fish, the king mackerel has a pointed snout, two dorsal fins plus a row of eight or nine dorsal finlets, and an anal fin plus eight to ten anal finlets. Keenly sought by anglers off the coasts of Florida and the Gulf of Mexico, king mackerel are taken on trolled or drifted bait, and on spinners and plugs.

The Spanish mackerel *(Scomberomorus maculatus)* is another popular gamefish in these waters. Most weigh 6 to 10 pounds, and the maximum is about 20 pounds. The Spanish mackerel has spots on its sides and no stripes on its back, unlike the striped but spotless king mackerel and the striped and spotted cero mackerel *(S. regalis)*, another Atlantic species which grows to 35 pounds.

MARLINS

M ost anglers would like to tangle at least once with one of the world's most sought-after gamefish – a marlin. Blue marlin *(Makaira nigricans)*, black marlin *(M. indicus)*, white marlin *(Tetrapturus albidus)* and striped marlin *(T. audax)* are all true big-game species.

The blue marlin is the most widely distributed, being found in warm and temperate waters all round the world. The white marlin is an Atlantic fish, and the striped occurs in the Indian and Pacific Oceans, as does the black marlin which is also found in the far southeastern corner of the Atlantic.

Like all marlins, the blue has an elongated upper jaw or 'bill', long, thin, thorn-like scales, ventral fins, and a huge, deeply-forked tail with a pair of keels at either side of its root. The dorsal fin is high and pointed, and the pectoral fins are never rigid as they are in the black marlin. The back is cobalt blue, while the belly and flanks are silvery white.

All marlin spawn in summer, and feed mainly on fish and squid. Cannibalism also occurs; a 448-pound marlin caught off Walker's Cay in the Bahamas was found to contain the partly-digested remains of another, 72 inches long. Blue marlin reach weights of over 1500 pounds, and black marlin slightly more; the maximum for striped marlin is around 480 pounds, about three times that of white marlin.

WHITE MARLIN
A sporting fish found from Nova Scotia to Brazil. Slender body, rounded lobe on dorsal fin, curved pectoral fin.

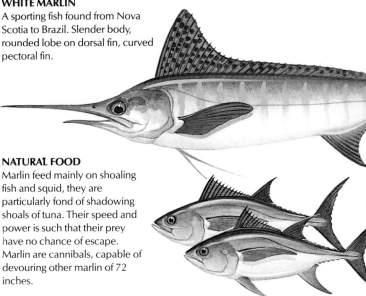

NATURAL FOOD
Marlin feed mainly on shoaling fish and squid, they are particularly fond of shadowing shoals of tuna. Their speed and power is such that their prey have no chance of escape. Marlin are cannibals, capable of devouring other marlin of 72 inches.

MULLETS

A ll the mullet family are re-garded as tricky fish to catch. Soft-mouthed, shy and extremely strong when hooked on light tackle, mullet are a match for any angler's skill.

The thick-lipped mullet *(Crenimugil labrosus)*, thin-lipped mullet *(Liza ramada)*, golden gray mullet *(Liza Aurata)*, the striped or black mullet *(Mugil cephalus)* and the white mullet *(Mugil curema)* are all very similar in appearance.

The body is torpedo-shaped, with a broad, rather flattened head and two dorsal fins, the first having four heavy spines. The color is gray-blue on the back, with silvery gray sides and white underparts; the golden gray variety has a conspicuous gold patch on the cheek and gill cover.

Mullet are found in all temperate and tropical seas. They are fond of brackish water, and in large estuaries they often penetrate well inland beyond the influence of salt water. They are mostly caught on ultralight float tackle, used with bread or tiny marine worms as bait. In some areas, they will also take tiny, worm-baited spinners, and this method works particularly well in estuaries.

Mullet can reach weights in excess of 10 pounds, although most rod-caught fish are only 3 to 5 pounds. They are an excellent food fish, and equally good as bait for big game fish, marlin in particular.

Striped Mullet

Golden Mullet

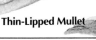
Thin-Lipped Mullet

MULLET VARIATIONS
Mullets have attractive heads with large, irregular shade patterns. Striped mullet have blunt heads and clear adipose eye-lids. Golden mullet have golden blotches on their cheeks and gill covers. Thin-lipped mullet are so-called because their top lip is less than half the diameter of their eye.

SILVER PIKE
The silver pike, found in Minnesota, was thought to be a variety of muskellunge but in fact is a mutant pike.

NATURAL FOOD
The muskie's diet consists of fish, snakes, crayfish, waterbirds and muskrats.

TECHNIQUE	ROD	REEL	LINE	TERMINAL TACKLE	HOOK	WEIGHT	BAIT
Baitcasting, spinning	6 to 8-foot heavy action baitcasting/spinning rod	Multiplier or fixed spool	12 to 15-pounds	12-foot strong wire trace, 20-pounds test			Plugs, spinner and buzz baits
Downrigger trolling	6 to 7-foot fast taper action	Multiplier	15 to 20-pounds	12-foot strong wire trace, 25 pounds test			Large spoons, plugs, minnows

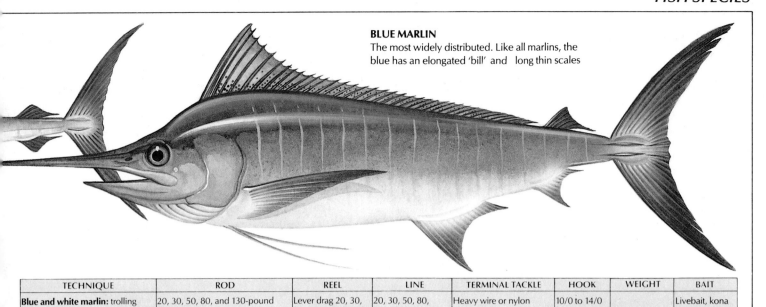

BLUE MARLIN
The most widely distributed. Like all marlins, the blue has an elongated 'bill' and long thin scales

TECHNIQUE	ROD	REEL	LINE	TERMINAL TACKLE	HOOK	WEIGHT	BAIT
Blue and white marlin: trolling livebait, trolling natural or artificial lures	20, 30, 50, 80, and 130-pound class rods	Lever drag 20, 30, 50, 80, 130 class/ 6/0,7, 14/0 star drag	20, 30, 50, 80, 130, nylon or Dacron	Heavy wire or nylon trace	10/0 to 14/0 flat forged		Livebait, kona head, mullet, mackerel

THICK-LIPPED MULLET
Most widely distributed of British mullet. The top lip is more than half the diameter of its eye.

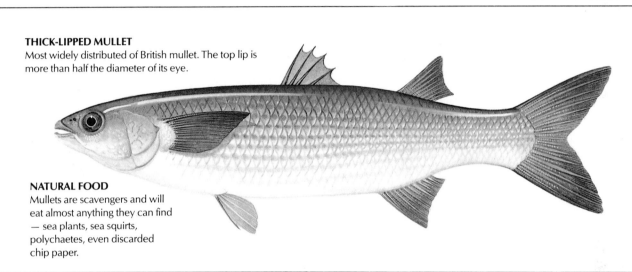

NATURAL FOOD
Mullets are scavengers and will eat almost anything they can find — sea plants, sea squirts, polychaetes, even discarded chip paper.

TECHNIQUE	ROD	REEL	LINE	TERMINAL TACKLE	HOOK	WEIGHT	BAIT
Bait or baited line	12-foot float or light spinning	Fixed spool	5-pound nylon	Shotted float, bar spoons	6-10 fresh water or 10 treble	Split shot	Worm, banana, macaroni, meat, sweetcorn

MUSKELLUNGE
Almost identical to the northern pike in appearance, the muskie is, however, bigger – up to 70 pounds and 5 feet.

LOWER JAW
The underside of the head showing the position of the pores on the ventral surface of the lower jaw.

MUSKELLUNGE *Esox masquinongy*

The muskellunge of North America is without doubt the king of the pike family. Although somewhat slimmer than its closest rival the northern (or Euopean) pike, the muskie grows to over 70 pounds and 20 to 30-pounders are not uncommon.

In build and fin structure the muskies are like all other pike, being long and sleek in the body with strong, tooth-filled jaws, and with the dorsal and anal fins set well back for short, controlled bursts of speed. The back is usually olive to bronze, with paler sides, but the markings vary considerably and usually differ from those of other pike.

Muskellunge most prefer clear streams, rivers and lakes with plenty of vegetation where they can wait for passing shoal fish.

Muskellunge are found in and around the Great Lakes, in eastern lakes such as Chautauqua Lake (NY) and down the Ohio drainage to Tennessee, and into North Carolina and Georgia. There are in fact three very similar varieties of muskellunge: the Great Lakes muskellunge (*Esox masquinongy masquinongy*); the tiger or northern muskellunge (*Esox masquinongy immaculatus*) of Minnesota, Wisconsin and parts of Michigan; and the Chautauqua or Ohio muskellunge (*Esox masquinongy ohioensis*).

PADDLEFISH *Polyodon spathula*

The paddlefish is a large, almost scaleless freshwater fish with a huge, paddle-shaped snout. It has a large, shark-like tail, and like the sharks its skeleton is mostly of cartilage. The head and mouth are large, but the eye is tiny, and the fish feeds on plankton and insect larvae by straining them from the water through large and numerous gill rakers. To do this, it swims with its mouth wide open, like a basking shark.

The body is a dusky blue to dark gray on the back and dirty white below, and the gill cover extends backwards as a long, pointed flap. The paddlefish is large for a freshwater fish, and has been known to reach 200 pounds and a length of 6 feet, but the average maximum is less than 100 pounds and most of those caught are less than 40 pounds.

The paddlefish's range is smaller than it was, but it's still quite widely distributed throughout the larger rivers and lakes of the Mississippi drainage. Spawning takes place in April and May, and as the eggs are laid on gravel beds in shallow, running water, lake-dwelling paddlefish often have to travel great distances to suitable streams in order to spawn. Paddlefish can be caught on small baits, but apart from the high quality of its flesh it isn't regarded as a particularly worthwhile catch.

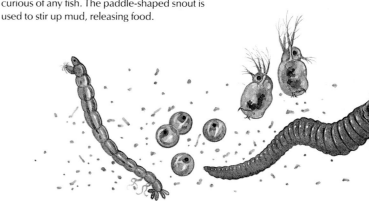

SNOUT
The upper jaw of the paddlefish is one of the most curious of any fish. The paddle-shaped snout is used to stir up mud, releasing food.

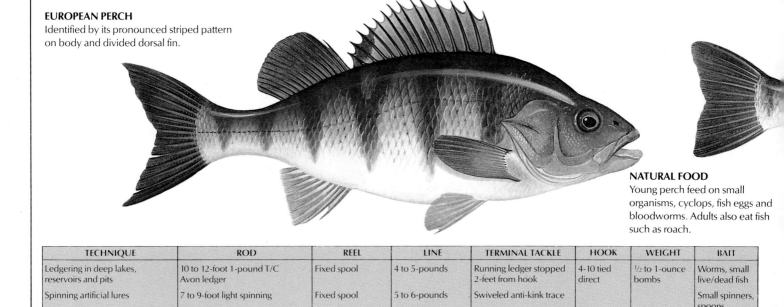

EUROPEAN PERCH
Identified by its pronounced striped pattern on body and divided dorsal fin.

NATURAL FOOD
Young perch feed on small organisms, cyclops, fish eggs and bloodworms. Adults also eat fish such as roach.

TECHNIQUE	ROD	REEL	LINE	TERMINAL TACKLE	HOOK	WEIGHT	BAIT
Ledgering in deep lakes, reservoirs and pits	10 to 12-foot 1-pound T/C Avon ledger	Fixed spool	4 to 5-pounds	Running ledger stopped 2-feet from hook	4-10 tied direct	½ to 1-ounce bombs	Worms, small live/dead fish
Spinning artificial lures	7 to 9-foot light spinning	Fixed spool	5 to 6-pounds	Swiveled anti-kink trace			Small spinners, spoons

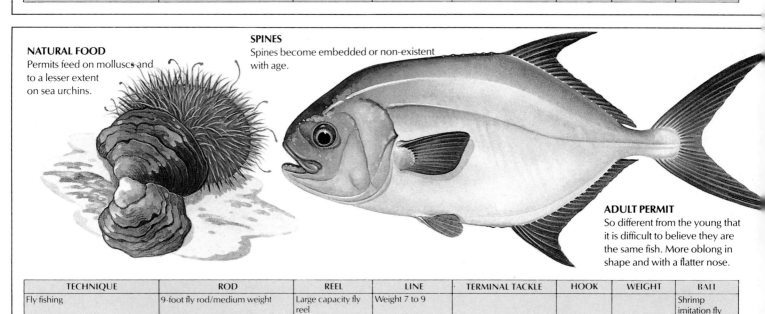

NATURAL FOOD
Permits feed on molluscs and to a lesser extent on sea urchins.

SPINES
Spines become embedded or non-existent with age.

ADULT PERMIT
So different from the young that it is difficult to believe they are the same fish. More oblong in shape and with a flatter nose.

TECHNIQUE	ROD	REEL	LINE	TERMINAL TACKLE	HOOK	WEIGHT	BAIT
Fly fishing	9-foot fly rod/medium weight	Large capacity fly reel	Weight 7 to 9				Shrimp imitation fly
Jig fishing	Medium-weight spinning rod	Large fly	Floating fly		Size 6 fly	None	Live crab
Bait fishing	Medium-weight spinning rod	Fixed spool	12-pounds nylon		Sizes 1/0, 2/0	None	Dead shrimp

PADDLEFISH

Large, scaleless, freshwater fish with strange, paddle-shaped snout. Known to reach 200 pounds.

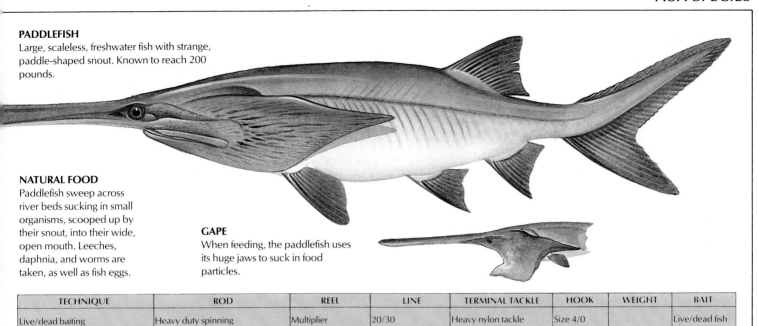

NATURAL FOOD
Paddlefish sweep across river beds sucking in small organisms, scooped up by their snout, into their wide, open mouth. Leeches, daphnia, and worms are taken, as well as fish eggs.

GAPE
When feeding, the paddlefish uses its huge jaws to suck in food particles.

TECHNIQUE	ROD	REEL	LINE	TERMINAL TACKLE	HOOK	WEIGHT	BAIT
Live/dead baiting	Heavy duty spinning	Multiplier	20/30	Heavy nylon tackle	Size 4/0		Live/dead fish

YELLOW PERCH
Closely related to the European perch, the yellow perch is regarded by some as a sub-species.

PERCHES

The European perch *(Perca fluviatilis)* is a freshwater shoalfish which is widely distributed throughout the British Isles and most of Europe and Asia, and is also found in southern Africa and in Australasia. The very similar, closely-related yellow perch *(Perca flavescens)* occurs in southern Canada and the central and eastern parts of the USA.

The body is oval in cross-section, and while young perch are quite elongated, they become chunkier and humpbacked as they get older. There are two separate dorsal fins, the first of which has strong spines, and the scales are very rough to the touch.

The color is dark olive along the back, with golden flanks marked by a series of vertical dark bars, and a white belly.

The perch lives on a diet of snails, crayfish, insects and small fish, including small perch. Its preferred habitats are clean, slow rivers and ponds, pits, lakes and reservoirs. The European perch grows to about 6 pounds in the British Isles and to 10 pounds or more elsewhere.

The white perch *(morone americana)*, which is related to the striped bass, is another popular North American panfish. More silver in color than the yellow perch, and without the vertical dark markings, it lives in salt, brackish and fresh waters along the eastern seaboard and inland to the Great Lakes.

JUVENILE PERMIT
Young permit have a deep body and elongated dorsal, anal and caudal lobes.

PERMIT *Trachinotus falcatus*

The permit, one of the great light tackle species, is a fish of the western Atlantic. The largest numbers are found off the coasts of southern Florida and the Bahamas.

Often called the 'great pompano', the permit differs from the common pompano *(T. carolinus)* by having fewer soft rays in the dorsal and anal fins. Another difference is that the permit has very large second and third ribs, which can be easily felt through the side of the fish.

The adult permit is oblong in shape, with a small mouth and a high, blunt forehead. The overall color is silvery with dusky fins, and some specimens have a touch of orange on the margin of the anal fin.

Permit are a shallow-water species, often travelling in schools over coral flats. They feed in much the same way as bonefish and in the same sort of waters, eating mostly shellfish, crabs, shrimps and sea urchins. Peak spawning time is May, and the major spawning grounds are believed to be about 200 miles from the Florida coast. The maximum weight is probably around 60 pounds, and most are taken on streamer flies or bonefish jigs. The mouth of the permit is as tough as leather, so to make sure of setting the hook it pays to make a series of strikes when a fish bites.

PICKERELS

The pickerels are small American members of the pike family. In overall shape and body structure they are similar to other pikes, and just as well-equipped with strong, sharp teeth.

The largest is the chain pickerel *(Esox niger)*, which grows to a top weight of around 9 pounds and a length of about 3 feet.As with other pikes, the body colors and markings provide excellent camouflage for a predator that likes to lurk in weedbeds to ambush its food as it passes.

The chain pickerel feeds on almost anything edible that comes its way, including fish, frogs, newts, crayfish and small rodents, and like all pikes the pickerel is a cannibal. It breeds in early spring, among vegetation in the shallows, and the fry feed on small creatures such as zooplankton and shrimp until they're large enough to take small fish.

The chain pickerel is widely distributed in the eastern USA, particularly the Atlantic states, and in Georgia and Florida, being most plentiful in waters where it isn't competing with (or being eaten by) larger pike.

There are two other species of pickerel, the redfin pickerel *(Esox americanus americanus)* found in waters of the Atlantic drainage, and the grass pickerel *(E. a. vermiculatus)* of the Mississippi drainage and the Great Lakes. These little pike (10 to 15 inches long) provide excellent sport on ultralight tackle.

REDFIN PICKEREL
A small pickerel, rarely more than 12 inches long.

NATURAL FOOD
Pickerels never feed exclusively on fish, as they are not large predators. They will take small animals such as caddis fly larvae, snails and fish larvae, including that of other pickerel.

PIKE *Esox lucius*

The northern pike is one of the most popular sports fish of Europe and North America, and in many areas it offers the anglers their best chance of catching a heavy fish. Pike can grow to over 4 feet long and 50 pounds, although fish of between 10 and 20 pounds are worthwhile catches.

In color, the pike is bronze to olive green along the back, with flanks of light olive patterned with blotches and spots of cream which create a highly effective camouflage. The fins are large and red to yellow in color, with dark markings, and the powerful forked tail gives the fish sudden and rapid acceleration when it ambushes its prey. The eyes are set high in the flattened head, which has strong, bony jaws.

Pike are found in most types of water, from deep, clear-watered lakes to shallow streams and ponds and even tidal rivers. Pike are essentially lazy fish, preferring to scavenge on dead food or to lie in ambush for a passing meal, but they will hunt if they have to. Their staple diet is live shoal fish, which may be up to a third or even half their own length, but they will also take rats, voles, frogs, mice and waterfowl. Spawning is in early spring, when the female, accompanied by one or more (much smaller) males, deposits her eggs in weedy shallows or on reed stems.

NATURAL FOOD
In European waters, pike feed almost wholly on fish, showing a particular fondness for roach. Dead roach is a popular pike bait.

IDENTIFICATION
Flat, broad snout, elongated body, bronze to olive green back, marked with cream spots and bars. Can grow to over 4 ft and 50 pounds.

JAWS
The pike has a complex bone structure and is well equipped with teeth pointing backwards for seizing and holding prey.

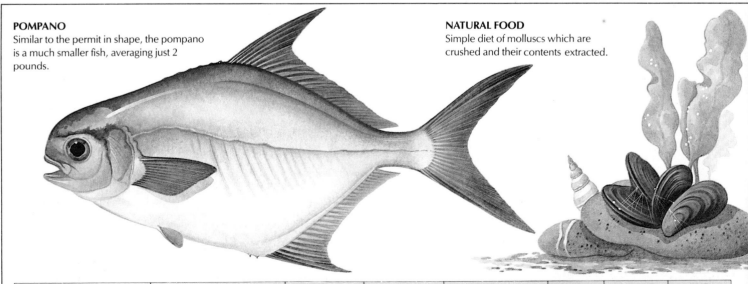

POMPANO
Similar to the permit in shape, the pompano is a much smaller fish, averaging just 2 pounds.

NATURAL FOOD
Simple diet of molluscs which are crushed and their contents extracted.

TECHNIQUE	ROD	REEL	LINE	TERMINAL TACKLE	HOOK	WEIGHT	BAIT
Spinning	Medium spinning rod	Fixed spool	10-pound nylon	Nylon trace	Size 8 treble	Light spinning/ bomb-shaped	Small spinner
Bait fishing	Medium spinning rod	Fixed spool	10-pound nylon	Nylon trace	Size 2 eyed		Fish strip

CHAIN PICKEREL
The chain pickerel is mottled green to bronze, with handsome and distinctive black, chainmail-like markings which give it its name.

MARKINGS
No markings on fin, unlike pike or muskie.

TECHNIQUE	ROD	REEL	LINE	TERMINAL TACKLE	HOOK	WEIGHT	BAIT
Popping surface lures through weedbeds	5½-foot baitcaster	Multiplier	6 to 8-pounds	Short wire trace			Small spinners buzz baits
Casting beside reedy shorelines	6 to 7-foot action spinning	Fixed spool	6-pounds	Short wire trace			Bar spoons, etc

TECHNIQUE	ROD	REEL	LINE	TERMINAL TACKLE	HOOK	WEIGHT	BAIT
Livebaiting with small fish	10 to 12-foot test curve pike or carp	Fixed spool	10 to 12	Sliding float below bead and stop knot	Two 8 trebles on 20-in wire trace	2 to 3 swan shots	4 to 6-inch roach, dace, etc
Lure fishing from boat or bank	7 to 9-foot 2-pound test curve medium-fast action spinning rod	Fixed spool	10 to 12-pounds	12-inch wire trace with snaplock swivel			plugs, spoons

POMPANOS

From an angling point of view, the two most important species of pompano are the common pom-pano *(Trachinotus carolinus)* and the African pompano *(Alectis ciliaris).* The common pompano, a fish of the western Atlantic, has a bluish-silvery back and silvery sides and is similar in shape to the permit *(Trachinotus falcatus).* However, the pompano has more soft rays in its dorsal and anal fins, and lacks the prominent second and third ribs of the permit. It is also much smaller than the per-mit, averaging about 2 pounds with a maximum of around 8 pounds.

The African pompano is found in the warmer waters of both sides of the Atlantic. Its back is bluish green, fading to silver-white on the sides and belly. Juveniles, and some adults, have a series of dark, vertical bars on the flanks, and some also have a dark blotch on the gill plate and on the front of the dorsal and anal fins. Young fish have almost diamond-shaped bodies, and elongated, thread-like rays extending from the front of the dorsal fin. These rays can be three or four times the length of the immature fish, but as the fish matures the rays become shorter, while the body shape itself changes. The adult fish have very jack-like bodies and high, blunt foreheads, and grow to a maximum weight of over 40 pounds.

AFRICAN POMPANO
A beautiful fish characterized by long wispy fin rays. The first seven dorsal rays and the first five anal rays are elongate.

PUMPKINSEED *Lepomis gibbosus*

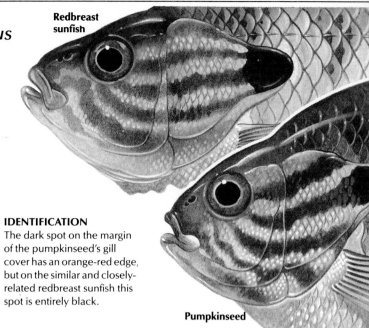

Redbreast sunfish

Pumpkinseed

Many consider the pumpkinseed to be the prettiest of all the North American panfish. This little fish, which grows to about 9 inches at most, is olive green overall with flecks and spots of yellow and blue, and bright blue lines running from the mouth to the edges of the gill plates. There's a red-tipped black spot on the upper corner of each gill plate, and the more brightly-colored males have distinctly red breasts.

The pumpkinseed spawns from May to late July or early August, the eggs being laid in hollows scooped out of sand or gravel beds, and the male guards the nest until several days after the fry

have hatched. The growth rate is slow, and most rod-caught fish are only a few inches long, but the pumpkinseed is very popular with young anglers.

It prefers shallow water with plenty of cover, so it's seldom found far from the bank, and although it's relatively easy to catch it puts up a good fight for a fish of its size. It can be caught on wet flies during spring, on grubs in summer, and on worms all year round.

The pumpkinseed, also known as the common sunfish, is found from the Dakotas and Iowa through to the eastern seaboard, where its range extends south to Georgia.

IDENTIFICATION
The dark spot on the margin of the pumpkinseed's gill cover has an orange-red edge, but on the similar and closely-related redbreast sunfish this spot is entirely black.

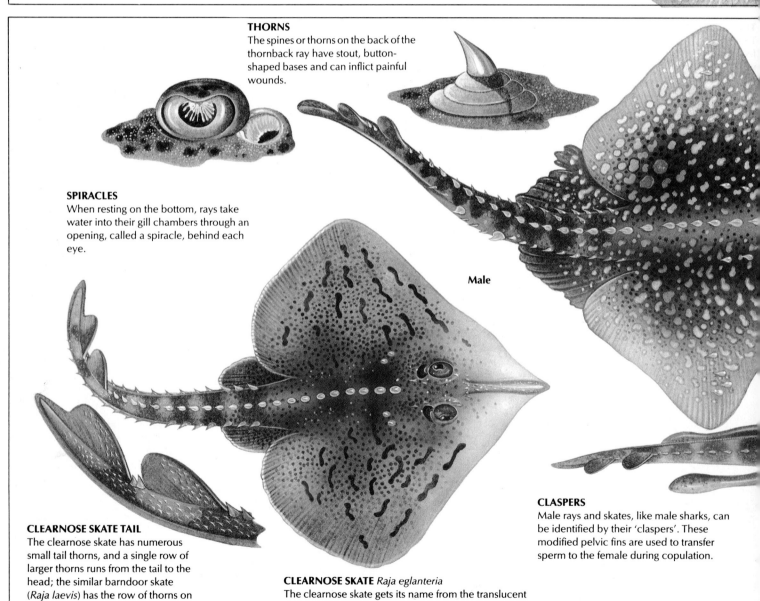

THORNS
The spines or thorns on the back of the thornback ray have stout, button-shaped bases and can inflict painful wounds.

SPIRACLES
When resting on the bottom, rays take water into their gill chambers through an opening, called a spiracle, behind each eye.

Male

CLEARNOSE SKATE TAIL
The clearnose skate has numerous small tail thorns, and a single row of larger thorns runs from the tail to the head; the similar barndoor skate (*Raja laevis*) has the row of thorns on its tail only.

CLEARNOSE SKATE *Raja eglanteria*
The clearnose skate gets its name from the translucent sides of its snout. It grows to about 6 pounds.

CLASPERS
Male rays and skates, like male sharks, can be identified by their 'claspers'. These modified pelvic fins are used to transfer sperm to the female during copulation.

TECHNIQUE	ROD	REEL	LINE	TERMINAL TACKLE	HOOK	WEIGHT	BAIT
Bottom fishing	Heavy beachcaster; 30 to 50-pound class boat rod	Multiplier 4/0 to 6/0	25/50-pounds	Heavy nylon trace or running ledger	Size 4/0 8/0	Bomb/pyramid	Whole or cut fish or squid

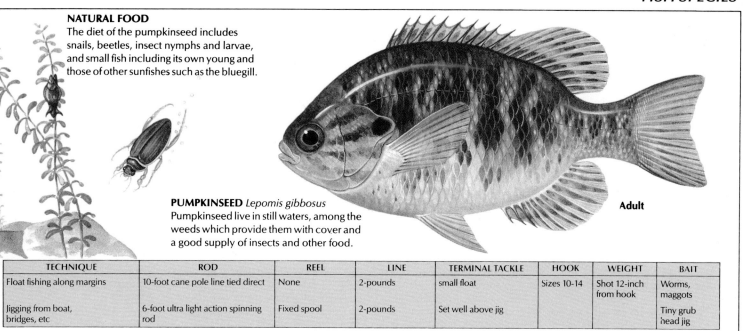

NATURAL FOOD
The diet of the pumpkinseed includes snails, beetles, insect nymphs and larvae, and small fish including its own young and those of other sunfishes such as the bluegill.

PUMPKINSEED *Lepomis gibbosus*
Pumpkinseed live in still waters, among the weeds which provide them with cover and a good supply of insects and other food.

Adult

TECHNIQUE	ROD	REEL	LINE	TERMINAL TACKLE	HOOK	WEIGHT	BAIT
Float fishing along margins	10-foot cane pole line tied direct	None	2-pounds	small float	Sizes 10-14	Shot 12-inch from hook	Worms, maggots
Jigging from boat, bridges, etc	6-foot ultra light action spinning rod	Fixed spool	2-pounds	Set well above jig			Tiny grub head jig

THORNBACK RAY *Raja clavata*
The thornback lives in depths of from 6 feet to 250 feet. Most of those caught weigh less than 15 pounds, but it can grow to over 40 pounds. Like all rays and skates, the thornback has powerful, flat teeth which grind up its food.

EGG CASES
The eggs of skates and of the oviparous rays are each enclosed in a tough casing which is attached to rocks and weeds. The empty cases, known as 'mermaid's purses', are often washed up on beaches.

Male

Female

COMMON SKATE *Raja batis*
The common skate, found in the north east Atlantic, the North Sea and the English Channel, grows to over 8 feet long and more than 200 pounds.

RAYS AND SKATES

The rays and skates are mostly bottom-dwelling fish species, although they do sometimes hunt in mid water. They are related to the sharks, and like them they have cartilaginous rather than bony skeletons. Their bodies are flattened, and the broad pectoral fins or 'wings' give them their characteristic diamond or circular shapes.

Their tails are long and thin, and while rays lack both caudal and anal fins, skates have small but noticeable caudal fins. Most rays, however, have at least one spine or barb near or at the base of the tail. These spines can inflict painful injuries, and in many species of ray they are also poisonous. Another general difference between skates and rays is that rays have smooth skins, while the skin of most skates carries small barbs or thorns.

As with sharks, the eggs of skates and rays are fertilized within the bodies of the females. All skates are oviparous, laying their eggs to hatch in the sea. Some rays, such as the thornback ray *(Raja clavata)* of the eastern Atlantic, are oviparous, but most are oviviparous, that is, the eggs develop and hatch within the mother and the young are born alive.

The thornback is the commonest ray in the shallow waters of the North Sea, the English Channel and the eastern Atlantic, and also occurs in the Mediterranean and the western Baltic. It gets its name from the rows of sharp spines on its back and tail – usually a long row running from the back of the head to the tip of the tail, with a smaller row on either side of it plus others on the tail and sometimes on the wings and snout. These spines are not poisonous, like those of the stingrays, but they are bacteria-ridden and so any wound they inflict on the unwary angler can become infected.

Most thornbacks are taken by boat anglers, usually in waters of less than 30 feet, but during the summer months many come close inshore and are taken by anglers fishing from the beach or rocks.

Rays and skates range in size from comparatively small fish such as the Atlantic guitarfish *(Rhinobatos lentiginosus)* and the clearnose skate *(Raja eglanteria)* which are normally under 2½ feet long and weigh only a few pounds, to the Atlantic common skate *(Raja (Dipturus) batis)* which can top 400 pounds and the manta *(Manta birostris)* of the tropical western Atlantic which grows to about 2 tons. These huge rays, over 20 feet long and almost as wide, feed and bask at or near the surface, and are strong enough to overturn a small boat with a flip of wing. The Pacific manta *(Manta hamiltoni)* is a few feet smaller and about half the weight.

Rays and skates feed mostly on molluscs, crustaceans, fish, squid and worms. Despite their ugly appearance and general lack of true fighting ability, they are popular with many anglers because they often feed when other fish are noticeable by their absence.

ROACH *Rutilus rutilus*

The roach may only be modest in size, but it's the most commonly-sought of all British and European freshwater fish. Roach attain a maximum weight of 4 to 5 pounds and a length of about 18 inches, but anything over 2 pounds is considered a noteworthy catch.

In cross-section the roach is oval, the adult fish being particularly humpbacked and deep-bodied, but shape varies from one environment to another. Roach in small rivers tend to be more streamlined, while those living in deep, rich reservoirs are always very deep-bodied.

The color along the back varies from gray to blue or green, with bright, silvery flanks and a clearly-defined lateral line. Winter roach have a bluish tint to their scales, while in summer they take on a more brassy look. The belly is always a creamy white.

Roach are abundant shoal fish, often shoaling in numbers of several hundred, and are found in every type of water from tiny streams to the tidal reaches of major rivers. They also thrive in still water, and are to be found in lakes, reservoirs and village ponds everywhere. They often shoal with other species, such as rudd and bream, and when they gather in late spring or early summer to spawn this often results in roach/rudd and roach/bream hybrids.

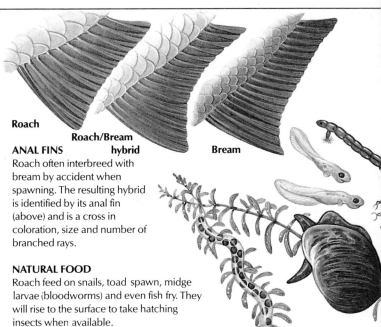

Roach

ANAL FINS   **Roach/Bream**   **hybrid**   **Bream**

Roach often interbreed with bream by accident when spawning. The resulting hybrid is identified by its anal fin (above) and is a cross in coloration, size and number of branched rays.

NATURAL FOOD
Roach feed on snails, toad spawn, midge larvae (bloodworms) and even fish fry. They will rise to the surface to take hatching insects when available.

RUDD *Scardinius erythrophthalmus*

The rudd is the prettiest of all British and European shoaling freshwater species. This gentle fish has a rather slim, oval cross-section and a small, neat head with a protruding jaw.

The back is medium olive, shading into beautifully-scaled flanks of bright, golden, buttery yellow with a sheen quite unlike that of any other freshwater species, and along the belly the color changes to a more creamy yellow. The fins are rather pert and of a brilliant orange-red color, and the tail is forked.

Rudd are sometimes confused with roach, with which they often hybridize. The points to look for are the richer color and protruding lower jaw of the rudd, and the more rearward position of its dorsal fin. When the rudd's dorsal is folded flat along its back, it easily overlaps a point directly above the front edge of the anal fin, whereas the roach's does not.

Rudd feed on scuds and nymphs in the bottom detritus or among weeds and reed stems, but in summer they can be seen at the surface, feeding on the rising pupae and the emerging flies.

Rudd are found mainly in still waters, but also thrive in slow-flowing rivers. They usually stay close to underwater vegetation, and they spawn in soft weeds or among rush or reed stems in warm shallows in late spring.

NATURAL FOOD
The rudd has a sharply upturned mouth, ideal for surface feeding. Rudd will take mayflies and damselflies from the surface as well as diving beetles and aquatic animals. In winter, or when insect activity is low, rudd feed on the bottom.

OLD RUDD
Old, large rudd are a rich bronze and become very deep-bodied.

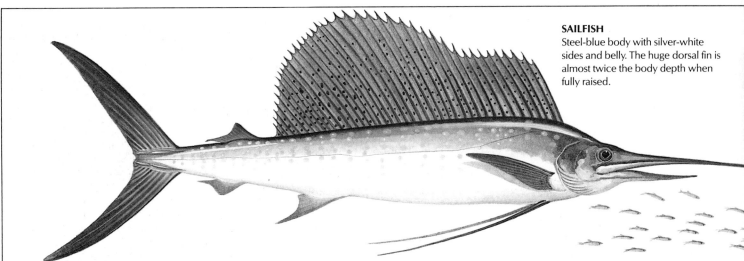

SAILFISH
Steel-blue body with silver-white sides and belly. The huge dorsal fin is almost twice the body depth when fully raised.

TECHNIQUE	ROD	REEL	LINE	TERMINAL TACKLE	HOOK	WEIGHT	BAIT
Trolling	20, 30, 50-pound class boat rod	20, 30, 50 lever drag multiplier	20, 30 50-pound nylon/Dacron	Heavy nylon/wire trace	8/0 flat-forged eye		Small Kona Head
Fly fishing	Heavy fly rod	salt water fly reel	Weight forward 10	20-pound fly leader	2/0		Streamer fly

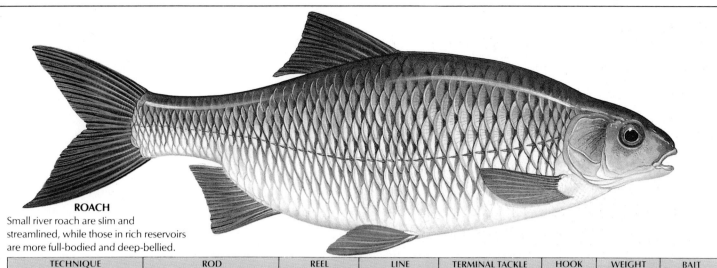

ROACH
Small river roach are slim and streamlined, while those in rich reservoirs are more full-bodied and deep-bellied.

TECHNIQUE	ROD	REEL	LINE	TERMINAL TACKLE	HOOK	WEIGHT	BAIT
Trotting in slow-flowing rivers with bait tripping bottom	12 to 14-foot match/float light tip action	Centrepin, fixed spool, closed face	2½-pound	Waggler/stick float	Sizes 14-20	4 no. 6 to 4BB	Casters, tares maggots
Quivertip ledgering in rivers watch tip for delicate bites	10 to 11-foot ledger with screw in quiver to built in quivertip	Fixed spool	2½-pounds	Fixed link or block end swimfeeder	Sizes 10-12	Swan shot link	Casters, bread-flake, maggots

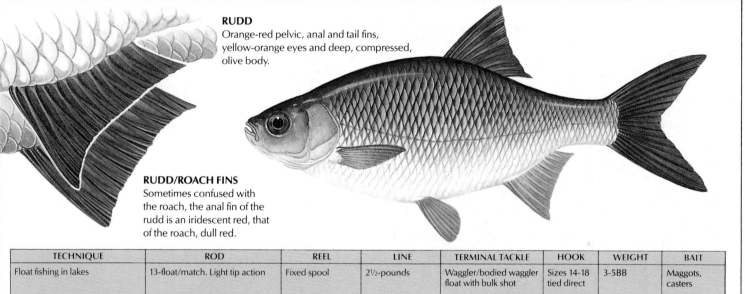

RUDD
Orange-red pelvic, anal and tail fins, yellow-orange eyes and deep, compressed, olive body.

RUDD/ROACH FINS
Sometimes confused with the roach, the anal fin of the rudd is an iridescent red, that of the roach, dull red.

TECHNIQUE	ROD	REEL	LINE	TERMINAL TACKLE	HOOK	WEIGHT	BAIT
Float fishing in lakes	13-float/match. Light tip action	Fixed spool	2½-pounds	Waggler/bodied waggler float with bulk shot	Sizes 14-18 tied direct	3-5BB	Maggots, casters
Ledgering in stillwaters	10 to 12-foot Avon action ledger	Fixed spool	3 to 4-pounds	Fixed paternoster with blockend swimfeeder	Sizes 10-16		Breadflake, casters

DEVELOPMENT
Sailfish eggs are shed in open water. Only a tiny proportion of the grotesque-looking young survive, though their growth-rate is several feet each year.

NATURAL FOOD
Sailfish feed mostly at mid-water on squid and a variety of pelagic fish species, such as anchovy.

SAILFISH *Istiophorus platyperus*

Although both the Atlantic and the Pacific sailfishes are considered to be a single species, the Pacific sailfish grows to over twice the size of the Atlantic fish. As a result, the IGFA lists them separately for record purposes. Commercially-caught Pacific sailfish of 275 pounds have been recorded, but rod-caught fish are smaller.

The outstanding feature of the sailfish is its huge dorsal fin, which when fully raised may be more than twice the body depth of the fish. This fin is normally a beautiful cobalt blue, with a sprinkling of black spots, while the body is steel blue on the back with silver-white sides and belly.

There is usually a series of vertical rows of pale spots along the sides, which tend to fade after the fish dies. The upper jaw is elongated into a long, slender spear, and the tail is symmetrical and deeply forked; the pectoral fins are longer than those of any other billfish.

Sailfish tend to travel in small, loose schools, feeding on squid and a wide variety of fish. They feed mostly at mid water, but on occasions when the baitfish shoals move to the surface, a school of feeding sailfish is a spectacular sight. Once hooked, on live or dead fishbaits, sailfish put up a dramatic, acrobatic fight which makes them very popular with light tackle anglers.

SALMON

The various species and sub-species of salmon are the most highly-regarded of all the fish that can be caught in fresh water, both for their angling value and for their flesh. The Atlantic salmon *(Salmo salar)*, for instance, can be guaranteed to put up a strong and often spectacular fight when hooked, and its flesh can be cooked or smoked to provide one of the finest of foods.

Although hatched in fresh water, the Atlantic salmon spends most of its life at sea, returning to fresh water only to spawn. In the sea, the salmon travel widely, and many make transatlantic migrations to feeding grounds off Greenland or in the Norwegian Sea.

Unfortunately, many of these isolated feeding grounds have been discovered and over-exploited by commercial fishing interests, and this has resulted in a marked decline in stocks throughout the known range of the Atlantic salmon.

Atlantic salmon normally return to their parent river after about 3 or 4 years at sea, although some return sooner. They often die after spawning, but many survive to make two or more spawning runs.

The Atlantic salmon spawn far upriver in November and January, the eggs being deposited in a redd, a nest scooped out in the gravel by the hen fish. Once buried in the gravel, the eggs remain in place until they hatch in late April or early May. The fry remain in the gravel for 3 to 5 weeks, until they're free of their egg sacs, and begin to feed actively as soon as they emerge.

At this stage, the small fish (or parr, as they are called) swim and feed in shoals, but as they grow they spread out along the length of the river. After some 3 to 5 years in the river, the parr, now about 6 inches long, lose their mottled colors and become silvery, ready for their journey to the sea.

In the sea, mature Atlantic salmon are normally green-blue on the back, with silvery white sides and underparts. This coloring changes as the fish approach the spawning stage, when they become brown or bronze with spots of red and black, and the fins darken. After spawning, many salmon die, but the few weak and emaciated survivors, known as kelts, slowly make their way downstream to the sea.

Although adult salmon are believed not to feed while they are in fresh water, they will none-theless attack a fly, spinner, plug, prawn or bunch of earthworms, possibly out of bad temper.

The Pacific salmon *(Onchorhynchus* spp), unlike their Atlantic cousins, all die after spawning. However, apart from this rather tragic wipeout of the parent fish, the life cycle of most of the species is comparable to that of the Atlantic salmon.

There are six species of Pacific salmon, one of which – the cherry salmon *(Onchorhynchus masou)* – is found only in Asian waters. Of the others, the chum salmon *(O. keta)* is occasionally encountered by anglers but mostly caught by commercial netting. This fish is commonest off Alaksa.

The king salmon *(O. tshawy-tscha)*, also called the chinook, is the largest of the Pacific salmon. The biggest recorded – a commercially-caught fish – weighed in at a staggering 126 pounds, but most rod-caught chinook are less than 20 pounds.

The other Pacific salmon species are the coho salmon *(O. kisutch)*, the pink salmon *(O. gorbuscha)* and the sockeye salmon *(O. nerka)*. A small, landlocked form of sockeye, the kokanee, was once found only in lakes from Oregon to Alaska, but has been introduced into lakes and reservoirs in many parts of the USA.

There is also a landlocked form of Atlantic salmon, found originally in New England and the Maritime Provinces of Canada but since introduced into other areas, known as the landlocked salmon in the USA and as the ouananiche in Canada.

In Europe, there is a landlocked relative of the Atlantic salmon known as the huchen *(Hucho hucho)*. The huchen, which originated in the Danube Basin, has been successfully introduced into rivers in eastern France. There was also an unsuccessful attempt to introduce it into the River Thames.

This huge fish, which is usually confined to the upper reaches of its resident river system, can attain a weight of over 45 pounds. The huchen has a greeny-blue back, silvery sides and white underparts, and the sides have a subtle pink sheen and delicate, X-shaped markings.

A voracious feeder, the predatory huchen is normally caught on spinners or wobbled deadbaits. Unfortunately, in many areas the huchen has been severely overfished, but efforts are being made to replenish stocks.

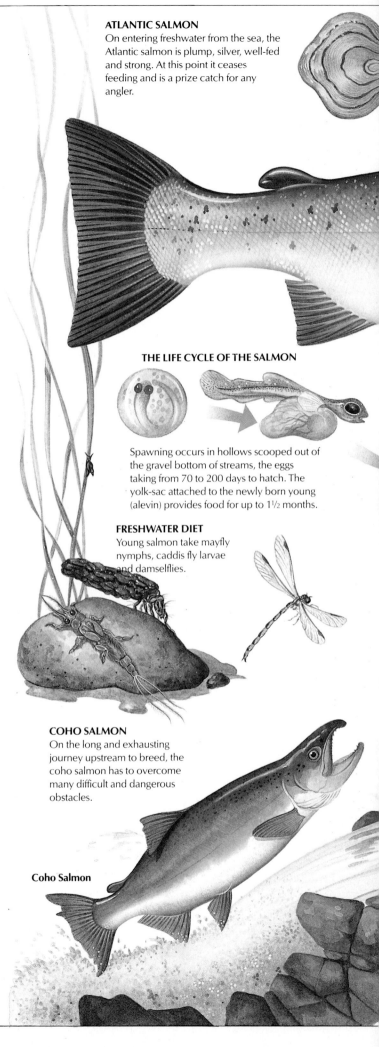

ATLANTIC SALMON
On entering freshwater from the sea, the Atlantic salmon is plump, silver, well-fed and strong. At this point it ceases feeding and is a prize catch for any angler.

THE LIFE CYCLE OF THE SALMON

Spawning occurs in hollows scooped out of the gravel bottom of streams, the eggs taking from 70 to 200 days to hatch. The yolk-sac attached to the newly born young (alevin) provides food for up to 1½ months.

FRESHWATER DIET
Young salmon take mayfly nymphs, caddis fly larvae and damselflies.

COHO SALMON
On the long and exhausting journey upstream to breed, the coho salmon has to overcome many difficult and dangerous obstacles.

Coho Salmon

SCALES
The age, condition and spawning history of a salmon is revealed by examining its scales.

JAWS
As the male salmon progresses upstream, it undergoes various changes. The lower jaw develops a hook or kype, and the skin becomes tougher and thicker, taking on a pink hue with numerous spots and blotches.

Atlantic Salmon

A young salmon, or parr, of between 6 months and two years old.

Between 2 and 5 years parr turn silver and as smolts move towards the sea, returning as adults to the stream of their birth to spawn.

KELTS
After spawning, the spent fish, or kelt, is exhausted, having lost 40 percent body weight since leaving the sea. Many die, but the survivors return to the sea, recover, and spawn again.

Kelt

CHINOOK SALMON
An inhabitant of rivers from southern California to Alaska, the black speckled chinook normally spawns from September to November.

Chinook Salmon

TECHNIQUE	ROD	REEL	LINE	TERMINAL TACKLE	HOOK	WEIGHT	BAIT
Fly fishing	12 to 16-foot rod	Fly reel	Fly line Weight forward	Heavy fly cast	Single or double	None	Salmon flies
Spinning	10-foot heavy spinning rod	Multiplier	20-pound nylon	15 to 20-pound nylon	Trebles	Wye lead	Plugs, Toby
Bait fishing		multiplier	20-pound nylon	15 to 20-pound nylon	Size 1 eyed	Bullet lead	Worms

SHADS

The shads are a group of marine fishes, related to the herring, which migrate into rivers to spawn. In Europe, the numbers of the once-plentiful twaite shad *(Alosa fallax)* and allis shad *(Alosa alosa)* have been greatly reduced by pollution and the destruction of spawning grounds.

Shads have fared better in North American waters, where the American shad *(A. sapidissima)* and, to a lesser extent, the hickory shad *(A. mediocris)* and the skipjack herring *(A. chrysochloris)* are of interest to anglers.

The American shad was originally found only in Atlantic waters and associated rivers from the Gulf of St Lawrence to the Florida Keys, but in 1871 it was introduced, with great success, to the California coast. Since then, its range has extended as far north as Alaska. In Atlantic waters, the shad can attain a weight of about 12 pounds, and those in the Pacific tend to grow even larger.

Most shads are caught when they come into the rivers to spawn, normally in March and April. The males mature about 3 or 4 years after hatching, but females may take twice this time.

American shad are a popular sporting fish, taken by trolling or spinning with small spoons, spinners or jigs, or by fly fishing with streamer flies.

EUROPEAN SHAD
The twaite and allis shad are so closely matched that the only distinct feature separating the two species is that the twaite shad has six to eight blotches on the dorsal area, whereas the allis shad has just a single dark blotch.

NATURAL FOOD
In freshwater, younger shad feed on a simple diet of small organisms such as cyclops, water fleas and rotifers. At sea, opossum shrimps form part of their diet.

SHARKS

The sharks, of which there are over 250 species, are an ancient group of fishes whose skeletons are composed of cartilage rather than bone. They do, how-ever, have bony teeth, and their tiny scales are formed from a similar material.

Sharks are commonly thought of as ruthless predators, and while many are – the white shark *(Carcharodon carcharias)*, for instance – others such as the 50-foot basking shark *(Cetorhinus maximus)* and the 70-foot whale shark *(Rhincodon typus)* are harmless plankton-eaters.

Like those of their relatives the rays and skates, the eggs of sharks are fertilized within the bodies of the females. Some species are oviparous, laying their eggs to hatch in the sea, but most are oviviparous – the eggs hatch within the mother, and the young are born alive.

One of the most commonly caught sharks is the blue shark *(Prionace glauca)*, which is distributed worldwide and can reach a weight of more than 450 pounds. The mako *(Isurus oxyrhincus)* is also a very popular game fish, and one which puts up a good fight when hooked. Other sporting sharks include the great hammerhead *(Sphyrna mokarran)*, the porbeagle *(Lamna nasus)*, the thresher *(Alopias vulpinas)*, the tiger shark *(Galeocerda cuvieri)*.

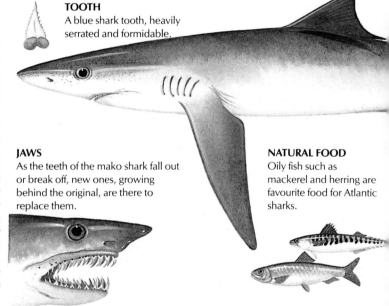

TOOTH
A blue shark tooth, heavily serrated and formidable.

JAWS
As the teeth of the mako shark fall out or break off, new ones, growing behind the original, are there to replace them.

NATURAL FOOD
Oily fish such as mackerel and herring are favourite food for Atlantic sharks.

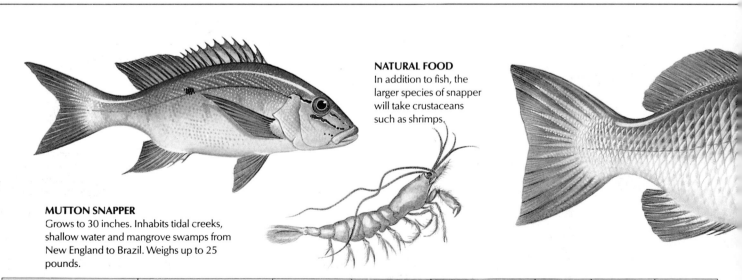

NATURAL FOOD
In addition to fish, the larger species of snapper will take crustaceans such as shrimps.

MUTTON SNAPPER
Grows to 30 inches. Inhabits tidal creeks, shallow water and mangrove swamps from New England to Brazil. Weighs up to 25 pounds.

TECHNIQUE	ROD	REEL	LINE	TERMINAL TACKLE	HOOK	WEIGHT	BAIT
Plug fishing	Heavy duty spinning rod	Small multiplier	15/20-pound nylon	Wire/heavy nylon trace	2/0 treble		Plugs
Bottom fishing	Heavy duty spinning rod	Medium fixed spool	15/20-pound	Wire/heavy nylon trace	2/0 eyed	Bomb/pyramid	Live/dead bait

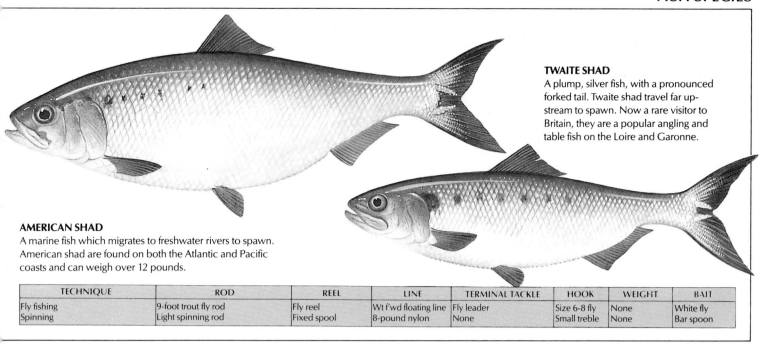

TWAITE SHAD
A plump, silver fish, with a pronounced forked tail. Twaite shad travel far up-stream to spawn. Now a rare visitor to Britain, they are a popular angling and table fish on the Loire and Garonne.

AMERICAN SHAD
A marine fish which migrates to freshwater rivers to spawn. American shad are found on both the Atlantic and Pacific coasts and can weigh over 12 pounds.

TECHNIQUE	ROD	REEL	LINE	TERMINAL TACKLE	HOOK	WEIGHT	BAIT
Fly fishing	9-foot trout fly rod	Fly reel	Wt f'wd floating line	Fly leader	Size 6-8 fly	None	White fly
Spinning	Light spinning rod	Fixed spool	8-pound nylon	None	Small treble	None	Bar spoon

BLUE SHARK
The blue shark is one of the commonest sharks in temperate and tropical seas.

PORBEAGLE SHARK
Male sharks are identified by their claspers. These, in fact, are not used to clasp during mating, but to penetrate.

PORBEAGLE TOOTH
Identified by its two cusps or additional points.

TECHNIQUE	ROD	REEL	LINE	TERMINAL TACKLE	HOOK	WEIGHT	BAIT
Blue: drift floating	50/80-pound class boat	9/0, 10/0, 12/0	50/80-pound nylon/Dacron	Heavy duty yacht rigging	10/0, 12/0, 14/0 offset		Fresh live/ dead fish
Mako: trolling	50/80-pound class boat	9/0, 10/0, 12/0	50/80-pound nylon/Dacron	Heavy duty yacht rigging	10/0, 12/0, 14/0 offset		Black Kona Head

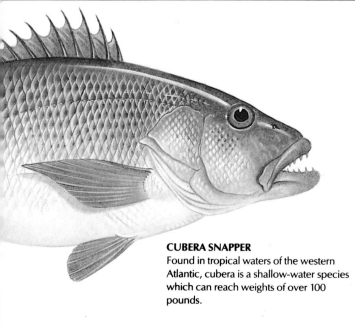

CUBERA SNAPPER
Found in tropical waters of the western Atlantic, cubera is a shallow-water species which can reach weights of over 100 pounds.

SNAPPERS

The snapper family includes such fish as the mutton snapper *(Lutjanus analis)*, red snapper *(L. blackfordi)*, dog snapper *(L. jocu)*, gray snapper *(L. griseus)*, lane snapper *(L. synagris)*, blackfin snapper *(L. buccanella)*, mahogany snapper *(L. mahogani)*, the yellowtail snapper *(Ocyurus chrysurus)* and the cubera snapper *(L. cyanopterus)*, which is the largest of them all.

The cubera snapper can reach a weight of over 100 pounds, and like most snappers it occurs in the tropical western Atlantic. In color, the cubera snapper is green to grey, with dark red eyes and sometimes a reddish tinge to the flanks. The cubera is a shallow-water species found close to submerged reefs and rock ledges at depths of from a few feet to a maximum of about 120 feet, and small specimens are also to be found in estuaries and salt lakes.

The cubera is a good sports fish which readily takes live or dead natural baits and will also attack artificial lures, in particular plug baits trolled close to the bottom.

Small cubera snappers have tasty flesh, but they aren't as commercially important as the gray snapper and the very popular red snapper. Gray snapper can be taken on a light tackle with live shrimp bait, but red snapper are usually taken with deadbaits on heavier tackle.

SNOOK *Centropomus undecimalis*

The snook is a popular salt-water game fish found along the coasts of Florida and Texas and throughout the West Indies, and in the tropical Pacific. Its most noticeable feature is the thick, black lateral line which runs from behind the shoulder to the very end of the tail, quite unlike that of any other fish.

The back is goldish brown to brown or dark gray, lightening quickly to silvery sides and a white belly. The head is very flat with a strongly-protruding lower jaw, and the snook has no teeth as such, just strong, sharp bristles along the jaw rims and on the tongue; the edges of the gill covers are very sharp.

The snook spends most of its time in shallow coastal waters, often venturing into estuaries, creeks, lagoons and mangrove swamps, and sometimes travelling well inland along rivers or canals into almost completely fresh water, a habit it shares with the tarpon.

The snook's diet consists of shrimp, small crabs and fish. It can be taken on artificial lures, but live bait, especially mullet, is one of the best ways to tempt a large snook; it should be set to fish shallow beneath a float. Most rod-caught snook are of 5 to 8 pounds, rising to 12 to 25 pounds in some areas, and the top weight is around 50 pounds.

NATURAL FOOD
Snook are a predatory species feeding on many types of fish, and they also take shrimps and small crabs, which make up an important part of their diet.

REDEAR SUNFISH
L. microlophus
The redear sunfish closely resembles the pumpkinseed, but it has a red or orange tip to its gill cover.

NATURAL FOOD
Redear sunfish have a marked fondness for snails, but they also take insect larvae such as those of the midge.

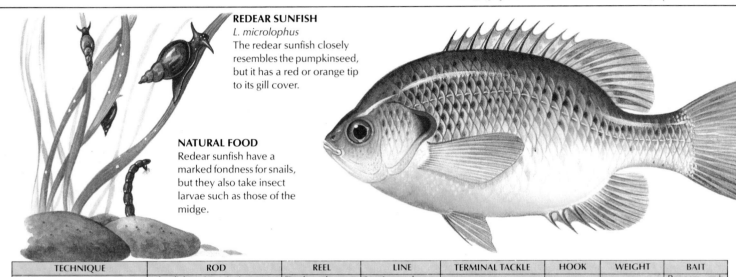

TECHNIQUE	ROD	REEL	LINE	TERMINAL TACKLE	HOOK	WEIGHT	BAIT
Surface poppers or jigs	6-foot light action spinning	Fixed spool	3 to 4-pounds				Poppers, grub tails, spoons
Float fish worm or fish baits	10-foot pole, line tied direct	None	2 to 3-pounds	Small float	6-12 tied direct	Shot 12-inches from hook	Worms, shrimps, caddis grubs

BARRED SURFPERCH
A. argenteus
The barred surfperch is brassy above, lightening to silvery on the sides with offset vertical bars of a dark red-brown.

NATURAL FOOD
Surfperches feed on crustaceans and molluscs, often very close inshore.

TECHNIQUE	ROD	REEL	LINE	TERMINAL TACKLE	HOOK	WEIGHT	BAIT
Light surf fishing	Surfcasting rod	Small multiplier	10 to 15-pound	Short nylon trace	1/0 eyed	Grip or bomb	Cut fish, crab
Bottom fishing	Spinning or 12-pound class boat	Small multiplier	10 to 15-pound	Short nylon trace	1/0 eyed	Grip or bomb	Cut fish, crab

SNOOK *Centropomus undecimalis*
The snook has a pike-like shape and is easily identified by the thick black lateral stripe along its side.

TECHNIQUE	ROD	REEL	LINE	TERMINAL TACKLE	HOOK	WEIGHT	BAIT
Lure fishing	6-foot surfcaster	Multiplier/fixed spool	10 to 12-pounds				Plugs, spoons
Fly fishing	9-foot fast tip action fly WF 8-9	Single action fly	Bass taper floating	12-pound cast			Streamers jigs

GREEN SUNFISH *L. cyanellus*
Many species of sunfish are very similar in appearance. One of the distinguishing features of the green sunfish is its large mouth, which extends back to below the mid point of the eye, unlike the mouths of, say, the redear sunfish and the redbreast sunfish (*L. auritis*).

SUNFISH

The sunfish are a family of over thirty North American freshwater species, including many of the fish most popular with American anglers such as bluegill, crappies, pumpkinseed and the highly-prized largemouth and smallmouth basses. Other commonly caught sunfish are the green, redbreast and redear sunfishes and the rock bass.

The green sunfish (*Lepomis cyanellus*) averages 5 to 7 inches long, with a maximum of about 9 inches. An inhabitant of streams, rivers and lakes, its main range is from the Mississippi valley east to the Alleghanies, west to Colorado and New Mexico and north to the Great Lakes.

The redbreast sunfish (*Lepomis auritis*) is a handsome, red-breasted fish which reaches a length of about 12 inches, although most are between 6 and 8 inches, and is found in the rivers, and sometimes ponds and lakes, of the Atlantic drainage. The redear sunfish (*Lepomis microlophus*) is larger, and can grow to over 4 pounds.

The rock bass (*Ambloplites rupestris*) is a sturdy, olive-green fish which is found mainly in waters from Manitoba to New England and south to Texas, and reaches a maximum of about 12 inches long and a pound in weight.

SURFPERCHES

STRIPED SEAPERCH *E. lateralis*
The striped seaperch is one of the most beautiful of the surfperches. It grows to a length of about 15 inches, and is found from California to Alaska.

Most of the 23 species of surf-perch are found in shallow water along the Pacific coast of North America. The exceptions are the pink seaperch (*Zalembius rosaceus*) which lives in deep waters of about 100 to 300 feet, and the tule perch (*Hysterocarpus traski*), is a freshwater fish found in rivers and one lake (Clear Lake) in central California.

Many surfperches are commercially important, and also provide shore anglers with some of their sport in California and elsewhere along the Pacific coast. The most important species for anglers is the barred surfperch (*Amphistichus argenteus*), which reaches a maximum of over 4 pounds; as with all surfperches, the females give birth to live young.

Other surfperches of angling interest include the black perch (*Embiotoca jacksoni*), calico surfperch (*Amphistichus koelzi*), pile perch (*Rhacochilus vacca*), rainbow seaperch (*Hypsurus caryi*), redtail surfperch (*Amphistichus rhodoterus*), rubberlip seaperch (*Rhacochilus toxotes*), shiner perch (*Cymatogaster aggregata*), silver surfperch (*Hyperprosopon ellipticum*), spotfin surfperch (*Hyperprosopon anale*), striped seaperch (*Embiotica lateralis*), walleye surfperch (*Hyperprosopon argenteum*) and the white seaperch (*Phanerodon furcatus*).

SWORDFISH *Xiphias gladius*

The swordfish or broadbill rates as the ultimate challenge to big game anglers, and this great, leathery, prehistoric-looking fish can be one of the most difficult of all the mighty ocean predators to tempt into taking a bait.

A totally unmistakable fish, the swordfish has a smooth, flattened bill, longer and wider than that of any other billfish. It also has a high, non-retractable dorsal fin and a large single keel on each side of the base of the big, crescent-shaped tail. Adult swordfish lack scales, and their coloring varies a good deal. The back can be dark brown, bronze, gray-purple, blue or even black, but the belly and sides are usually a dirty white and the fins are dark. The eyes are large and dark blue.

Swordfish are distributed worldwide in temperate and warm waters, and are probably more common than many people realize. They are, however, rather solitary fish and are rarely seen in pairs, and are often found at extreme depths.

The swordfish has a very soft mouth, and many hooked fish are lost when the hooks tear out, but once hooked it puts up a strong, savage fight. Swordfish can be taken on slowly-trolled fish or squid bait, and fishing at night using squid in conjunction with a chemical light stick can be very successful.

Close-up of remora showing the disc above the head

NATURAL FOOD
In midwater, swordfish take clupeidae and pelagic squid.

TARPON *Megalops atlantica*

The tarpon is thought by anyone fortunate enough to have landed one to be one of the most exciting sports fish in the world. They fight ferociously when hooked, hurling themselves as much as ten feet out of the water in an attempt to get free.

The distribution of tarpon covers many tropical and subtropical waters around the world, with the largest concentrations being in and around the Gulf of Mexico, the Florida Keys and Everglades, Surinam, Costa Rica and many of the Caribbean islands.

The tarpon is a deep-bodied fish, with compressed flanks and huge, tough scales. The back is a dark gray, often with a blue or green tinge, quickly turning to burnished silver along the flanks, and the belly is milky white. The fins are large and powerful, and the last ray of the dorsal is distinctively elongated.

Although tarpon are occasionally caught by offshore trolling, they are essentially a fish of estuaries and tidal creeks and channels. They love to explore mangrove swamps, lagoons and shallow rivers, which is where they spawn in the spring.

Tarpon can reach lengths of over 8 feet and weights of over 300 pounds, though most of those taken by anglers are in the 20 to 80 pound range.

FIGHTING TARPON
A ferocious fighter, the tarpon will leap clear of the water when hooked, making repeated attempts at escape.

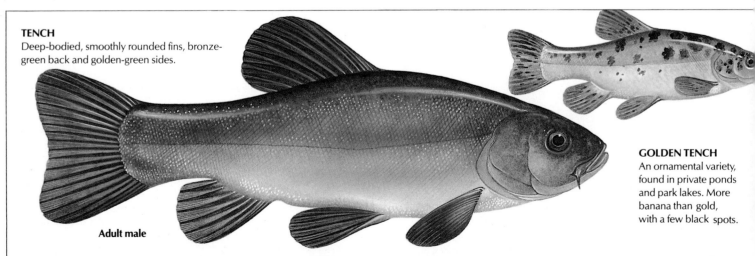

TENCH
Deep-bodied, smoothly rounded fins, bronze-green back and golden-green sides.

Adult male

GOLDEN TENCH
An ornamental variety, found in private ponds and park lakes. More banana than gold, with a few black spots.

TECHNIQUE	ROD	REEL	LINE	TERMINAL TACKLE	HOOK	WEIGHT	BAIT
Float fishing, lift method	12 to 13-foot medium action	Centrepin, fixed 2½ to 4-pounds spool	Peacock quill float fixed bottom end			1 AA shot	Breadflake, sweetcorn
Ledgering	10 to 12-foot Avon 1¼-pounds test curve ledger	Fixed spool	6-pounds	Fixed paternoster with open-ended feeder	10-14 on 4-pound link	Only on feeder	Maggots casters

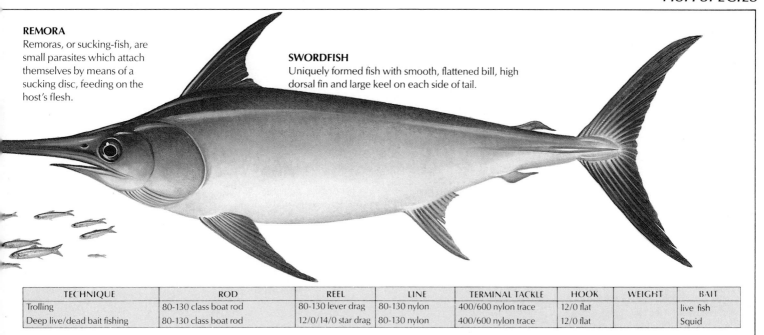

REMORA
Remoras, or sucking-fish, are small parasites which attach themselves by means of a sucking disc, feeding on the host's flesh.

SWORDFISH
Uniquely formed fish with smooth, flattened bill, high dorsal fin and large keel on each side of tail.

TECHNIQUE	ROD	REEL	LINE	TERMINAL TACKLE	HOOK	WEIGHT	BAIT
Trolling	80-130 class boat rod	80-130 lever drag	80-130 nylon	400/600 nylon trace	12/0 flat		live fish
Deep live/dead bait fishing	80-130 class boat rod	12/0/14/0 star drag	80-130 nylon	400/600 nylon trace	12/0 flat		Squid

TARPON
A deep-bodied fish with unusual elongated rays on the dorsal fin.

NATURAL FOOD
Tarpon feed on fish fry found among plankton, small open-water fishes such as anchovy, and shrimps.

TECHNIQUE	ROD	REEL	LINE	TERMINAL TACKLE	HOOK	WEIGHT	BAIT
Float fished live bait	9 to 10-foot powerful spinning, 2½-pounds test curve	Fixed spool/ multiplier	15/18-pounds	20-inch wire trace slider float. Fish bait midwater	Single size 1/0 treble	Swan shot	5-7-inch fish, crab
Fly casting	9 to 10-foot powerful fast taper reservoir fly 9/10	Large fly holding 200 yds	Bass taper floating size 9-10	12-inches 70-pounds mono			Bucktail streamer

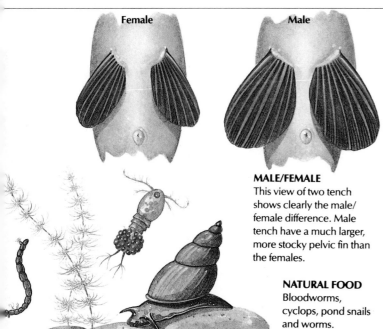

Female

Male

MALE/FEMALE
This view of two tench shows clearly the male/female difference. Male tench have a much larger, more stocky pelvic fin than the females.

NATURAL FOOD
Bloodworms, cyclops, pond snails and worms.

TENCH *Tinca tinca*

The tench is a popular European cyprinid, most commonly found browsing through thick vegetation in lakes, pits, reservoirs and lowland rivers. It has a thick-set body, bronze-green along the back and golden-green on the sides, sometimes more gold than green. There is even a rare variety called the golden tench, which is distinctly banana-colored with a few black specks, and rather pointed, pink-tinted fins instead of the rounded, brown-gray fins of the common tench, with which it is unlikely to be confused.

The scales of the tench are tiny and set flat against the body, and covered in a thick layer of protective slime. The eyes are tiny and orange-red, and the mouth, which is semiprotrusible, has a tiny barbule at each corner and thick, rubbery lips.

The tench is found in Britain, Europe and much of Asia, and was introduced into many Irish waters in 1958. In Europe and Asia it's valued as a food fish, and commercially fished for and farmed. Its natural diet consists of bloodworms, annelid worms, crustaceans, small molluscs and algae, and it loves burying its snout in thick silt and weedbeds to feed. The tench can attain a length of 26 inches and a weight of over 12 pounds, but most good rod-caught fish weigh only 2½ to 6 pounds.

TROUT

O f the many species of trout, the brown trout *(Salmo trutta)* and the rainbow trout *(Salmo gairdneri)* are probably the most widely known.

In shape, the brown trout is an elongated fish. The wrist of the tail is deep, and the upper and lower tail fin rays seem to flow into the outline of the body. The tail itself is broad and normally square-cut, although younger fish occasionally have a slightly concave tail outline which usually vanishes when the fish reaches maturity.

The color of the brown trout varies considerably from one locality to another. In tiny, often acid, streams, they are mostly brownish in color with a sprinkling of black and rust red spots. Fish from rich chalk waters are much brighter, having a golden brown back and buttercup yellow sides, and only rarely have red spots.

Brown trout that live in large lakes and reservoirs are different again, normally having an overall silver appearance and minimal spotting. The exception to this are the huge brown trout that live a cannibal existence in deep, peat-water lochs. These giants are dark gold in color and the spots are very pronounced.

Brown trout spawn in winter, normally between October and January, the eggs being deposited in gravel redds dug by the females. The eggs hatch after 6 to 8 weeks, depending on the water temperature, and the fry remain in the gravel for a further 4 to 6 weeks before beginning to feed.

Like all trout, brown trout feed on insects and crustaceans, but the larger the fish grows the more predatory it becomes, until eventually it feeds almost exclusively on fish; cannibalism is common. Under the right circumstances, brown trout can reach a weight of over 30 pounds.

The sea trout is a migratory form of brown trout which leaves its parent river to spend much of its life in salt water, but returns to it to spawn. Sea trout normally grow faster than their non-migratory brethren, and when fresh-run they have a decidedly silver appearance.

The brown trout, a native European fish, was introduced

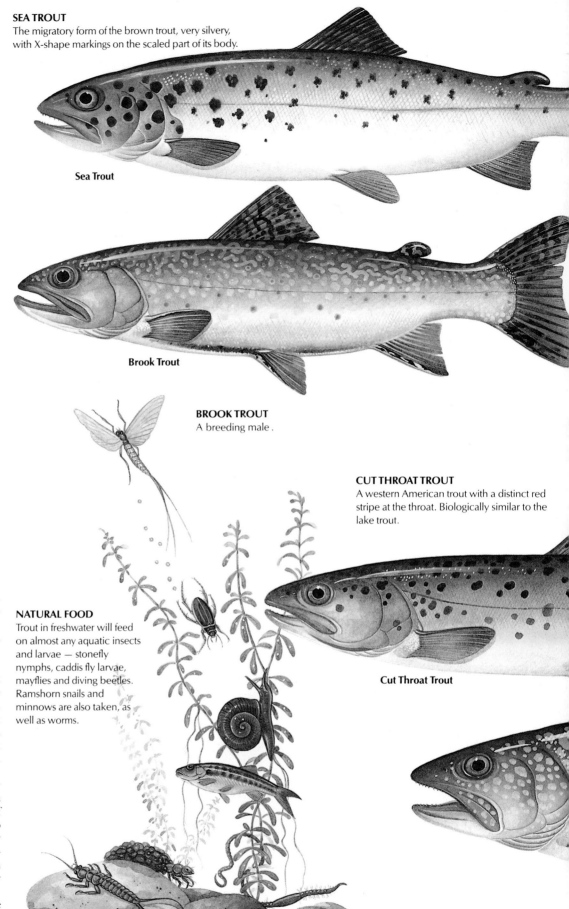

SEA TROUT
The migratory form of the brown trout, very silvery, with X-shape markings on the scaled part of its body.

Sea Trout

Brook Trout

BROOK TROUT
A breeding male .

CUT THROAT TROUT
A western American trout with a distinct red stripe at the throat. Biologically similar to the lake trout.

NATURAL FOOD
Trout in freshwater will feed on almost any aquatic insects and larvae — stonefly nymphs, caddis fly larvae, mayflies and diving beetles. Ramshorn snails and minnows are also taken, as well as worms.

Cut Throat Trout

TECHNIQUE	ROD	REEL	LINE	TERMINAL TACKLE	HOOK	WEIGHT	BAIT
Fly fishing	8, 9, 10, 11-foot fly	Fly reel	Floating/sinking fly	Fly leader	Fly hooks		Wet/dry flies
Spinning	9-foot medium spinning	Fixed spool	Floating/sinking fly	Fly leader	Trebles		Spinners
Trolling/bait fishing	9-foot medium spinning	Fixed spool	10/15-pound nylon	Nylon tackle	Trebles 10-2 f/water	Split shot	Live/dead fish

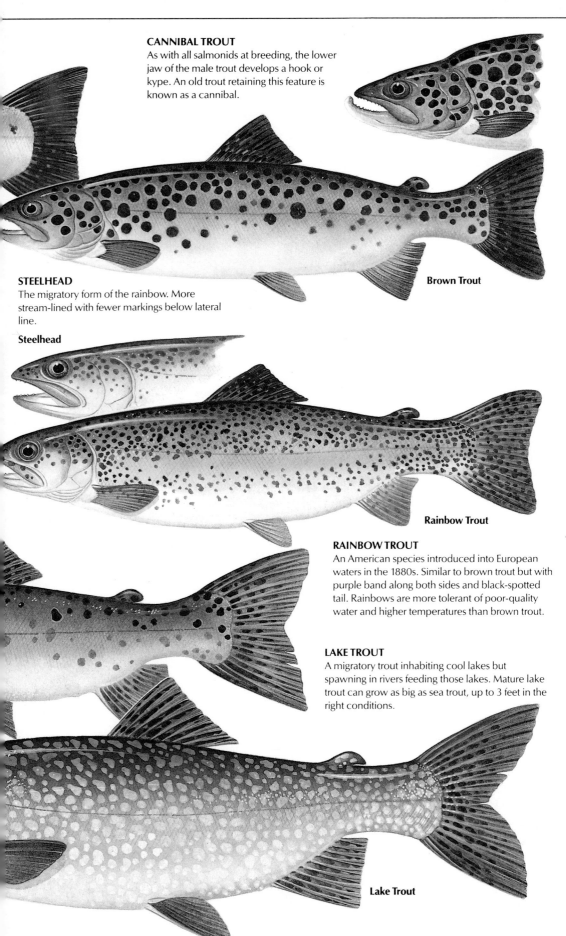

CANNIBAL TROUT
As with all salmonids at breeding, the lower jaw of the male trout develops a hook or kype. An old trout retaining this feature is known as a cannibal.

STEELHEAD
The migratory form of the rainbow. More stream-lined with fewer markings below lateral line.

Steelhead

Brown Trout

Rainbow Trout

RAINBOW TROUT
An American species introduced into European waters in the 1880s. Similar to brown trout but with purple band along both sides and black-spotted tail. Rainbows are more tolerant of poor-quality water and higher temperatures than brown trout.

LAKE TROUT
A migratory trout inhabiting cool lakes but spawning in rivers feeding those lakes. Mature lake trout can grow as big as sea trout, up to 3 feet in the right conditions.

Lake Trout

into North American waters in 1883; the following year saw the beginning of the introduction of rainbow trout to European and other waters from its original range in western North America.

The rainbow trout is slightly more hardy than the brown trout, and can withstand higher water temperatures and poorer water quality. The growth rate of the rainbow is extremely rapid when adequate food is available, one reason why it's now probably the most widely farmed fish in the world. On trout farms, rainbows can reach 20 to 30 pounds in just 4 or 5 years.

Interbreeding with other species and subspecies of trout, plus selective breeding on trout farms, has led to a wide range of color variations in rainbow trout. The most common coloring, though, is blue-brown on the back, silvery white on the underside and iridescent magenta on the sides. Some varieties are heavily spotted, while others show few or no spots and are an overall silver color. Like the brown trout, the rainbow has a migratory form which spends most of its time in the sea. This migratory rainbow is known as the steelhead trout.

The brook trout *(Salvelinus fontinalis)* was originally a native of the northeastern part of North America, but like the rainbow it has been introduced into waters throughout the USA and Canada and in Europe. Although the brook trout has the typical trout shape, it is actually closely related to the char.

Like most of the trout types, the coloring of the brook trout is exemely variable, but a typical pattern is olive to brown on the back, silvery white below, with light green sides dappled with creamy spots and tiny magenta blotches.

Fish farmers have successfully crossed male brook trout with female brown trout to produce a hybrid known as the tiger trout. Tigers are often highly colored, voracious fish that hit a fly or lure like an express train.

Trout can be caught on fly, bait and spinners, but fly fishing is generally regarded as the most sporting and most satisfying technique. When hooked, most trout put up a tremendous fight, sometimes jumping repeatedly in an attempt to shake the hook free.

TUNAS

The tunas, which are members of the mackerel family, are of great importance to commercial fishermen as well as to anglers. The largest, the bluefin tuna *(Thunnus thynnus)* is also one of the largest bony fishes in the sea, growing to over 1500 pounds. The bluefin is distributed worldwide and is highly migratory, travelling in huge schools over great distances; tagged fish have been recorded as travelling 5000 miles in just 50 days.

The bluefin is dark blue-black on the back, paling to silvery white on the lower flanks and belly. Its pectoral fins are rather short, especially when compared to those of the albacore *(Thunnus alalunga)*. This fish, which is dark steel blue with yellowish blue sides and a white belly, has elongated, sickle-shaped pectoral fins and is also known as the longfin tuna as a result.

Other tunas include the blackfin tuna *(Thunnus atlanticus)*, yellowtail tuna *(Thunnus albacares)*, bigeye tuna *(Thunnus obesus)*, little tuna *(Euthynnus alleteratus)*, the little tunnies *(Euthynnus lineatus* and *E. affinis)* and the skipjack tuna *(Katsuwonus pelamis)*. All tunas are predatory, and can be caught by drift fishing with live or dead baits (live mackerel or dead herring), or by trolling with rigged natural or artificial baits.

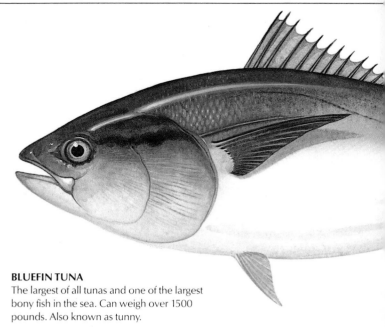

BLUEFIN TUNA
The largest of all tunas and one of the largest bony fish in the sea. Can weigh over 1500 pounds. Also known as tunny.

WAHOO *Acanthocybium solandri*

One of the world's great game fish, the wahoo puts up an explosive fight and is a challenge to any angler on light to medium tackle. The wahoo is a member of the mackerel family, and is found worldwide in subtropical and tropical waters. Although it can grow to over 150 pounds, anything over 60 pounds can be regarded as a fine catch.

The body is long and slim, and the long head has a pointed, cylindrical snout and large, strong teeth. The first dorsal fin is long, with 21 to 27 spines, and it folds down into a groove along the fish's back. The second dorsal and the anal fin are very small, and behind the second dorsal a row of finlets leads to a strong, tuna-like tail.

The color of the back is a deep, almost electric blue, the sides are bluish gray and marked with vertical, dark blue bands, and the underparts are white.

Wahoo normally travel in small groups, eating just about any baitfish or squid that crosses their path. They are commonly taken on trolled deadbaits, such as mullet, and on feathers and other artificial lures. Livebait, fished from a drifting boat, is also effective.

Wahoo are very susceptible to infestation by a trematode parasite, numbers of which are usually present in their stomachs.

TEETH
Typical of predatory species, the wahoo has a large mouth with numerous razor-sharp teeth.

NATURAL FOOD
Wahoo feed on shoaling fishes such as members of the herring family.

FIRST DORSAL FIN
The pattern of the walleye is smudged and vague, that of the zander regular. The walleye also has a black spot, not present on the zander.

WALLEYE
Similar to the zander, but the lower lobe of the caudal fin is pale or white.

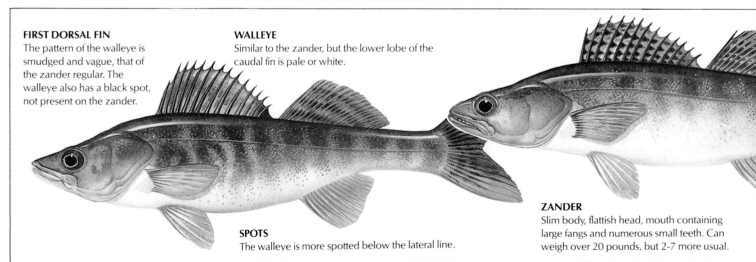

SPOTS
The walleye is more spotted below the lateral line.

ZANDER
Slim body, flattish head, mouth containing large fangs and numerous small teeth. Can weigh over 20 pounds, but 2-7 more usual.

TECHNIQUE	ROD	REEL	LINE	TERMINAL TACKLE	HOOK	WEIGHT	BAIT
Spinning	8-foot medium action spinning	Fixed spool	6-8-pounds	Short fine-wire trace			Bucktail lead heads
Ledgering live or deadbait	10 to 11-foot medium action ledger, 1¼-ounce test curve	Fixed spool	6-8-pounds	20-inch wire trace with running bomb	Two size 10 trebles	1-ounce bomb	Small live/ dead fish

ALBACORE
Distinguished from the bluefin by its very long pectoral fin. Dark steel-blue with yellow blue sides. Also known as the longfin tuna.

NATURAL FOOD
A predatory species, all tunas feed on pelagic squid and shoaling fish such as sardines.

TECHNIQUE	ROD	REEL	LINE	TERMINAL TACKLE	HOOK	WEIGHT	BAIT
Trolling	80-130 class, full roller rings	Lever drag multiplier	80-130 class nylon	400-600-pound nylon	10/0-12/0 flat		Kona Head
Live/dead baiting	80-130 class, full roller rings		80-130 class nylon	400-600-pound nylon	10/0-12/0 offset		Live mackerel dead hearing

WAHOO
Long, torpedo-shaped body, pointed, cylindrical snout and large, strong teeth. Can weigh over 150 pounds.

TECHNIQUE	ROD	REEL	LINE	TERMINAL TACKLE	HOOK	WEIGHT	BAIT
Trolling	30 to 50-pound class	6/0 star drag or 30-50 class multiplier	30-50-pound nylon	Heavy wire tackle	Sizes 8/0-10/0 flat		Kona Head Natural bait mounted for trolling

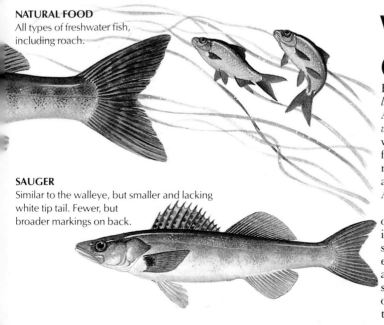

NATURAL FOOD
All types of freshwater fish, including roach.

SAUGER
Similar to the walleye, but smaller and lacking white tip tail. Fewer, but broader markings on back.

WALLEYE, ZANDER AND SAUGER

Only very slight genetic differences separate the European zander (*Stizostedion lucioperca*) from the North American walleye (*S. vitreum vitreum*). The zander and the walleye are members of the perch family, and both are often referred to as 'pikeperch', a term also applied to the North American sauger (*S. canadense*).

The zander and walleye are outwardly very similar. The body is elongated and round in cross-section, with a flattish head. The eye is large, and the powerful jaws and the roof of the mouth carry strong, sharp teeth. The color is olive on the back and sides, fading to metallic white on the belly, and the back and sides are marked by darker bands. The fins are large, and the tail of the walleye has a white tip, absent in the zander, on its lower fork. Both fish can reach weights of over 20 pounds, but 2 to 7 pounds is more usual and anything over 10 pounds is noteworthy.

Sauger are smaller, only 1 to 3 pounds in most waters, although Missouri fish can reach 8 pounds.

All the pikeperches live in rivers, lakes and reservoirs (although the sauger are found in only the very biggest), staying close to the bottom where they hunt in packs for small shoalfish, feeding mostly from dusk till dawn.

WEAKFISHES

The weakfishes are members of the corvina family, most of which live in the Pacific off the coasts of Central and South America. The weakfish (*Cynoscion regalis*) itself, however, is a very popular gamefish of the eastern Atlantic, occurring in inshore waters from Massachusetts to Florida but commonest from Chesapeake Bay to New York. A slim, well-shaped fish, it gets its name from its delicate mouth, which tears easily when hooked.

In appearance, the weakfish is similar to its relative the spotted seatrout (*C. nebulosus*) which is found in the same waters. Both fish average about 4 pounds in weight, although the weakfish can top 19 pounds and the spotted seatrout 16 pounds. Two other seatrout, the sand seatrout (*C. arenarius*) and the silver seatrout (*C. nothus*), which occur further south, are much smaller and generally weigh well under a pound.

In contrast, the white seabass (*C. nobilis*), another relative of the weakfish and not a true sea bass, can reach weights of over 80 pounds, although most are only 15 to 30 pounds. The white seabass is a Pacific species, found from Alaska south to Chile.

All these fishes are good table fish, and the spotted seatrout and the white seabass both have commercial importance.

NATURAL FOOD
Weakfish are predators feeding on shoaling, silvery fishes and molluscs. Noted for their taking flashing, artificial baits.

WHITEFISHES

MOUTH SHAPE
The many species of whitefish are so similar that fin ray counting is sometimes the only means of identification. With the lake and mountain whitefish, however, there are obvious differences in mouth shape and head size.

Lake Whitefish

Mountain Whitefish

The whitefishes of Canada and the northern USA are a group of freshwater species related to the trout and salmon. For anglers, the most important of them are the lake whitefish (*Coregonus clupeaformis*), mountain whitefish (*Prosopium williamsoni*), inconnu (*Stenopus leucichthys*), round whitefish (*Prosopium cylindraceum*) and the eight species of ciscoes (*Coregonus* spp).

The lake whitefish, which also enters rivers, is a popular gamefish which averages about 4 pounds but can reach over 20 pounds. The mountain whitefish is smaller, most being around 2 pounds with a maximum of 5 pounds or so, and is usually sought in the winter months when its flesh is at its most tasty. Round whitefish are even smaller, rarely exceeding 2 pounds, but the inconnu is to reach 50 pounds.

The ciscoes, found in New England and the Great Lakes Basin, are also popular with anglers and mostly reach about 2 pounds in weight. Like the lake, mountain and round whitefish, the ciscoes feed mainly on insects and crustaceans, and provide good sport for fly fishermen during the summer mayfly hatches. Inconnu can also be taken on flies, but as they are a predatory species, fishing for them with spinners or spoons is more likely to bring results.

NATURAL FOOD
Tautog come inshore at high tide to prise mussels off rocks.

TAUTOG
Rounded head, blunt nose and thick lips; green-brown to charcoal and up to 25 pounds weight.

TECHNIQUE	ROD	REEL	LINE	TERMINAL TACKLE	HOOK	WEIGHT	BAIT
Bottom fishing	Light surf or heavy spinning rod	Multiplier/ medium fixed spool	12/15-pound nylon	Running ledger/ paternoster	Size 1/0 or 2/0	Pyramid/bomb	Worm, crab shellfish

SPOTTED SEATROUT
Not a trout at all but with markings and the torpedo-shaped body similar to the sea trout.

WEAKFISH
A slim, well-shaped marine fish. Its name derives from its delicate mouth which tears easily when hooked. A popular gamefish.

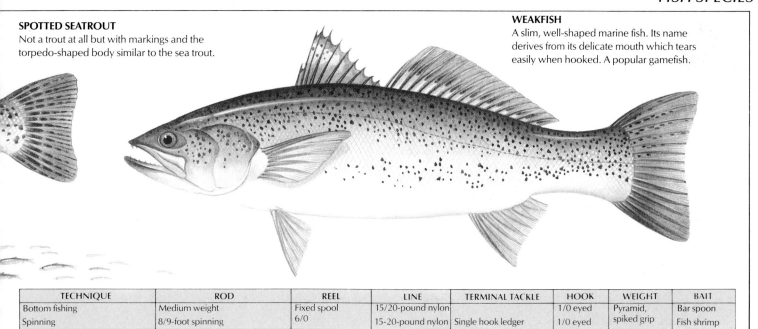

TECHNIQUE	ROD	REEL	LINE	TERMINAL TACKLE	HOOK	WEIGHT	BAIT
Bottom fishing	Medium weight	Fixed spool	15/20-pound nylon		1/0 eyed	Pyramid,	Bar spoon
Spinning	8/9-foot spinning	6/0	15-20-pound nylon	Single hook ledger	1/0 eyed	spiked grip	Fish shrimp

WHITEFISH SPECIES
The most important angling whitefishes are the lake, mountain, inconnu and round whitefish, together with the eight species of ciscoes.

LAKE WHITEFISH
A popular freshwater gamefish, which despite its name is also found in rivers. Averages about 4 pounds, but capable of reaching over 20.

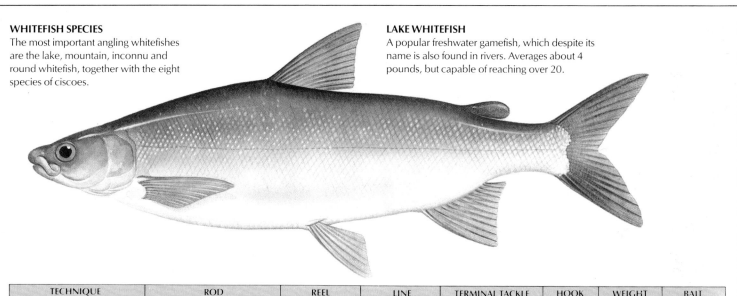

TECHNIQUE	ROD	REEL	LINE	TERMINAL TACKLE	HOOK	WEIGHT	BAIT
Fly fishing	8-foot fly rod	Single action fly reel	Floating or sinking 5/6	Tapered leader			Small wet or dry flies

PHARYNGEAL TEETH
Ballan wrasse have a set of secondary, pharyngeal or throat teeth, used to crush food against the bony palate.

BALLAN WRASSE
When the mouth of the ballan wrasse is open and the lips extended for feeding, the blunt and crushing teeth are exposed. These are ideal for crunching molluscs and crustaceans.

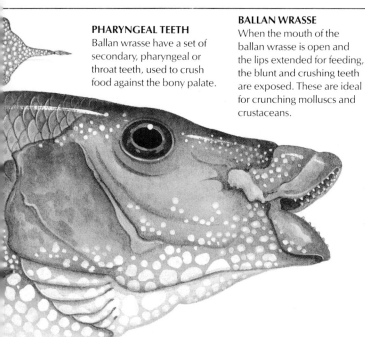

WRASSES

Although the wrasse family of saltwater fishes includes some 450 species, the majority of them are tropical and comparatively few species are found in temperate waters. In the Pacific, the temperate wrasses include the California sheephead *(Pimelometopon pulchrum)* and the senorita *(Oxyjulis californica)*. The principal temperate Atlantic wrasses are the tautog *(Tautoga onitis)* and cunner *(Tautogolabrus adspersus)* of the north west, and the ballan wrasse *(Labrus bergylta)* and cuckoo wrasse *(Labrus mixtus)* of the north east.

The tautog is commonest from Nova Scotia to South Carolina, and has a rounded back, blunt nose and thick lips. In color, tautog range from green-brown to charcoal gray, but like all wrasses they can alter their color to match their surroundings, The ballan wrasse ranges in color from yellow to green or red, and like the tautog feeds mainly on molluscs and crabs. Unlike most saltwater fish, the ballan wrasse lay their eggs in nests, which they build by jamming pieces of sea-weed and debris into rock crevices.

The ballan wrasse can grow to a weight of over 8 pounds, and the tautog up to 25 pounds, although weights of around 3 pounds are more usual for rod-caught tautog. Other wrasses of the north east Atlantic include the rainbow wrasse *(Coris julis)* and the corkwing *(Crenilabrus melops)*.

TECHNIQUES

One of angling's great strengths is that the basic techniques are easily learnt, which makes the sport more accessible, to more people, than most others are. Another is that once the basics have been mastered, there are so many subtleties involved in fishing that the dedicated angler never stops learning about it, and gaining increasing pleasure from it.

Unfortunately, because there is so much that can be learnt, many anglers tend to concentrate on one particular type of angling, and rarely try their hand at anything very different from their chosen method. This is a pity, because every kind of fishing has much to commend it and can offer great enjoyment to those who practise it.

Fly fishing, for example, is generally accepted to be the most refined and artistic form of angling, and because of this it's often regarded by lure and bait fishermen as rather mysterious and far from easy. In fact, the vast majority of anglers who try it find that they can soon master the basic techniques of casting and retrieving a fly, and are surprised at just how quickly they can learn to catch fish on it; to become an expert, though, takes a little longer.

Fly fishing – using the submerged wet fly or the dry fly which floats on the surface – is primarily a freshwater technique. However, saltwater fly fishing is growing in popularity as a method of catching shallow-water species such as pollack and bonefish. For this, you need a basic knowledge of fly casting, corrosion-resistant tackle, and a good understanding of the feeding habits of the fish you're after and how to work the fly to attract their attention. Saltwater fly fishing can even be used to catch small shark that come close inshore, if the fly is attached to a short wire leader and cast to within a few inches of the snout of the essentially short-sighted fish.

The more usual methods of fishing from the shore, though, are surfcasting, using long, two-piece rods with multiplier or fixed spool reels, and saltwater spinning, which employs lighter rods and fixed spool reels. Most other saltwater fishing is done from boats – from dinghies close inshore, and from larger boats (usually chartered) further out in deep water. Charter boats, generally purpose-built, are also used for big game fishing, hunting ocean giants like billfish and tuna.

Trolling, one of the basic big game fishing techniques, can be used to good effect when fishing for smaller saltwater species such as sea bass and pollack, and on fresh waters it's a very good way to get at fish living in the depths of large lakes and reservoirs. Downrigger trolling from motorboats, using heavy weights to keep the terminal tackle down where the fish are, is often the only way to take species such as lake trout in really big waters, but in shallower waters lines can simply be trailed behind a rowed boat or a canoe.

Most freshwater angling methods can be used from a boat, but the majority of freshwater fishing is done from the shore or bank or by wading in shallow water. The techniques can be divided into three main categories: fly fishing, lure fishing and fishing with hookbaits.

Fly fishing, one of the oldest forms of sports fishing, is popular all over the world, but there are distinct regional preferences for either lure fishing or bait fishing. This is partly due to local traditions, but mainly to the types of fish predominant in the region. In North America, because so many of the popular sports fishes – such as the basses — are predatory, the majority of anglers fish with artificial lures. In Europe, on the other hand, there are comparatively few predatory species – mostly trout, pike and perch – and so most of the fishing is with hookbaits for fish such as carp, tench and roach.

As a result, the major American freshwater techniques are spinning and baitcasting, using spinners, spoons, plugs, jigs and other artificial lures. These neat, effective methods, using light and relatively uncomplicated tackle, are as yet sadly underrated in Europe. Conversely, there is much scope for the wider use of European-style ledgering and float fishing techniques in North America. They're all described in this chapter, so why not try them?

BAITCASTING

Baitcasting was originally a technique which used natural baits (hence its name) and fixed spool reels, and although this method is still used, most anglers today use the term to refer to the art of throwing an artificial lure, using a baitcasting (revolving spool or multiplier) reel. And an art it certainly is. Making a lure land exactly where you want it to, cast after cast, takes considerable skill and good quality, well-balanced tackle.

Whether you're using a single or a double handed rod, it should fit your hand like a comfortable old glove. With the shorter, single handed rod, for instance, your index finger should hook comfortably around the trigger, with your thumb snugly yet firmly over the spool.

The reel should be full of monofilament line wound on under firm tension, line which is not old, kinked or abraded. If your line's in good condition you'll lose fewer big fish on the strike, and you'll also cast more fluently.

Before you start casting, set the star drag and the cast control of your reel to suit the lure you're using. The star drag should be set so that the spool will only give line to the firm pull of a good fish. To set the cast control, put the reel in free spool and adjust the control so that the lure will drop slowly to the ground under its own weight. This will give you an approximate starting setting: when you start casting, you might find that you need to tighten the control some more for wind resistant plugs, or loosen it off quite a bit for denser models.

The weight of the lure will also determine your casting drop, the distance from the lure to the rod tip before you start your cast. For a ½ to ¾ ounce plug, a drop of about 6 inches should be enough.

BASIC OVERHEAD CAST

plug pulls on rod tip

reel in free spool

1

stop rod at 11 o'clock position

rod flexes

THE BAITCASTING REEL
As with other reels, the secret of successful casting with the baitcasting (or multiplying) reel is careful preparation. You may consider the effort a chore, but the rewards will be trouble-free performance and improved casting.

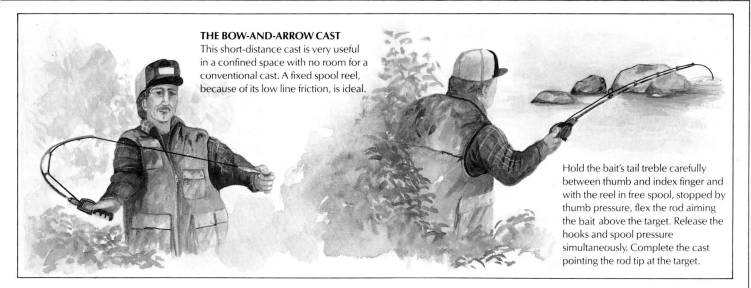

THE BOW-AND-ARROW CAST
This short-distance cast is very useful in a confined space with no room for a conventional cast. A fixed spool reel, because of its low line friction, is ideal.

Hold the bait's tail treble carefully between thumb and index finger and with the reel in free spool, stopped by thumb pressure, flex the rod aiming the bait above the target. Release the hooks and spool pressure simultaneously. Complete the cast pointing the rod tip at the target.

Heavier plugs might need slightly less than this, but lightweights such as spinner baits, plastic worms, weedless spoons or jigs and bucktails, will need from 10 to 30 inches.

There are other occasions when casting with a longer drop is advisable, for example to avoid snap up when you're using ultralight tackle, or when you're fishing with soft naturals such as worms, crayfish, small fish and strip baits. Sharp, short casting would only throw them off.

When you're using a single handed rod, the easiest cast is probably the simple overhead flick cast. Pick the spot you want the plug to land at, then with the reel in free spool and your thumb on the spool, rotate your wrist so the reel handles are pointing up and bring the rod smartly back until you feel the weight of the plug flexing the rod.

Now in one positive, fluid movement, flick the rod forwards as though you're hitting a nail with a hammer, and ease your thumb pressure off the spool when you feel the plug pull. With your thumb pressure completely off the spool, and the plug racing towards its target, gentle thumbing of the spool will stop it overshooting the mark. As soon as the plug hits the water, clamp your thumb down firmly, then swap the rod to your other hand and put the reel into gear by winding.

Keep the rod tip pointing at the plug during the retrieve to maximize the chances of setting the hooks when a fish hits, and lift the rod high into the strike. Working the plug, particularly if it's a surface lure, does of course take the rod tip a little to either side as you twitch, freeze, twich again, bob, or jerk the lure to give it

lifelike movement. So be careful not to allow an acute angle between the rod and the plug, or the fish will be lost simply because the hooks never went fully home on the strike.

Over-the-shoulder and side casting use the same basic routine, but although good methods for cutting through strong winds, they lack the accuracy of standard overhead casting.

For flipping plugs into awkward spots such as beneath low, overhanging branches or under piers, a flip-type cast works best. Stand sideways-on to the target spot, holding the rod out in front of you with the tip a little lower than the butt. Now whip the rod tip quickly round in a circle (like stirring paint).

When the plug's moved through about 2/3 of the circle, take your thumb off the spool so

that the plug flies off towards the target, and gently follow through with the rod tip.

Another useful technique for getting to awkward spots, or for casting when you're surrounded by dense vegetation, is the 'bow and arrow' or 'catapult' cast.

Start with the plug on a drop of about 2/3 the length of the rod. With your left hand, hold the last hook tightly by the bend with your thumb and index finger (be careful here), with the reel in free spool and held by your right thumb. Pull back on the plug to bend the rod like a bow, aim the plug at the target, then let it fly. At the same time, release the spool and follow through to point the rod tip at the target.

With longer, double handed rods, the casting techniques are basically the same, but with the left hand gripping the butt of the rod at around chest height.

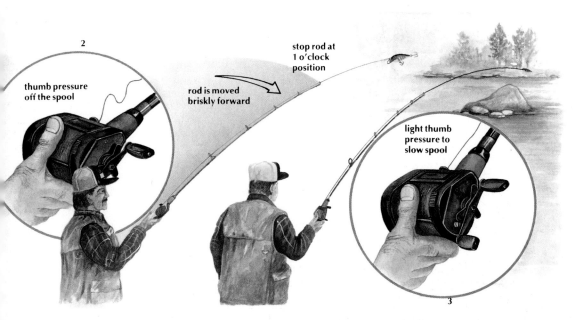

2 thumb pressure off the spool

rod is moved briskly forward

stop rod at 1 o'clock position

light thumb pressure to slow spool

3

THE OVERHEAD CAST
1. With the reel correctly adjusted, the lure on the correct drop for its weight and the thumb locking the spool, start the cast by bringing the rod briskly back and stopping it at about the 11 o'clock position.

2. When you feel the pull of the lure on the rod tip, flick the rod forwards as if you're hammering a nail. Stop the rod at the 1 o'clock position and remove your thumb pressure as the lure pulls line out.

3. As the lure drops towards the water apply thumb pressure to brake the spool. As the lure hits the water clamp your thumb firmly on the spool to prevent overrun and the resulting tangle of line.

BIG GAME FISHING — DRIFTING

Big game fishing takes many forms, ranging from simple drift fishing for shark up to complex trolling techniques developed for species such as billfish and tuna.

Drift fishing consists of fishing a natural live or dead fishbait from a boat which drifts with the wind and tide flow. This technique was developed primarily for shark fishing, but it's been effectively adapted for catching broadbill swordfish as well.

For shark, the boat is taken out to an area known to hold them, the most usual species for deepwater sport fishing being mako, porbeagle, blue and hammerhead. Once the shark grounds are reached, the engines are cut and the boat begins to drift.

The first job now is to create a 'smell lane' through the water to attract hungry shark to the baits. This is known as chumming or rubby-dubbying, and the easiest way to do it is to hang a mesh bag full of minced fresh, frozen or rotting fish over the side of the boat. Each time the boat rises and falls on a swell the bag pumps up and down in the water and releases additional bait particles into the water. To make the trail more attractive, the minced fish can be 'hotted up' with fish oil or blood.

If you know the shark are feeding close to the surface, hang the bag over the side on which the rods are to be placed. If the sharks are down deep, you should hang the bag on the opposite side to the rods, so that the released bait particles drift under the boat and are deflected downwards by the keel, laying a deep trail to attract shark up from the depths.

Drift fishing tackle is always kept as simple as possible: a rod, reel, line, leader (trace) and bait. For anglers who like to watch a float, a partially inflated balloon can be used both as a bait support and as a bite indicator. It should be allowed to slide on the reel line until stopped at the required depth by a rubber band half-hitched to the line.

Most shark drifting boats use four rods fished at staggered distances and depths. Baits are normally fished at about 25, 30, 60 and 70 feet; whichever bait it taken first indicates the feeding level of that particular species of shark on that particular day. However, even when a deep set bait is taken, you should still keep one bait working close to the surface. An individual shark will often come in close to the surface intent on attacking the chumming bag, and will usually stop to pick up any bait in its path.

The choice of bait is wide, as almost any fish can be used as shark bait, but oily fish such as mackerel, sardine or bonito are probably the best. The method of hooking the bait depends a great deal on its size. Small fish like sardine are best fished in bunches, each fish being threaded on the hook via its eye sockets.

Mackerel, unless large, are best fished in pairs, tandem fashion, to create the illusion of a big bait. Bonito are large enough to be fished singly, but as shark are highly adept at chopping big baits in half, pass the wire trace through the body of the bait so the hook protrudes through the gill slit.

Although shark are often regarded as greedy, rather stupid creatures, there are occasions (and species, such as mako and great white) when they show a distinct cunning. Because of this, take great care not to alarm the fish during the initial stages of the take or strike. At the first indication of a bite, pick the rod up and hold it so that the tip

Below *Boating a shark with a flying (breakaway) gaff.*

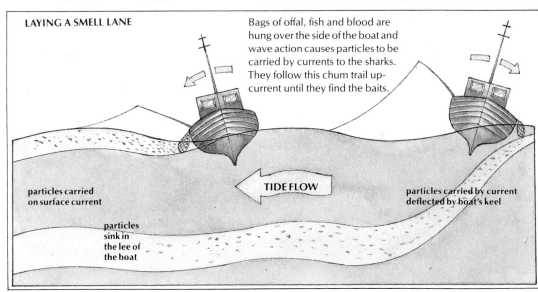

LAYING A SMELL LANE

Bags of offal, fish and blood are hung over the side of the boat and wave action causes particles to be carried by currents to the sharks. They follow this chum trail up-current until they find the baits.

particles carried on surface current

TIDE FLOW

particles carried by current deflected by boat's keel

particles sink in the lee of the boat

points directly down the line into the sea. At the same time, put the reel into free spool and control it by thumb pressure only. This allows the shark to take line freely without feeling any suspicious drag.

Normally, the fish will take the bait and run out a few yards of line, then stop and begin to

Below *Casting to a small school of tarpon from a drifting boat.*

swallow the bait before moving away again. As this second run begins, put the reel into gear so that you can strike the moment the line goes tight, and then play the fish out in the normal way.

The basic technique for broadbill swordfish is similar to that for sharks, except that swordfish are normally fished for at night with the bait exceeding 1000 feet. The two major baits for swordfish are livebaits and squid,

although there are many local variations. In Portugal, for example, the bait is normally a live Ray's bream hooked once through the back. Elsewhere, the technique is to fish a whole dead squid in conjunction with a chemical light stick, which is either pushed into the mantle of the squid or attached to the leader directly above the bait.

The light stick is simply a light plastic tube containing two

separate chemicals, and it's activated by bending the tube so that the chemicals mix. The mixed chemicals react and give off a steady, greenish light for up to twelve hours.

When the stick is inserted into a natural squid, it makes the bait glow with a natural-looking phosphorescence that broadbill swordfish find highly appealing. Broadbill normally take a fish bait savagely.

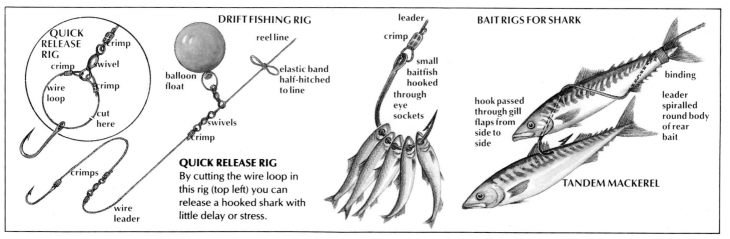

QUICK RELEASE RIG
crimp
crimp
swivel
wire loop
crimp
cut here
crimps
wire leader

DRIFT FISHING RIG
reel line
balloon float
elastic band half-hitched to line
swivels
crimp

QUICK RELEASE RIG
By cutting the wire loop in this rig (top left) you can release a hooked shark with little delay or stress.

leader
crimp
small baitfish hooked through eye sockets

BAIT RIGS FOR SHARK
binding
leader spiralled round body of rear bait
hook passed through gill flaps from side to side

TANDEM MACKEREL

BIG GAME FISHING — TROLLING

Although shark and other fish are regularly caught on bait presented from a drifting boat, other species are better taken on moving baits. The more active ocean predators like marlin, sailfish, wahoo and tuna show little interest in static baits, but they're likely to strike at a moving bait. Because of this, these species are fished for by trailing baits behind a moving boat, so that the baits resemble the living food on which the big game fish prey.

This trailing, or 'trolling' as it's known, is a highly selective way of showing baits to fish over a wide area. Most big game boats fish four rods at a time, with two directly over the stern and two on specially designed outriggers that keep their lines away from the sides of the boat. These are called 'rigger lines', while the central rods, whose baits are fished closest to the boat, are known as 'flatlines'.

Normally, all lines are staggered to present baits over a wide area, and to create the illusion of a small shoal of frantically swimming bait fish. Strangely enough, the baits fished closest to the boat often produce the most strikes. This is particularly true of solitary fish like marlin, which seem to be attracted by the wake of the boat itself.

The choice of bait for trolling is up to the individual angler and the boat captain. Most anglers prefer to leave the decision to the captain, whose experience is usually far greater than theirs. Traditionally, bait choice would be specially mounted or rigged natural baits, mackerel, balao (ballyhoo), mullet or ladyfish being the most favoured bait

species. In more recent years, many boat captains have switched bait preferences from naturals to artificial lures, in particular the Kona Head type which originated in Hawaii.

Initially, these baits were hand carved from hardwood and wrapped with an improvised skirt. Nowadays, many companies specialize in producing a wide range of head shapes and plastic skirts in a host of color combinations. These lures are all known as Kona Heads, but are often marketed under various trade names.

Most baits are fitted with two differently colored skirts, usually to simulate a specific fish color: blue on white for mackerel and tuna, for example, or yellow and green for dorado, and pink and red for shrimp.

In operation, each bait is mounted on a wire or preferably heavy nylon leader fitted with one or two flat forged hooks. Hooks with offset points are useless for lure fishing, because they have a tendency to spin and wrap up the tail of the bait's plastic skirt. A bait tangled in this fashion catches nothing.

Normally, the strike drag on the reel is set before fishing begins. With both the lever drag and star drag types of multiplier it's usually set on the quayside, using a spring balance to check the poundage. When a fish strikes a bait, the initial power of the rod and the setting of the drag should be enough to set the hooks. The drag setting depends on the weight class of the rod and the breaking strain of the line. For instance, for an 80 pound class outfit the drag would be set at 28 pounds.

As a technique, trolling is a highly efficient way of catching fish. Unfortunately, though, many strikes fail to produce hooked fish. This is particularly true when trolling for billfish with artificial baits. The hardness of the fish's mouth, and the rapidity with which artificial baits are tasted and rejected, lead to a high incidence of lost fish – one marlin hooked for every three strikes could be regarded as the norm. Frustrating as this may seem, the beauty of the Kona Head style lure is that under most circumstances it raises more billfish than do natural lures.

With tuna, missed strikes are a rarity. The tuna's mouth is very different from that of the marlin, and tuna also have a tendency to gulp a bait straight down. More tuna are lost through tackle breakage than pulled hooks. The

drawback to tuna is that they invariably school, and when one bait is taken the chances are that the other lines will produce strikes within seconds.

Some fish, like wahoo and sailfish, seem to prefer natural baits to artificial lures, wahoo being particularly good at cutting a bait in half on the strike.

As a method, trolling – especially with artificial lures – has much to recommend it. It's clean, the baits are easy to rig.

Right Trolling is the best way to fish for species such as marlin, tuna and sailfish, using either natural baits or artificial lures.

Below Shark are usually caught by drifting, but they can also be taken on slowly-trolled strip or whole fishbaits. This one is a 186-pound whitetip shark.

TROLLING WITH LURES

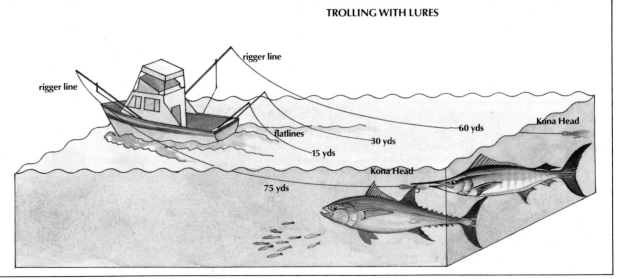

BIG GAME TROLLING

Trolling is a very effective method, but with marlin the ratio of strikes to hooked fish is only 3:1. Marlin often hit the lures nearest the boat, perhaps attracted by the wake. The tuna's way of hitting a lure means that it is rarely missed. Tuna strikes on all lures at once are common.

rigger line

rigger line

flatlines

15 yds

30 yds

60 yds

75 yds

Kona Head

Kona Head

Kona Head

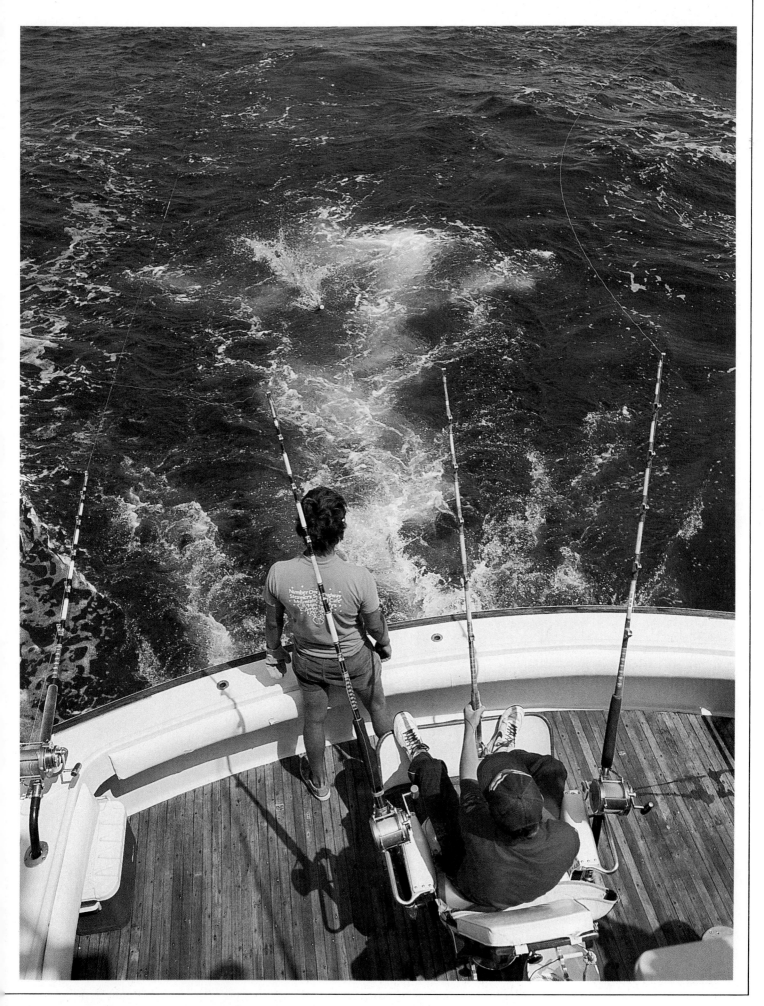

BOAT FISHING

Boat fishing in salt water falls into two main categories: inshore dinghy or small boat fishing and offshore big boat fishing. Dinghy fishing is an inexpensive way to reach marks that are beyond the reach of the shore caster but inside the grounds worked by larger boats. Often, dinghy anglers can get to saltwater creeks, estuaries and reefs that are rarely, if ever, fished.

One of the best techniques to use for this small boat fishing is the fish-finder rig, which works well in waters down to 30 feet, from an anchored boat. For this style of angling an 8 to 10 foot rod and a fixed spool reel should be used, and the leader and sinker (or lead) are critical factors.

The leader should never be less than 3 feet long, and it could be longer depending on the type of bottom you're fishing over, the shorter leader being ideal for fishing over rocks or other solid snags. Over a flat sand or mud bottom, use a longer leader to allow the bait to swirl around in the tide flow.

A nylon leader is best, made up with a single size 1/0 or 2/0 hook and a swivel. Slide the lead, which should be bomb shaped, directly over the reel line, then knot the reel line to the leader swivel. This lets the lead slide easily on the main line, and the swivel acts as a stop to keep the lead from sliding down to the hook. For bait, use worm, fish, squid or crab.

Cast the tackle uptide and well away from the boat. The lead should be just heavy enough to take the bait to the bottom but not heavy enough to anchor it in one position; you rarely need to use a lead of more than one ounce. The idea is that the bait should travel slowly down the tide until it reaches a position directly astern of the dinghy.

Hold the rod at all times, as bites may occur anywhere along the search path of the bait, and once the bait comes to rest astern of the boat, retrieve the tackle and recast it. By changing your casting distances you can thoroughly search out the sea on either side of the anchored boat.

Offshore fishing in deep water is different. The boat is anchored over a known mark but the tackle is much stouter and heavier, the light inshore tackle being changed for a larger boat outfit, such as a 30 or 50 pound class rod and a 4/0 or 6/0 size multiplying reel.

Make up the terminal tackle as before, but with a wire or heavy nylon leader and a 6/0 or 8/0 hook. The lead size depends on the strength of the tide flow, but you may need anything from 6 ounces up to 2 pounds or more; it should be just heavy enough to hold bottom. The leader length depends on the type of fish you're after: for cod or conger a 3 foot leader is ideal; for tope, turbot or bass you need a 6 or even 8 foot leader.

The technique is simple. With the reel out of gear but braked gently with your right thumb, drop the terminal tackle down until you feel the lead touch bottom. At this stage the reel is still in free spool but clamped firmly by your thumb. After the lead has been in position for a moment or two, raise the rod tip to lift the lead, and release a yard or two of line. This has the effect of trotting the line back a yard or so with the tide flow. Each time the lead comes to rest, leave it there for a few moments and then repeat the process if no bites are registered. When you feel a bite, give the fish a yard or so of slack line and then put the reel in gear ready for the strike.

Fishing over wrecks is usually carried out from a drifting boat, the boat skipper setting up the drift so that the boat passes directly over the wreck. This technique calls for little finesse but a good deal of muscle. Most wrecks are fished with either an artificial or a natural bait, the most popular artificial being a rubber eel of the red gill type

Fishing from a boat, whether close inshore or further out, will usually provide good sport.

fished on a long leader.

Once the boat's drifting, you lower the terminal tackle until the lead bumps the wreck. As soon as this happens, crank the reel handle at high speed to get the tackle clear of the wreck and activate the bait or rubber eel. Strikes on this sort of rig, mostly from pollack, coalfish, cod and suchlike bottom fish are extremely savage.

When you're fishing a natural bait, keep the leader short – about 2 feet being ideal. Again, lower the terminal tackle until the lead touches the wreck, then crank the reel handle two or three times to lift the bait above the wreckage. Bites are normally indicated by a slow pull on the rod tip. This method often produces large catches of big fish such as ling, cod, conger and very occasionally a big turbot or halibut.

After each drift the boat is re-positioned, and this allows a brief breathing space to repair or totally replace your terminal tackle. On a good day you might lose a dozen sets of tackle; on a bad, losses can be astronomical.

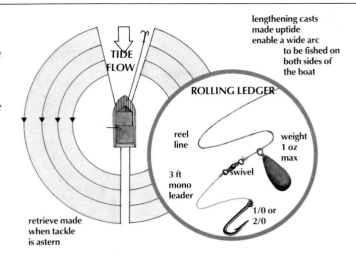

UPTIDE ROLLING LEDGER

The seabed beyond the range of the shore angler but inshore of the charter boat grounds is a lightly-fished area which the dinghy fisherman is ideally situated to explore. The uptide rolling ledger enables the fisherman to search a large area of the bottom to either side of his boat. Casts are made uptide and the ledger allowed to swing round until it's dead astern. Repeat casts at different distances give thorough coverage.

OFFSHORE FISHING

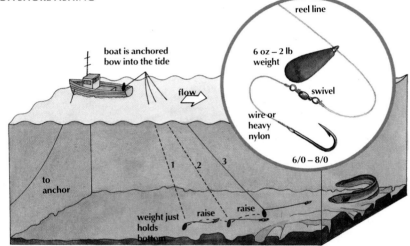

OFFSHORE RIG
This rig is similar to that used for uptide fishing, but scaled up for the rougher ground and potentially much larger fish you can expect to catch over deep water marks.

This form of fishing is done at anchor over the chosen mark, using tackle similar to the uptide rolling ledger rig, but much stronger. With the reel out of gear, feed out line until the weight touches bottom. Brake the spool with your thumb, raise the rod and let out a yard or two of line as the weight drops back on the tide. Repeat until you get a strike, then give some slack, put the reel in gear, and hit the fish hard.

SIMPLE DRIFT RIG

Rigs for drift fishing over wrecks or reefs are best kept fairly simple. This minimizes the inevitable tangles and lost tackle, and the subsequent frayed tempers.

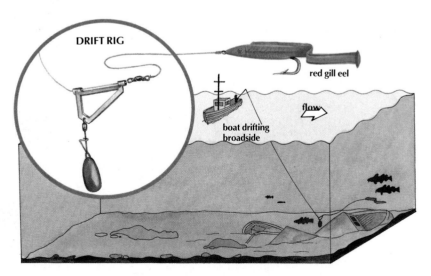

DRIFT FISHING OVER WRECKS

Using a rig similar to that illustrated above, offshore wrecks can be fished 'on the drift', with the boat drifting with the current directly over the mark, rather than at anchor. All rods fish from the downtide side to reduce the risk of lines tangling or chafing on the keel.

The tackle is lowered until the weight touches the wreck, then it is cranked at high speed to activate the lure. Strikes are savage. When the drift is completed, the boat is taken back uptide on the motor and repositioned for another drift down the current and over the wreck.

FEATHERING AND PIRKING

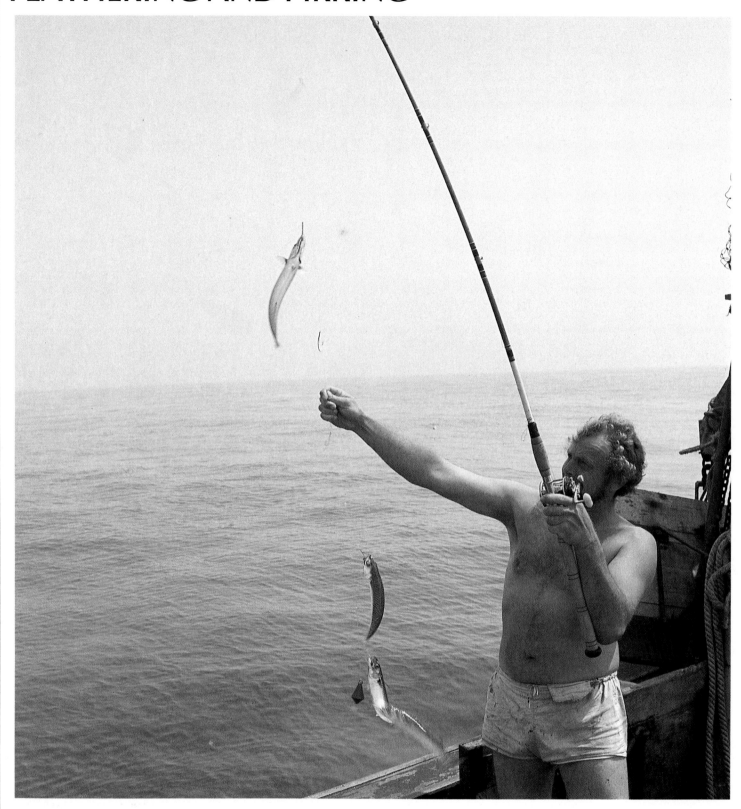

Many sea fish are totally pre-datory, and such fish fall readily to artificial lures. Some lures are highly sophisticated, but others, like feathers (streamers) and pirks, are more basic.

Feathers – hackle feathers pulled from the neck of a domestic cockerel – are one of the simplest of all lures. They can be used in the natural state or dyed in various colors, and are simply lashed to the shank of a flat forged, tinned sea hook. The origins of feathering lie in the traditions of commercial fishing, where they are used to catch cod, pollack, coalfish and mackerel in quantity.

Feathers are fished from boats and used in long strings, leaders carrying six or a dozen separate hooks being normal. The idea is to give the impression of a shoal of small, brightly colored fish or sand eels. Feathers (and pirks) can be worked up and down as well as across or through a tide flow.

The technique is simple, the string of feathers being worked above a dipsey sinker. You just lower the sinker to any position between the seabed and the surface, and animate the feathers by raising and lowering the rod

Above *Fishing with a strin of feathers will get you good catches of shoaling mackerel, and also of other predators such as cod.*

top at regular intervals.

Every angler will develop an individual feathering routine, and almost any routine will catch fish, with the possible exception of really rapid rod movements.

Feathering is particularly

useful when mackerel are shoaling in vast numbers. Bites often come as the feathers are lowered; sometimes the line will appear to go slack, a sure indication that a quantity of mackerel have taken the feathers. The apparent slackness is created by the fish taking the feathers and swimming upwards, dragging the sinker behind them.

Such a bite normally indicates a full string or 'full house' of prime mackerel, and since you can find yourself with a number of fish on the line at the same time, you should use a 30 to 50 pound rod. When fish are less abundant, most bites will be signified by a light rattling pull on the rod tip.

Larger fish such as cod and pollack normally take the feathers savagely, firmly hooking themselves in the process. If you're expecting to catch these bigger fish you should cut back on the number of feathers on the leader, three being the maximum it's safe to use.

Commercial fishermen will never use blue colored nylon for making up feathered leaders, as they believe that blue line drives fish away from the feathers.

A variant on the feathers is a short length of brightly colored electrical sleeving slid over the bend of the hook. These plastic 'feathers' may seem to hold little fish appeal, but in use the plastic has proved deadly with shoaling mackerel. The beauty of the plastic is that it's very durable; feathers, being soft, are often totally destroyed by the fish.

The pirk or diamond jig is an equally basic lure which can be extremely good for cod and pollack, and when baited for ling and halibut. Pirk baits are an updated version of the scraped lead lures used by Grand Banks cod fishermen, though most commercially made pirk style baits now originate in Scandinavia.

The pirk is basically a single piece of chromed metal fitted with a large treble hook. The shape of the pirk varies from one manufacturer to another, but all incorporate the same wicked style of hook. Commercial fishermen call the bait a 'ripper' or 'iron murderer', apt names considering how many fish are foul hooked in the head or belly on one or more prongs of the huge treble. Sporting anglers normally replace the treble with a large, well sharpened single hook.

Pirk baits are worked in the same way as feathers, but without a sinker, as the weight of the lure is enough to take it down to the bottom. Fish obviously mistake the pirk for a natural food.

When you're fishing for ling or halibut, you can enhance the attraction of the pirk by baiting the large single hook with a fillet of fish or a chunk of squid or cuttlefish. A pirk baited in this way can be deadly, and wreck fishermen make spectacular ling catches on baited pirks. For big fish, mount the pirk on a heavy wire or nylon leader. Line of normal breaking strain will be cut through instantly by a ling's sharp teeth.

Pirks come in a variety of sizes and weights, ranging from tiny lures for catching live bait up to huge metal slabs weighing in at over 2 pounds. The small lures are for shallow or tide-free water, the largest for deep, tide-ripped water. These large lures can be extremely expensive, and to cut costs many anglers prefer to make their own. You can save a good deal of money by making pirks at home, particularly if you go wreck fishing which can be a costly exercise in terms of lost lures.

Sometimes, anglers and manufacturers go to extreme lengths to bend and shape pirk baits in the hope of making them move more in use. The truth of the matter is that a hungry fish feeding in deep water doesn't have the time to be picky about the way its lunch moves. Food is food, and a straight pirk will be taken as savagely as the most carefully bent 'tuned up' lure.

FEATHER RIGS

Whether it's to be used as a quick method of collecting baitfish such as mackerel for shark or other predator fishing, or as a fishing technique in its own right, the feather string is easily made.

1 tie in two suitably bright spade hackles
hook size to suit species sought

2

pull both ends of line tight and trim

3

Feathering and pirking is often done over rough ground, which means that large amounts of tackle can be lost. Luckily, these simple lures are easily made from readily obtainable materials, and instead of using lead weights you can use scrap metal attached to the line by weak links of light line or even thread ('rotten bottom'). Then if the weight snags, you won't lose your lures as well.

swivel — reel line

feathers tied either to loop links or stand-off loops

THE PATERNOSTER LOOP LINK

swivel

lead weight or scrap metal

PIRK

length of chromed metal tube

hammer ends flat

drill holes in flattened ends

part-fill with scrap lead or nuts and bolts

smooth edges with coarse file

attach split rings

finish off with a swivel and a single or treble hook

FLOAT FISHING — 1

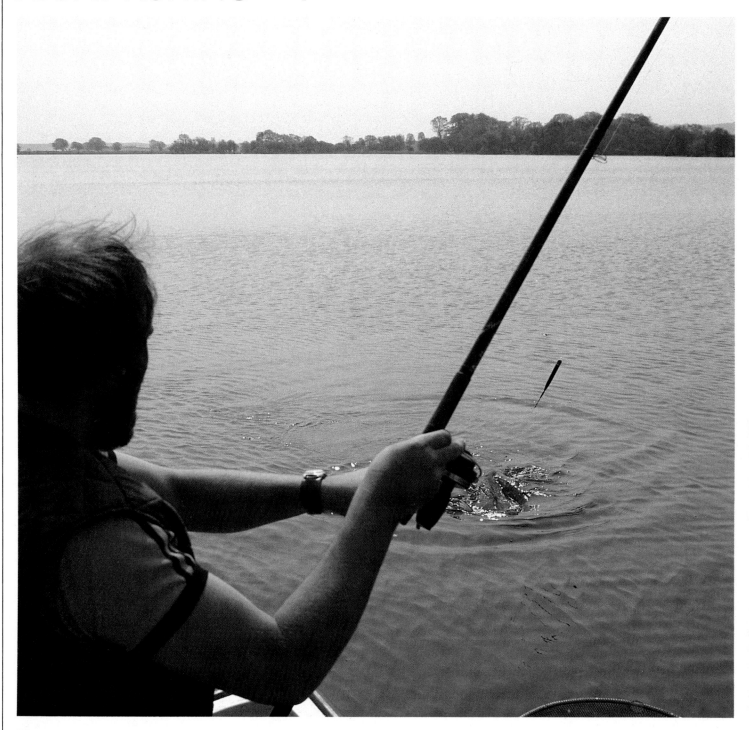

Fishing with a float (a bobber) is the most widely used angling method in the UK and Europe. Almost any freshwater fish can be caught by float fishing, and the float is the most sensitive type of bite indicator yet invented.

Despite the vast range of shapes and sizes of floats, they all fall into one or another of two distinct functional categories: floats which are attached to the line at their bottom end only, and floats attached at both top and bottom.

Fishing with a float attached bottom end only allows some or all of the line between the rod tip

and the float to be sunk beneath the surface, so that the float (and consequently the bait present-ation) is hardly affected by wind or surface drift.

With a float (usually a stick type) attached top and bottom to the line by silicone rubber float bands, you can trundle the bait along close to the bottom, even in deep water. The bait will travel at the same speed as the midwater flow, which is nowhere near as fast as the surface currents.

For accurate casting at close range, use one-handed spinning tackle with an underarm or sideways flick, and feather the

line to a standstill (with your forefinger against the rim of the spool) so the terminal tackle doesn't land abruptly. Aim for a spot several feet beyond your swim, and quickly dip the rod tip a few inches below the surface once the float touches down. Then wind in a few rapid turns to sink all the line and draw the float to the position you want it before lifting the rod tip.

The overhead cast is best for long range work of twenty yards or more. Grip the rod butt firmly in your left hand with your right hand firmly over the tip of the reel seat. With the bale arm open,

Above *Playing a fish caught on float tackle, rigged with the float fixed to the line at both the top and bottom ends.*

hook the line around your index finger so that it's taking the weight of the terminal tackle.

Start with the rod pointing upwards directly in front of you, and then tilt it backwards over your right shoulder so that the tip flicks the float tackle out behind you. Now, in one smooth stroke, punch forward with your right arm and pull in with your left, keeping the rod in a straight, forward line. As before, aim for a

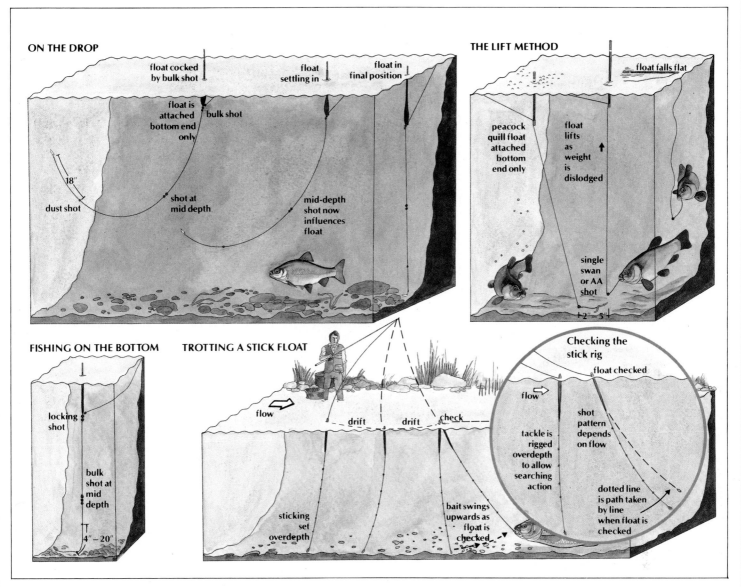

ON THE DROP

float cocked by bulk shot

float settling in

float in final position

float is attached bottom end only

bulk shot

18″

dust shot

shot at mid depth

mid-depth shot now influences float

THE LIFT METHOD

float falls flat

peacock quill float attached bottom end only

float lifts as weight is dislodged

single swan or AA shot

2″ – 5″

FISHING ON THE BOTTOM

locking shot

bulk shot at mid depth

4″ – 20″

TROTTING A STICK FLOAT

flow

drift

drift

check

sticking set overdepth

bait swings upwards as float is checked

Checking the stick rig

float checked

flow

tackle is rigged overdepth to allow searching action

shot pattern depends on flow

dotted line is path taken by line when float is checked

---

spot beyond your swim. When the tackle lands, close the bale arm, sink the rod tip and get the line sunk quickly.

For most stillwater float fishing, the float is attached bottom end only by passing the line through the eye and locking it into position at the required depth (distance from float to hook) with one or more shots an inch or so either side of the eye.

To present a falling bait ('on the drop'), group most of the shots on both sides of the float's bottom eye, leaving a tiny shot fixed at around mid-depth and another (a dust shot) 18 inches from the hook. After casting, let the bulk shot cock the float and then count how many seconds afterwards first the middle shot and then the dust shot take to sink the float tip to its final position.

A few practice casts and count-downs will soon show you how long it's taking for the float to settle. Then if a fish takes the bait

while it's dropping, the tip won't settle when it should, and that's when you should strike. Once the bait has reached the end of its fall and hangs in the water, bites will register with the float going under.

To present the bait just on the bottom (use a hookless weight or plummet to plumb the exact depth) when bites aren't expected on the drop or at higher levels – such as when the water temperature is low – get it down quickly by regrouping some of the bulk (locking) shots at mid-depth. Try the bottom shot at various positions between four and twenty inches from the hook until bites come.

To fish on the bottom with large baits like breadflake, pastes and corn, for species such as catfish and carp which tilt nose-downwards to suck up the bait, use a lift method rig. A very buoyant peacock quill float is ideal for this, fixed bottom end

only with a float band, rather than locking shots, because this rig works best with just a single large shot (a swan or AA shot) fixed two to five inches from the hook. If more shots are needed they should be fixed at mid-depth.

Set the float several inches deeper than the swim so that it lies flat on the surface, then gently wind in line until it cocks. The instant a fish sucks up the bait and dislodges the shot, the float will lift or pop out of the water and lie flat. Strike as soon as the float starts to lift.

Depending on the type of circumstances, river fishing demands either waggler floats, attached bottom end only, or stick type floats attached top and bottom. Shotting patterns can vary from just a couple of tiny shots down the line for fishing a slow flow, to bulk shot fixed within three feet of the hook for deep, fast rivers.

The technique is simply an extension of stillwater control, except that the float moves ahead of the bait and line is given from the spool, with the bale arm open, as the float 'trots' downstream.

Cast the float a little downstream of you rather than directly opposite, and start the trot through by allowing line to pull from the spool under gentle pressure from your forefinger. After each coil goes, return finger pressure to the spool rim so that when you get a bite, you can strike and hold the line tight until the bale arm comes round to gather it as you wind. Bottom end only floats should be adjusted to present the bait just off, or actually dragging, the bottom.

Set stick type floats a little deeper than the swim, and cast with an underarm swing, controlling the float gently as it settles and is pulled downriver by the current. Apart from slightly overshotting the float, the secret

FLOAT FISHING — 2

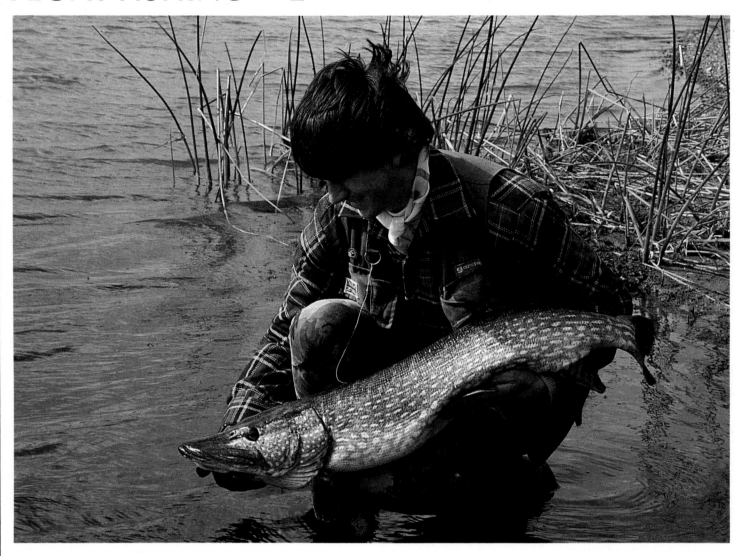

of trotting with stick type floats is in holding back hard on the float every so often, encouraging the bait to swim enticingly upwards.

In still water, float ledgering (bottom fishing with a float and fish-finder rig) is useful for presenting a bait at long distances where a light tackle rig can't be cast. Use a long peacock quill waggler, attached bottom end only with a float band. All the casting weight should be concentrated in either a running dipsey or a swan shot link ledger, and stopped some six to twelve inches from the hook by a BB shot. In depths greater than the length of the rod, use the slider float style with a stopknot.

If set too shallow, the ledger should easily sink the float, so in effect the rig becomes its own depth gauge. Set the float so that it lies half cocked or flat on the water. Sink the line after casting, and put the rod on two rests with the tip above the surface. Then gently wind the reel until an easily visible amount of the float tip is showing, and wait for the fish to

bite.

Float ledgering in running water (often called stret pegging) is more difficult because of current pressure against the line, so you can't fish directly out as in still water. Sit or stand facing downstream and place the bait only a few yards out.

Make up a rig similar to that for still water, but fix the float top and bottom. Set it at least three feet overdepth, allowing current pressure to bow the extra line to reduce water resistance, and cast directly downriver to the desired spot.

Once the ledger has settled, put the rod horizontally into rests and gently take up the slack. The float is more sensitive when it's pushed well up the line so that it lies flat on the surface. Bites will register as gentle twitches of the float, quickly followed by its disappearance beneath the surface at a steep angle.

Slider float fishing is a versatile technique, its uses ranging from casting light float rigs with small baits into deep, far-off swims, to

presenting live or dead fishbaits at prearranged depths. You can also use it to offer baits on or just below the surface for species like carp.

To rig up a bodied waggler or antenna float for fishing deep water, thread the line through the eye of the float so that it can slide. Then tie the hook on, and make a sliding stopknot.

Form a loop with 12 inches of reel line, leaving one end twice as long as the other. Hold the loop tightly against the line at the required depth, and wind the short end five times around both the reel line and the long end, then feed it through the loop. Remember to wet the line before tying the knot, and when you're moving it to a new position, or the line might break through frictional heat.

Pull the knot tight, and cut off both ends to at least 1½ inches long so that they will easily fold through the rod rings for casting or playing a fish. Rig the bulk shot no more than five or six feet from the hook, so that the float slides

Returning a good-sized pike – caught on a deadbait float rig – safely to the water.

down and rests against them for casting regardless of preset knot depth, and pops up to the surface against the stopknot when it's in the water.

Sink the line to minimize drag, and remember to leave the bale arm open for a few seconds so the line can feed through the eye of the float as the bait sinks. Then carefully wind in the slack and expect the same kind of bites as with fixed floats.

Bottom end sliders can be set to offer a livebait well away from the bottom and over weedbeds at any prearranged depth fished static, or fished with or across the wind on the drift. Even deadbaits, mounted horizontally and suspended beneath a slider, can be made to 'come alive' by casting well across the wind and encouraging a belly of line to zoom them along with the waves.

To anchor deadbait on the bottom beneath a slider in still

water, with the line between float and rod sunk, simply pinch on enough swan shots to cock the float immediately above the wire trace, and set the float slightly overdepth. This will prevent the float from shooting under every few seconds in rough conditions and giving false bite indications.

To present a livebait in this way, rig up a running paternoster with the bomb link set however many feet above the bottom you wish to fish. The main benefit from a slider in these situations is that regardless of depth, the strike is very much more direct than with a large fixed float.

Close-range livebaiting in calm conditions, in both still and running water, can be most effectively presented with tubed sliders and a greased line. A good example of this is fishing for pike in still water, with a deadbait on the bottom in lee of the bank or boat. Set the float to at least twice swim depth so that when it comes to rest against the stopknot it will lie completely flat on the surface. When a pike sucks up the bait it will feel no resistance, because the float won't go under but simply follow the fish across the surface of the water.

A similar rig can be used in running water, but with the bait anchored down on the bottom by a dipsey running above the leader. Cast directly downstream, and the float won't be pulled under by even the strongest flow, provided it's been set far enough over swim depth.

Small, self-cocking controller sliders are great for presenting surface baits. You simply watch the line near the float or close to the rod, or just keep an eye on the bait itself. Baits fished on the drop work well too.

To rig a controller, fix up a link about three feet long with a swivel on one end and the hook on the other. Then tie the reel line to the swivel, after first threading on the float followed by a tiny bead to stop the float eye jamming over the swivel. The controller simply slides up and down the line as you play a fish, and it can be made heavy enough to be cast to most far-out spots.

FLOAT LEDGER RIG FOR STILL WATER   **RUNNING WATER — STRET PEGGING**

The float ledger rig for still water is useful for presenting baits at long distances. The rig for stret pegging has the float set at least 3 feet overdepth to allow for the effect of the current.

DEEPWATER FISHING WITH SLIDING FLOAT   **BOTTOM END SLIDING FLOAT — STILLWATER DEADBAIT RIG**

For deepwater fishing with a sliding float, use a bodied waggler or an antenna float. A good way to present deadbaits in still water, for fish such as pike, is to use a bottom end sliding float rig.

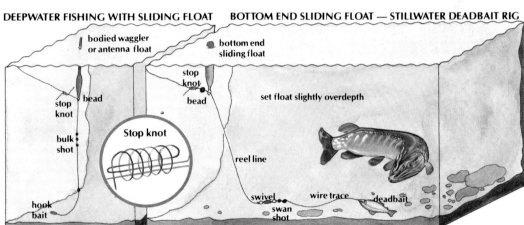

TUBED SLIDING FLOAT — STILLWATER DEADBAIT RIG

An alternative to the bottom end sliding float rig for stillwater deadbaiting is the tubed sliding float rig. The float is set at double the swim depth so that it lies flat on the surface.

SLIDING CONTROLLER FLOAT RIG

Sliding controller float rigs are ideal for presenting surface baits such as floating breadcrust, and can also be used for baits fished on the drop.

FLY CASTING

In many fly fishing situations, especially for trout, it only needs one good cast to catch one. It therefore pays to develop all the skill and dexterity with your tackle that you can muster. Even if you don't catch anything, you will get a great deal of satisfaction and pleasure from just casting well and being by the water.

In the early stages of learning to cast it's essential to master the basics. All good casting is done with a combination of wrist and forearm movement. Some novices develop too much wrist action while others think that sheer, brute strength will enable them to wave the rod about to good effect, using only body power.

For most of us, the hammer-and-nail analogy has proved to be the best way of visualizing the way to handle a single handed fly rod. If you're using a hammer to knock in a large nail, you don't use it with a totally stiff wrist. Nor do you use wrist action only with no forearm movement. Instead, you bring the hammer back with forearm movement and return it in much the same way. But just before the hammer hits the nail you flick your wrist forwards to add extra impetus to the forearm power stroke. You should use the same sort of action when casting with a single handed fly rod.

In overhead casting, all good forward casts begin with a good back cast. This is essential to load the 'spring' of the rod, so that when it's driven forward there will be a release of that spring to drive the line and fly towards the target.

When you're learning to cast, the first thing to do is to practise this wrist/arm action. It may help to sit on a small stool, with the rod in your right hand. Place your right elbow on your right knee, and keep it there while flicking the line back and forth to get the right rhythm.

The rod should be raised and flicked with your thumb coming up alongside your right eye. But if you find that you're tending to bring the rod too far back, angle your arm slightly to the left, so that when you raise the rod your thumb comes up to your nose. Then, if you're doing it all wrong, the rod will bang you on the forehead at the precise moment that it should be stopped anyway.

Following some practice, casting a modest length of line becomes easy. But beware of trying to cast too much line, for this is when faults start to creep in. You may let the rod go too far back and have the line catch the ground behind. Alternatively, you may develop a tendency to push during the final forward cast. This push will do nothing to give more power (and thus greater distance), as it merely kills the spring of the rod.

Greater distances are best achieved by what is termed 'shooting line'. This is best done by holding spare coils of line in your left hand and releasing them at the precise moment of the application of power in the forward cast. With practice, some remarkable lengths of line may be shot in this fashion; but it's not a technique you can master in the first five minutes.

Once you've gained some experience you'll want to try some other types of casting. The roll cast, for instance, is most useful for laying out a line under trees or for merely recasting in the same direction without bringing the line and fly behind you in a back cast.

Instead of lifting the line off the water in a back cast, just bring it feathering back slowly until the rod is just past the vertical behind you and the line is sagging down from it at your side. Then, with a powerful flick forwards and upwards (you should exert power as if trying to break your rod), send the line rolling out like a large 'O' and follow through by bringing the rod tip down to almost water level.

Modifications of this cast are most useful when you're fishing under trees or in places where a back cast is impracticable or impossible. Known to salmon anglers as the Spey casts, they are easily achieved with the longer single handed rods and involve something akin to a roll cast with a change of direction.

The type of Spey cast you should use will depend on which bank you're fishing from. The single Spey cast, for instance, is best done from the left bank (looking downstream), while the double Spey cast is most used on the right bank. Both entail an initial positioning of the line in front of or slightly upstream of where you're standing before the final roll out.

Whenever you're making overhead casts, however, it's important to be able to place the line and fly accurately at the required distance to cover a fish. Differing techniques will be needed for dry fly and wet fly fishing, and there is also a most useful distance cast known as the double-haul cast.

Casting in a wind poses many problems, but it can sometimes be made easier by casting with the rod held horizontally and down near the water. Most times a headwind will cause the leader and fly to curl back and thus upset your plans. The late application of power in the forward cast will sometimes ensure that the line and leader just unfurl in time to alight on the water before the wind can do its damage; but sometimes it's better to find a more sheltered spot or move to a position where the wind is more helpful.

Right Being able to cast well and to present your fly accurately is one of the joys of fly fishing.

THE BACK CAST
rod flexes under
pull of line
straightening behind

THE BASIC OVERHEAD CAST
This is best approached in two stages: the back cast and the forward cast, both shown here in two colours

THE BACK CAST
It is impossible to make a good cast forward without first making a good basic back cast.
With the rod in the 2 o'clock position (1) and the wrist cocked downwards, the line is held firmly in the free hand. The rod is accelerated briskly to the 12 o'clock position (2). Now flick the wrist backwards taking care not to allow the rod to drift beyond 11 o'clock (3).

THE FORWARD CAST

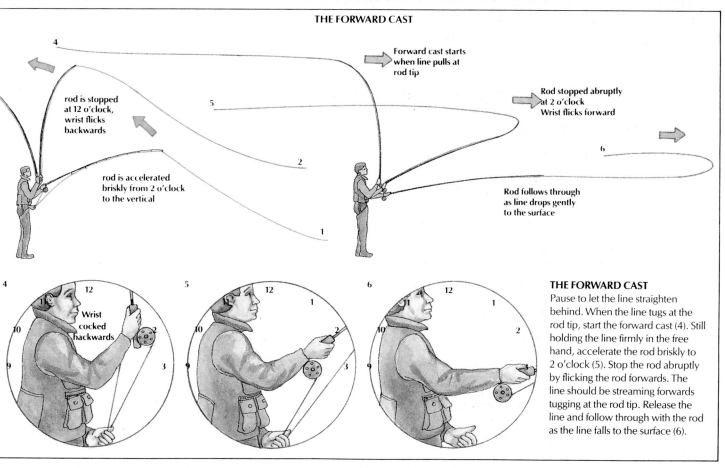

Forward cast starts
when line pulls at
rod tip

Rod stopped abruptly
at 2 o'clock
Wrist flicks forward

4

5

6

2

1

rod is stopped
at 12 o'clock,
wrist flicks
backwards

rod is accelerated
briskly from 2 o'clock
to the vertical

Rod follows through
as line drops gently
to the surface

4

12
11
Wrist
cocked
backwards
10
9
3
2

5

12
11
1
10
9
3
2

6

12
11
1
10
9
2

THE FORWARD CAST
Pause to let the line straighten
behind. When the line tugs at the
rod tip, start the forward cast (4). Still
holding the line firmly in the free
hand, accelerate the rod briskly to
2 o'clock (5). Stop the rod abruptly
by flicking the rod forwards. The
line should be streaming forwards
tugging at the rod tip. Release the
line and follow through with the rod
as the line falls to the surface (6).

FLY FISHING — DRY FLIES

Much mystique has been built up about dry fly fishing over the years, but hatches of fly are less likely to be dominated by just one species than they were a hundred years ago, and the fish (thanks to hatchery breeding) are more catholic in their diet anyway. However, there is still a lot to be said for the challenge of pursuing trout with a dry fly which has been carefully chosen to match the hatching flies, although it can be argued that skilful, accurate presentation counts for more than precise fly selection.

There are many factors which can affect your chances of a catch. For instance, most of the bigger fish in the water didn't get that way by being easily hoodwinked by anglers' flies; it always pays to have an eye for color and size and to know the times of the season, or the day, when a specific species of fly might hatch. Also remember that fish will |sometimes| feed more greedily on one species of fly than another. Other factors to take into account include the direction and quality of the light and its effect on fish vision, and the more subtle effects of drag, often undetected by you but not by the fish you hope to delude.

Most times on running water you should try to cast upstream to the rising fish. This will ease your problem of remaining unobserved and help place your fly over the fish without instant drag being induced to scare it away.

It often pays not to cast too far upstream of the fish, for the simple reason that there is then more time for drag to be induced before the fly gets into the taking zone. When fish prove very difficult it's sometimes a good plan to cast into the receding ripples from a previous rise. This requires great accuracy and dexterity, but it will often get you a fish which is now taking on impulse, before it's had time to give the fly or its movement some critical examination.

This method will often work wonders when there is more than one fish in the same taking position. This is when greed

Above right A brown trout taken on a dry fly tied to imitate an adult cranefly or daddy-longlegs.
Dry flies, designed and tied so that they float on the surface, are used mainly on streams and rivers, but are also useful on still waters. On running waters, it's usually best to cast them upstream.

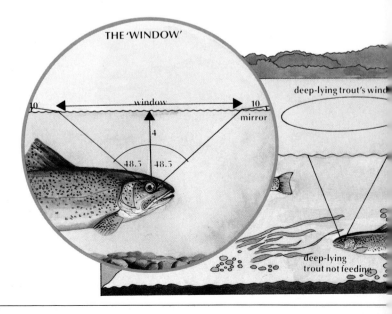

THE TROUT'S VISION (WINDOW)
A trout's view of the world beyond the water depends on the laws of refraction. Light rays passing vertically into the water are not bent, but the amount of refraction increases as the angle from the vertical increases, until at about 10° from the horizontal they are bent to about 48.5° to the vertical. 10° is the lowest angle at which useful light penetrates to the trout. This gives the trout a field of view (or 'window') of about 160° (180°−20°). The area of surface through which it cannot see is called the 'mirror'. A simple calculation shows that the trout's window diameter is proportional to its depth in the ratio of 9:4, and so the deeper the trout is lying, the larger its window.

DRY FLY PRESENTATION

THE 'WINDOW'

window

mirror

deep-lying trout's wind

deep-lying trout not feeding

TYING A DETACHED BODY FLY

1 Place a rewiring needle, eye first, in the fly vice.

2 Tie in a slim bunch of deerhair or bucktail by the butts , and make a whip finish.

3 Take the thread down the needle in firm, open spirals, whip finish, then return in open spirals to the butts. Whip finish. Cut away the waste thread. Give the body, not the tails, a coat or two of liquid PVC.

4 When dry, slip the body off the needle and trim the tails.

5 Leave five or six hairs to simulate the natural mavfly.

6 Partially insert 3-inches of nylon monofil into the hollow body. Place a drop of fast-setting adhesive on the stalk just ahead of the body. Push it quickly into the body. Leave to set.

7 The nylon is tied in on top of the preferred hook.

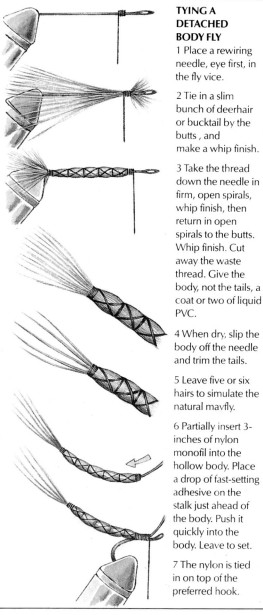

comes first, and in a mad dash to get the fly first, the fish will often throw all caution to the winds.

Most times, of course, a large trout in a stream will occupy its own well-defended territory and will seek to drive off other small fry or fish which try to intrude. Trout born and accustomed to life in the wild are essentially very territorial creatures. Those with hatchery origins, which spent a lengthy period being pampered with artificial feeding, tend to form into schools at first rather than establish territories, and it may be some time after their release into the wild before they abandon this habit.

In the clear chalk streams, a territorial trout can easily be identified as it cruises up and down its pitch sipping in the hatching duns. Chalk streams, because of their origins, are much more alkaline than rain-fed rivers. As a result, they have abundant weed growth which harbors a large number of natural insects, and for this reason the chalk stream trout are invariably larger than other river trout and much easier to see.

Trout which have got used to the plentiful supply of food in a chalk stream can be very selective in their feeding habits, but so, too, can fish in other waters. So being able to recognize the natural flies and choose an artificial to match them is a skill worth learning.

Although it's usually best to catch a dry fly upstream when fishing running water, there's nothing to stop you casting it across or downstream if you prefer. However, if you do this, there's more chance of your being seen, and of imparting drag to the fly before the fish has time to intercept it. If you do cast downstream, try to cast a slack line which may, for a few seconds, present your fly well without any drag. It will also avoid covering the fish with your leader.

Dry fly fishing is practised mostly on flowing water, but it may also be used to good effect on still waters. Here the technique is merely to cast the fly out and wait hopefully for a cruising fish to come and take it, sometimes giving the fly an occasional twitch to attract the fish's attention. But the use of the dry fly is essentially a tactic for the chalk streams or those rivers with only a modest rate of flow, where it provides one of the most exciting of all forms of trout fishing.

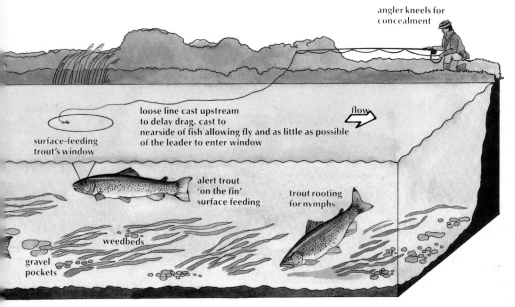

angler kneels for concealment

loose line cast upstream to delay drag. cast to nearside of fish allowing fly and as little as possible of the leader to enter window

flow

surface-feeding trout's window

alert trout 'on the fin' surface feeding

trout rooting for nymphs

weedbeds

gravel pockets

FLY FISHING — WET FLIES

The dry fly technique is one of the more interesting ways of catching fish, but many anglers will argue that successful wet fly fishing demands greater expertise and so provides greater satisfaction. However, both methods have their own type of challenge, and both may be very easy at times or test the patience of a saint at others.

Unlike the dry fly, which is fished floating on the surface, the wet fly or nymph is used below the surface. In general, sparsely dressed wet flies are preferable to the bulkier patterns.

Nowadays, a lot of wet-fly anglers fish with an imitation nymph cast upstream and then manipulated so that it drifts close to a fish which has been seen taking nymphs. At other times, perhaps when the fish may not be seen so easily, you can cast across and downstream and let your fly swing round in the current until you feel the pull of a taking fish. However, it's usually better to work the fly a bit to make it more attractive.

This is especially true if you're fishing with more than one fly on the leader, for instance with three flies, each separated by about twenty inches of leader monofilament and mounted on what are known as droppers. This team of flies can be trailed behind a moving boat, but when cast across and downstream they will merely dangle in the current, tethered by the line, with no natural-looking movement.

To work a team of flies in a lively way you should cast with a slack line and let the flies sink well down. Then, as the current takes them downstream, lift the line slightly just before the full drag of the stream takes effect. The tail fly will obviously swim at a greater depth than the top one, and it will be largely a question of a fish's mood at that moment whether it's more interested in the tail fly or the top or middle one.

During the cold water of the early season, for example, it's often the tail fly which attracts most trout. But it only needs a bright spell around lunchtime and a spasmodic surface hatch of natural flies for the fish to be more interested in taking the top fly or even a dry fly.

One very successful method of fishing with wet flies is to stand at the head of a pool or run, cast the flies out and across, and pay off as much line from your reel as is needed for the flies to reach the tail of the pool. Then slowly handline the flies back towards you and through the deeper water. This is a good way of enticing deep-lying trout in cold water and, depending on current strength, may be practised with either a sinking or a floating line.

On shallow rivers you might find it helpful to use a full, white floating line for the simple reason that it can be seen better than a sunken green one. Quite frequently, the first indication that a fish has intercepted your fly will come as a brief hesitation at the end of the floating line before you feel a pull. Constant alertness to what's happening to the end of your line will often get you more fish than if you just wait for a good pull. You may only detect a subtle hesitation or twitch at the end of the line, but when you do you should strike instantly.

In very deep water, though, it often pays to fish with either a full sinking line or one with a sinking tip. It's also wise to use patterns of fly which have been tied to sink well down, rather than those with more buoyancy which are intended for low water conditions.

For nymph fishing, where you want to get your fly down to a trout's level in the shortest possible time, use those with a piece of lead wire tied to the hook shank before the nymph is dressed. Known as leaded or weighted nymphs, these are ideal for chalk streams as well as for many of the large rain-fed rivers with deep runs and pools.

The real advantages of wet fly fishing are to be realized at those times preceding a surface hatch or when all surface activity has ceased. There will also be specific times of the season when surface activity will be minimal but when the fish are feeding hectically on or near the bottom of the river.

If you're fishing in still water you can use the same sort of techniques as for rivers, but you'll need to work the fly more to take account of the lack of current to make it move. When you're after rainbow trout rather than browns you'll often need to replace the small, sparsely dressed flies with larger, often bolder patterns. But there will be occasions when small flies will win the day.

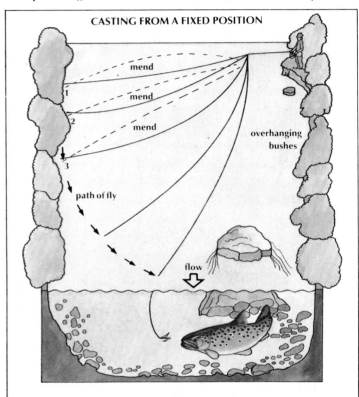

CASTING FROM A FIXED POSITION

When you're unable to move downstream, judicious use of the mend or upstream bow can get your fly to where you want it.

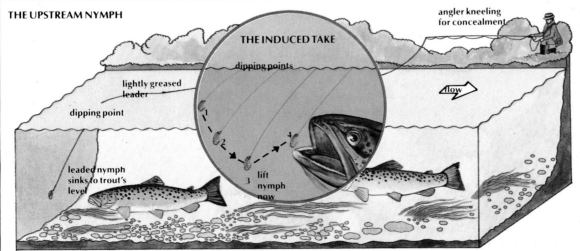

THE UPSTREAM NYMPH

THE INDUCED TAKE

This nymph fishing ploy, developed by the famous keeper Frank Sawyer on England's Hampshire Avon, is intended to trigger a response from a trout which has previously declined the drifting nymph. As the nymph reaches the trout it is made to dive sharply by lifting the rod or drawing in line by hand, often inducing the fish to take involuntarily hence the term 'induced take'.

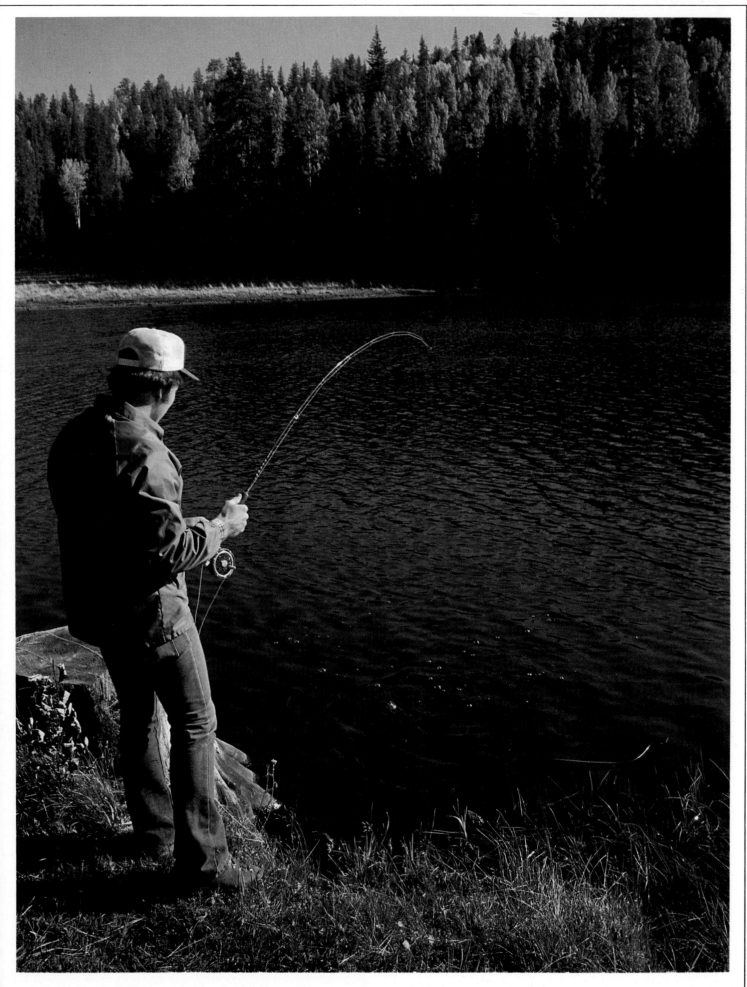

Above *Wet flies and nymphs are fished below the surface of the water, and are more sparsely dressed than the floating dry fly patterns.*

FLY FISHING—SALTWATER

Fly casting for saltwater fish is not like casting for trout or even salmon. The tackle and casting techniques are broadly the same, but the type of fly or lure used is very different. Most trout flies, for instance, are tied to 'match the hatch', in other words the fly tier has gone to a great deal of trouble to produce a pattern to imitate the actual insect life of the water to be fished.

By comparison with this selective approach, saltwater fly fishing is a rough and ready style of angling. Saltwater fish are opportunists, and their food comes in many forms and many shapes and sizes. The angler's problem is not in finding a fly that exactly reproduces a real shrimp or sandeel, but in finding one that will trigger an aggressive feeding response in whatever species of fish is sought.

Many species of fish can be induced to strike at a fly, up to and including large game fish such as sailfish. Mostly, though, it's the smaller inshore species that respond to fly-style lures. Bass, bluefish, bonefish, mackerel, pollack, permit, tarpon and a host of other species fall readily to fly gear, the trick to saltwater casting being to fully understand your tackle and the movement and preferred habitat of the fish you're after.

Choice of tackle is of vital importance. Most experienced saltwater fly fishermen prefer long rods, the ideal weapon being a 9½ to 10 foot, two piece boron or graphite rod capable of throwing weight forward lines in the 9 to 10 class rating. The reel should be a specially constructed, fully anodized saltwater fly reel. Failing this, you can use a good-sized salmon fly reel, but whichever reel you use it must be capable of taking a minimum of 200 yards of 20 pound backing line as well as the bulky fly line.

Tapered leaders of the type tied and used for trout fishing have little practical advantage for saltwater use. Sunken rocks, coral beds or sharp-edged shellfish have little respect for a fly leader. The trick is to cut costs by purchasing individual spools of nylon monofilament of various breaking strains, and cutting off a 9 or 10 foot length whenever you need a new leader.

By cutting costs in this way, you might even catch more fish. If a leader costs very little, you don't have to worry about losing it and you can happily fish amongst the really rough stuff where most fish are found. Fear of losing costly tackle cuts many anglers' success rates to a dismal minimum.

If you can use a fly rod well enough to cast 60 feet or more in an accurate line, the only difficulty you're likely to encounter lies in the choice of fly and the way you work it through the water. For shallow water or surface feeding fish you should use a floating fly line, but for depths of over 6 feet a high density fast sinking line is preferable.

Flies (except surface bugs) remain the same irrespective of the type of fly line you use, but the choice of fly depends a great deal on the species of fish, the time of day and the water conditions.

Take evening fishing for pollack, for example. During most of the daylight hours pollack live and feed close to the bottom. Then, as the light intensity begins to fade, they come up to feed close to the surface. Under these circumstances, any fly working through the surface layers is seen by the fish as a dark, moving silhouette. For this reason, black/brown or dark colored flies seem most effective.

The movement of the fly is often as critical as its color. With flies working on or just under the surface the trick is to create the illusion of a terrified and totally isolated bait fish. A natural fish finding itself in such a vulnerable situation panics and heads at speed for the nearest cover.

To imitate the movement of a bait fish you can retrieve the fly in two ways. A long pull of line at medium speed will make the fly shoot forwards at an even speed. To a hunting predator this will look like a natural fish heading for safety. Effective though this style of retrieve is, an even better technique is to retrieve line with a very fast, very short chopping stroke of the hand, each pull taking in no more than six inches of line. This odd but high speed retrieve will give the fly a sort of panicked motion that few predatory species can resist.

For bottom fish such as bonefish or permit, both shallow water feeders, use a very slow style of retrieve. Both these species are browsers, living on shrimp and crab which they pick up directly from the sea bed. Most of their food is located by the little cloud

Right *Fly fishing in saltwater is an interesting alternative to surfcasting or saltwater spinning.*

KNOTS

THE NEEDLE KNOT

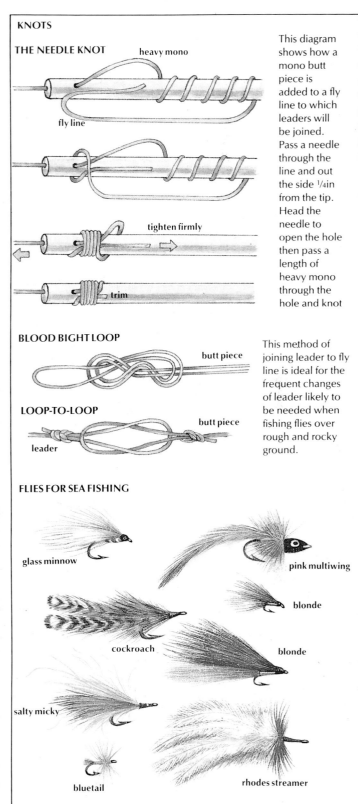

heavy mono

fly line

tighten firmly

trim

This diagram shows how a mono butt piece is added to a fly line to which leaders will be joined. Pass a needle through the line and out the side ¼in from the tip. Head the needle to open the hole then pass a length of heavy mono through the hole and knot

BLOOD BIGHT LOOP

butt piece

LOOP-TO-LOOP

butt piece

leader

This method of joining leader to fly line is ideal for the frequent changes of leader likely to be needed when fishing flies over rough and rocky ground.

FLIES FOR SEA FISHING

glass minnow

pink multiwing

blonde

cockroach

blonde

salty micky

bluetail

rhodes streamer

of sand or mud which is stirred up as the shrimp or crab crawls over the bottom.

A fly tied over a lightly weighted body can be inched back over the bottom to simulate this movement. The weighted body of the fly helps it to dig into and stir up the sand or silt, and is essential to this type of fishing.

For large fish like tarpon or sail-fish, the fly should be tied in streamer fashion to imitate a reasonable-sized bait fish. Flies tied from fine hair material give a bulky appearance without being too heavy to cast. This sort of fly should be worked at speed through the surface layers, and most big game fly casters wait until a fish has been sighted before attempting a cast.

KNOTS

Whenever you're fishing with mono or Dacron line, you'll have at least two knots on your line – the knot tying the line to the reel spool, and another fixing the hook to the line. It's very likely that you'll have other knots as well, such as fly dropper knots, or knots attaching swivels or leaders to the reel line.

Because each knot is a potential weak point in the line, it's advisable to keep the number of knots to a minimum, use a suitable knot for the job, and tie it carefully. Even the best of knots will have only around 90 percent of the strength of the line it's tied in, a point worth remembering, especially when you're joining two lines of different strengths. In practice, the knot might well have as little as 80 percent of the strength of the weaker line.

When you're learning to tie a knot, it's best to start by trying it out on a piece of string, which is easier to handle than nylon line and, being thicker, makes it easier for you to follow the formation of the loops, turns and tucks involved in making the knot.

To reduce the risk of damaging the line when you're tying a knot, wet it well to minimize friction before pulling it tight. Use a firm, steady pull when you tighten it, and trim off any loose ends so that they won't catch in the rod rings or create an unwanted disturbance in the water.

The knots illustrated here include knots for joining terminal tackle, such as hooks, swivels and lures, to the line; knots for joining line to line and line to leader; and knots for forming loops in lines or leaders. All of them are easy to tie, and are reliable and well-proven. They can be used with either nylon monofilament or Dacron, for freshwater or saltwater use.

The blood knot and the clinch knot can be used for attaching eyed hooks or swivels, and the spade end whip is for tying spade-end hooks to lines. The Domhof knot is for snelling eyed hooks, the Palomar is for attaching hooks, swivels or lures, and the spool knot is for tying line to spool.

For joining line to line or line to leader, the knots shown are the full blood knot, the water knot (or surgeon's knot), and a knot for tying a shock leader to a line. Finally, the knots for forming loops in lines or leaders are the double overhand loop (or the surgeon's end loop) and the blood bight.

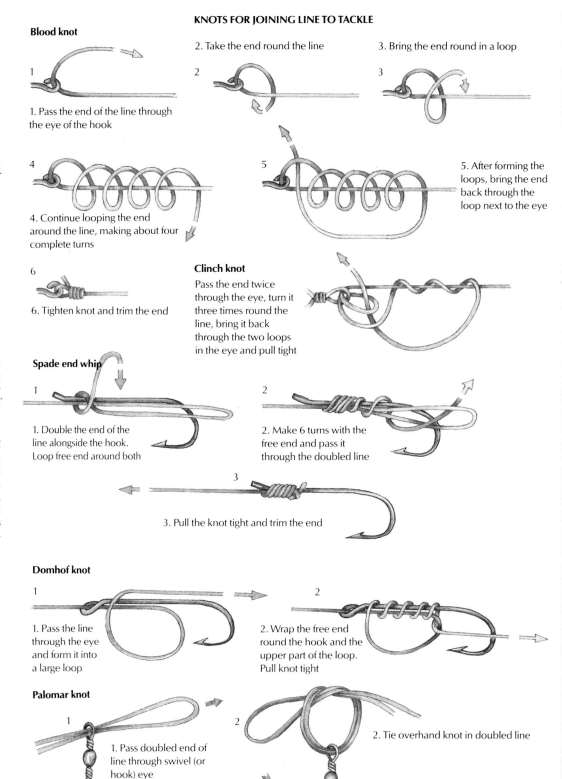

Blood knot

1. Pass the end of the line through the eye of the hook

KNOTS FOR JOINING LINE TO TACKLE

2. Take the end round the line

3. Bring the end round in a loop

4. Continue looping the end around the line, making about four complete turns

5. After forming the loops, bring the end back through the loop next to the eye

6. Tighten knot and trim the end

Clinch knot

Pass the end twice through the eye, turn it three times round the line, bring it back through the two loops in the eye and pull tight

Spade end whip

1. Double the end of the line alongside the hook. Loop free end around both

2. Make 6 turns with the free end and pass it through the doubled line

3. Pull the knot tight and trim the end

Domhof knot

1. Pass the line through the eye and form it into a large loop

2. Wrap the free end round the hook and the upper part of the loop. Pull knot tight

Palomar knot

1. Pass doubled end of line through swivel (or hook) eye

2. Tie overhand knot in doubled line

3 Pull the looped end over the swivel

4. Pull tight and trim

Spool knot

The most effective knot for tying the line to the reel spool

KNOTS FOR JOINING LINES

Full blood knot

1

1. Overlap the ends of the two lines. Take one end and wind it around the opposing line. Bring it back through the first loop.

2

2. Repeat the process with the free end of the other line

3

3. Wet the knot, pull it tight and trim it

Water knot (surgeon's knot)

1

1. Overlap the line and leader by 6 inches

4

4. Pull the knot tight and trim the ends

2

2. Form a loop, treating the line and leader as a single line

3

3. Make an overhand knot, pulling entire leader through the loop. Repeat 4 times

Shock leader knot

1

1. Double the ends of the leader and the line back six inches, and pass the line loop through the leader

2

2. Form the doubled line into a loop

3

3. Pass the end of the doubled line around both strands of the leader and through its loop

4

4. Repeat three more times

5

5. Holding the looped end, pull the line and its tag end

6

6. Pull both strands of line with one hand and the leader with the other, to tighten knot

KNOTS FOR FORMING LOOPS

Double overhand loop (surgeon's end loop)

1

1. Double the end back along the line

2

2. Tie an overhand knot

3

3. Repeat the overhand knot

4

4. Pull tight

Blood bight

1

1. Double the end back along the line

2

2. Turn double end around the line

3

3. Pass looped end through the turn

4

4. Pull tight

LEDGERING

Ledgering generally lacks the sensitivity of float fishing, but it's a very versatile technique because you can cast the bait great distances and present it on the bottom of deep lakes and fast-flowing rivers.

Whether you're casting long range in still water or anchoring the bait down on the bottom of a river, the first thing to decide is the amount and type of weight to use. As a general rule, if more than four swan shots are needed, switch to the neatness and more accurate casting of the dipsey.

In the simple running ledger, the weight is stopped 12 inches (this can be varied) from the hook by a single BB shot or a plastic ledger stop. For a more versatile and sensitive rig, fix the weight at the end of a link, as with the fixed paternoster ledger. Use a size 10 swivel as the junction, tying just 10 inches of line (to carry the weight) to one end, and both the reel line and the hook link (which for small hooks can be much lighter than the reel line) to the other.

The actual length of the hook link can vary between just 4 inches, for hitting tiny 'twitch' bites, and several feet, for presenting the bait on the drop (used mainly in still water). However, 16 inches is an ideal hook link length to start with.

When you're fishing for predators or carp, you often need to give the bite time to develop before striking. To allow the fish to take several feet of line without becoming suspicious, use a sliding link ledger rather than a fixed paternoster. Simply add a swivel to the weight link so that it slides above the junction swivel, allowing the reel line to run through if a fish takes the bait.

These are the three basic rigs for ledgering in both still and running water. Having chosen your rig, though, you next need to decide what type of bite indication will work best in the prevailing water and weather conditions.

For tackling fast water, you can use a simple running or fixed paternoster, with the rod tip itself acting as the bite indicator. For accuracy, use an over-the-shoulder cast (as in float fishing), closing the bale arm as soon as the ledger plops beneath the surface. Once the tackle has swung down in the current and settled into the desired position (if it won't settle, simply add more weight), watch the rod tip for bites.

You can either hold the rod, or put it on two rod rests with the tip angled upwards and pointing slightly downstream. This reduces the water pressure on the line and stops the tackle from being swept into the bank.

In slow water, or if you're trying to watch the rod tip for bites in a strong wind, keep it angled low down. Any movement of the tip is much easier to see if it's only a couple of inches above the water.

For more sensitive bite indication, screw a quiver tip into the tip ring (some rods have built-in quiver tips, which are even better) so that even the slightest twitch or knock will be easily seen. In a very gentle flow, a spring tip gives still greater sensitivity.

With both rod tip and quiver tip (or spring tip) indication, bites can register in two ways. If the bait is pulled directly downstream, the tip knocks and bends round accordingly. But should the fish move across the current or even upstream with the bait, the ledger will be dislodged and the tip will actually spring backwards before the weight resettles.

Once the ledger has settled after casting, and the tip has curled round gently to the pull of the current, you should strike instantly at any of these indications.

In still water, particularly over dense weedbeds where the operation of a running ledger would be impeded, the fixed paternoster is more commonly used. With this type of rig, the rod should be angled downwards on two rests and pointing at the bait, allowing the line to move freely through the rings when the fish pulls.

RUNNING LEDGER

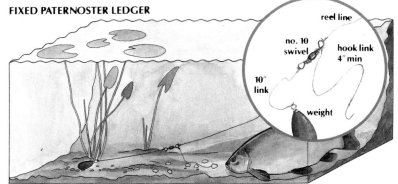

reel line

BB shot

nylon loop carries swan shot

shot to hook 12"

The running ledger can be weighted with up to 4 swan shots, mounted on a nylon loop and stopped about twelve inches from the hook by a BB shot or a plastic ledger stop.

FIXED PATERNOSTER LEDGER

reel line

no. 10 swivel

hook link 4" min

10" link

weight

The fixed paternoster ledger consists of a size 10 swivel with the reel line and hook link tied to one eye, and the link carrying the weight attached to the other.

SLIDING LINK LEDGER

bead

swivels

weight link

weight

The sliding link ledger has the reel line and hook link joined by a swivel, with the weight link fixed to a swivel sliding along the reel line.

BOLT LEDGER

6" from backstop to swivel

swivel

2 oz bomb

backstop

The bolt ledger has a 2-ounce weight sliding on the 6 to 10 inches of line between the backstop and the swivel joining the hook link to the reel line.

Above *An angler holding the line between his fingertips so that he can detect the lightest of bites.*

The easiest type of bite indicator to use here is the bobbin, which simply clips to the line between the reel and the butt ring, but this type can be blown about by the wind, giving false indications. Butt bite indicators, or the similar 'monkey climber' type, are more stable, or you can use an electronic bite indicator.

The swing tip, which screws into the tip ring and hangs down in front of the rod, allowing valuable slack to a biting fish, is perhaps the most sensitive of indicators – but its flapping about during the fight is distracting to many anglers.

Although primarily developed for carp fishing in still water, the shock or bolt ledger rig can be effective for other species such as tench. It works on the principle of making the carp bolt at the shock of suddenly feeling the weight of a heavy sinker. Instinctively, the carp closes its mouth and flees, hooking itself as it goes.

Once the carp is on the move and the line is going steadily out (use a minimum of 12 pounds test) the rod is picked up and the run struck.

To rig for this method, use a 2 ounce dipsey stopped at around 10 inches from the hook by a junction swivel, with a ledger stop on the reel side of the dipsey about 6 inches above the swivel. This is called the backstop, and it's what makes the carp tow the heavy dipsey, by stopping the line from running freely through it.

After casting and tightening up, put the line into a monkey climber on a 10 inch drop, leaving the bale arm open. Alternatively, the bale arm may be used closed with the antireverse off, and the reel will simply backwind when a run occurs instead of line peeling from the spool.

PLAYING AND LANDING — FRESHWATER

Playing a fish, especially on light, well-balanced tackle, is one of the most enjoyable parts of freshwater angling, and there's far more subtlety involved than even experienced anglers give themselves credit for. Consistent success can only come through practice and experience.

First of all, though, you need to appreciate just what your tackle is capable of, for instance how much the line can be stretched before it breaks, and what sort of curve your rod will take. Dacron line, for example, has next to no inherent stretch, while the stretch in monofilament nylon might be as much as 25 percent. It's important to use well-balanced tackle, that is, with the breaking strain and elasticity of the line matched to the power and action of the rod, and a good, smooth-acting reel.

Before you make your first cast at the beginning of a fishing session, check the adjustment of the reel's slipping clutch. If you're using a fixed spool reel put the antireverse on, or put the reel in gear if it's a multiplier (baitcaster). Then adjust the drag until it's just possible to pull line from the spool by hand.

With the drag properly set you'll be able to put maximum pressure on the fish, knowing that the clutch will slip and give line before the strain on the line reaches breaking point. Remember to check the clutch setting every so often while you're fishing, because temperature changes and prolonged use can greatly affect it.

Each time the fish runs allow both line stretch and the rod tip to absorb the lunges together. When the fish starts to slow down, lower the rod tip so that you can wind and gain line. Then pump the rod back up again into a nice full curve and wait for the fish's next move, either another run or an opportunity for you to gain still more line by pumping again.

There will be occasions when a fish powers towards snags and you have to forget the clutch, clamp down and just hang on, throwing caution to the wind. It's only when this sort of make-or-break situation crops up that you find out exactly what you, and more importantly your tackle, are capable of.

Rods will sometimes bend into the kind of curve no tackle dealer would wish to let you try out in the shop, while the elasticity of monofilament line allows it to cope with some seemingly impossible loads. So don't be afraid to really work your tackle, and play the fish with a controlled, firm hand whatever the outcome.

The time will come, however, when you hook into something so large that playing it seems immediately to be a hopeless task. Yet no matter how light your outfit, if it's well balanced and you have plenty of clear water in which to play the fish, success will be yours.

One of the best ways to control a powerful fish and make it change course is to use sidestrain. From an upright bend, you lower the rod tip down to or even below the surface and towards the direction in which the fish is headed.

Now, if you apply powerful sideways pressure in the opposite direction, the fish will eventually have no choice but to kite towards the line of strain. A strong fish, once pulled off course, will then try another run in the opposite direction. When it does this, repeat the sidestrain from the new angle. Go on doing this until the fish tires and can be coaxed towards you.

More fish, especially big ones, are lost during landing than at any other stage of the ganme, usually because the fish isn't fully played to a standstill. The angler tries to grab hold with the fish held on a short line, but the fish fights back, the hook flies out or the line breaks, and the fish is free.

So the first rule to remember, whether you intend netting your catch or picking it out by hand, is to wait until it's completely beaten and not still thrashing Then you won't suffer from hooks in your fingers, blood spurting from bite wounds, or hurt pride.

When catching really large fish, or small to medium sized fish on extra light tackle, a landing net is always the best way to get them out of the water. Wait until the fish is beaten, then draw it over the net, already sunk beneath the surface. If the fish is heavy, don't lift the rod by the handle because the rim could bend; draw the net towards you and grab the mesh itself for hauling out.

Where the water is very shallow in the margins the fish may be beached. This is often better than netting for fish caught on plugs or snap tackle, where flying hooks are bound to get entangled in the mesh of the net. Simply ease the fish up into the shallows and onto its side in one long, positive movement.

Taking the fish from the water by handing out will, now and again, cost you a lost fish. Nevertheless, it's an easy operation which allows you to unhook the fish and return it to the water in the shortest possible time. You can even unhook the fish while it's still in the water.

Draw the fish alongside the boat or bank, and reach down slowly. For pike, use a gloved left hand and slip your fingers into its left gill casing. Then clamp down firmly with your thumb, and lift. Be particularly careful of any loose hooks if the fish tries to twist or flap, which they usually do.

To pick out a bass or other less toothy fish, get a firm thumb and forefinger grip on its lower lip, if protruding, or simply pincer your hand around its neck immediately behind the gill case and lift it out.

Alternatively, if you aren't going to keep the fish or photograph it, reach down and flip the hooks out with long-nosed artery forceps while it's still in the water.

Above *It's vital to play the fish to a standstill before you try to land it, otherwise you'll risk losing it at the last minute.*

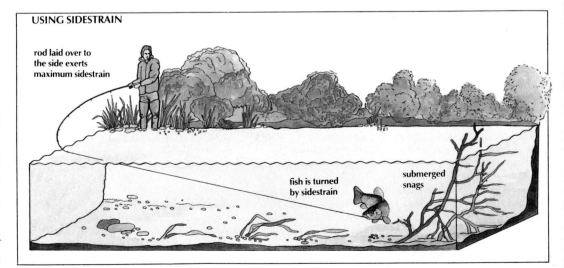

USING SIDESTRAIN

rod laid over to the side exerts maximum sidestrain

fish is turned by sidestrain

submerged snags

LANDING TECHNIQUES

Never try to land a fish which is full of fight by making wild lunges with the net. Wait until the fish is completely played out and on its side, then draw it steadily over the net.

wrong

right

tailing

lipping

The salmon angler need not be encumbered with gaff or net as nature has provided the salmon with a perfect landing aid – a 'wristed' tail.

This method enables you to unhook without taking the fish from the water or damaging its natural protective mucus with a landing net.

PLAYING A FISH

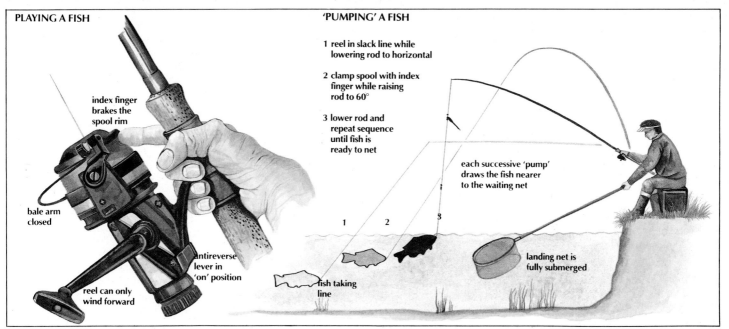

index finger brakes the spool rim

bale arm closed

antireverse lever in 'on' position

reel can only wind forward

'PUMPING' A FISH

1 reel in slack line while lowering rod to horizontal

2 clamp spool with index finger while raising rod to 60°

3 lower rod and repeat sequence until fish is ready to net

each successive 'pump' draws the fish nearer to the waiting net

landing net is fully submerged

fish taking line

PLAYING AND LANDING — SALTWATER

When you're playing a fish from the shore, the general tactics – pump-and-wind and the use of the reel drag and sidestrain – are similar to those used in freshwater fishing. If the water's calm and flat, you can play the fish to a standstill and draw it in to beach it. But when waves are running, you should bring the fish in on a good wave rather than try to pull it in against the undertow.

If you're boat fishing for small to medium-sized fish, the tactics are again the same, but for large fish such as shark, tuna or billfish a very definite playing technique is needed. These fish usually make a long initial run for freedom the second they feel the hook and the restricting rod pressure. During this first run you should make no attempt to turn the fish, because that usually results in a broken line and a lost fish.

The technique for these big game fish is to keep the rod up to absorb sudden shocks and let the reel drag work in the normal way, to slow the fish down. Even the largest of fish will only take 200 to 300 yards of line before slowing down and starting to circle.

Once this point is reached, you should begin to pump the fish hard to regain as much line as possible; at this stage the boat should be backing down on the fish to allow you to gain line more easily. The real battle begins when the fish goes deep. That's when you'll have to use your back, arm and leg muscles to try to raise the fish by applying maximum rod pressure.

Watch your rod tip at all times; as the fish lifts, the tip will come up, and when it reaches the 12 o'clock position drop it back down, at the same time winding in the slack. This pump-and-wind action often has to be repeated hundreds of times, depending on the size and type of fish on the hook, so always use a shoulder harness, clipped to the lugs on the reel rim, to take some of the strain off your arms.

At all times keep your left hand solidly on the foregrip of the rod. This is important, for should the line part under continuous pressure, your left arm will act as a brake to stop the rod from flying back in your face. Once the fish is finished and the double line swivel is against the rod tip, you should wait until the mate and skipper have 'wired' the fish. At this stage the drag system should be wound back a fraction, so that

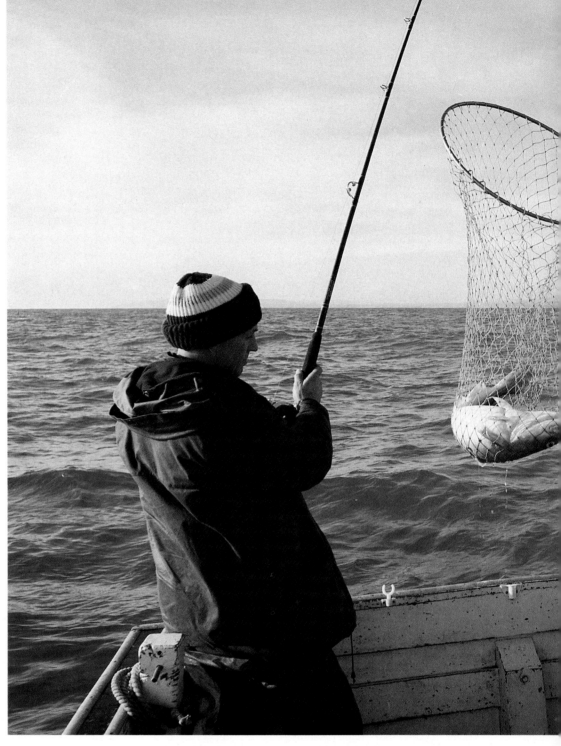

should the fish make a sudden dive the reel will be free enough to give line without breakage occurring.

Landing or boating a fish takes skill and a variety of specialized tools. Most very big fish, from cod, ling and conger up to shark, tuna, and billfish, are gaffed, the size and style of gaff depending on the size and type of fish. For fish of up to 100 pounds, a fixed head gaff – one which has been securely lashed to a strong handle – is best. Never use screw-threaded gaffs,

because they have an unpleasant tendency to unscrew themselves in use, and this can lead to lost fish. Fish like shark, conger or moray eels, which often twist at high speed when they're pulled out of the water, soon show up any weakness in a gaff.

For fish of over 100 pounds a flying or breakaway gaff is essential. This works on the harpoon principle, in as much as the gaff head detaches from the handle, leaving the angler or boatman attached to the fish by

rope and wire. The reason for using a breakaway gaff is to avoid accidents: big fish often go into a final frenzy when first gaffed, and a flailing gaff handle could easily break a man's arm or head.

When you're surf fishing for striped bass or other large fish you can use a fixed gaff. But when you're fishing from piers or harbor walls, landing fish can be something of a problem because of the drop between where you're standing and the water surface. In these situations you need a

THE FLYING GAFF
The flying gaff is used for large fish such as sharks and conger eels which, if gaffed on a fixed head, are powerful enough to break the arm of an unwary deckhand with their violent contortions as they are brought aboard.

THE DROP NET
A drop net is the only feasible method of landing a fish from such places as steep rocks, sea walls or piers. Lower the net into the water and bring the played-out fish over it. Then lift the net, and with the fish enmeshed lay the rod to one side and haul up the fish.

drop net.

This consists of a large, round frame to which a heavy net bag is fixed. Four cords tied to the rim of the net are centrally secured to a suitable length of heavy cordage, which allows the net to be dropped down and held just below the surface. You guide the fish over the net frame, then raise the net to get the fish into the bag. Once the fish is safely inside the net you can pull it up.

For boat fishing where it's easy to reach down into the water, you

Above Large fish need the gaff, but smaller ones can be safely boated with a good-sized net.

can use a normal landing net. Where possible it should be sunk in position before the fish is actually ready to be netted. The sight or sound of a net being pushed into the water is often enough to send a big fish into a final bid for freedom. By positioning the net beforehand this final spasm can often be avoided.

POLE FISHING

The art of pole fishing is to cast, hook and land fish (sometimes even quite large ones) on a long, multi-sectioned pole, to which the line is fixed at the tip. There is usually no reel, guides or any method of giving line.

One of the pole's greatest advantages is that due to its extreme length, the bait can be dropped easily into spots that would be difficult to get to with running tackle outfits. With a pole, you can put the bait into holes between weedbeds, or immediately beyond thick marginal rushes or reeds, or straight down the drop-off into deep water, and retrieve it again with little risk of tangled line or a snagged hook.

Tiny gaps between lily pads, where a light bait could never be presented on conventional gear, are no problem with a pole, and neither is holding a float well out in a powerful flow with the bait down on the bottom. With conventional gear, the angle between the rod tip and float would soon have the float swinging into the side.

Holding the float back gently in a flow is where the long pole really excels. A long line/short rod casting outfit pulls the float off course every time it's checked, except when literally fishing beneath the short rod tip at your feet. But as the pole tip is held directly above and slightly behind (upstream of) the float when trotting or laying on, it can be sent down the current as steadily as a truck when fishing well overdepth with the bait preceding the float. Thanks to the short amount of line between pole tip and float (two to five feet), there is no way the float can be dragged under by the current.

To cast with a pole, get comfortably seated and grip it with your hands well apart – left hand on the butt, the right about two feet higher – and swing the tackle out underarm or over the shoulder.

After casting, short poles (up to 15 feet long) can be held in the right hand, supported along the forearm and controlled just like a conventional rod. With all longer poles, though, a completely different technique is needed. This grip seems odd at first, but when you get used to it, it's actually quite comfortable.

As the float lands, lower the pole tip and swap over hand positions, bringing the butt to rest across your right knee. Your left hand now supports the pole immediately in front of your knee, with your right hand holding the butt tightly.

When you get a bite, simply twist your right hand quickly clockwise, steadying the pole with your left. This will lift the pole tip swiftly to set the hook.

Little fish can be swung into the hand if the line's long enough; if not, sections can be removed from the pole (if take-apart) until a suitable swing length is reached. With telescopic poles, you simply twist to unlock each section in turn and telescope it into the butt. When playing large fish, the pole is slowly reduced in length until the fish tires and is eased towards the landing net.

Poles are very effective for presenting tiny, leadheaded jigs to species such as crappies or perch, holed up in reeds or in very colored water close to the boat or bank.

Originally, crappie poles were long Tonkin canes with the line tied direct to the tip, similar to the first cane roach poles used in southern England on rivers like the Thames and the Lea. Modern crappie poles are made of graphite or fiberglass, 10 to 12 feet long, with the line threaded through the middle and out the tip. At the butt section, the line passes out through a tiny hole in the sidewall where it is retained on a winder or keeper.

Some crappie poles are even rigged with reels and guides. Fishing with this rod can't really be classed as pole fishing, which is all about fixed line fishing. That's the particular skill which makes pole fishing so different from any other method.

Once you've mastered the basic technique of pole fishing, you can control even the lightest terminal tackle with great accuracy and delicacy, because you can keep the pole tip directly above the float. The line hangs down vertically from tip to float, and so the bait can be twitched, lifted, jiggled, bounced or made to fall repeatedly 'on the drop', quickly and under the full control of the angler. Whether in still or running water, the pole offers a quality of bait presentation which can seldom be attained with any other type of rod.

If the line is long enough, small fish such as this roach can be simply swung into the hand once the hook is firmly set. For larger fish you need a landing net.

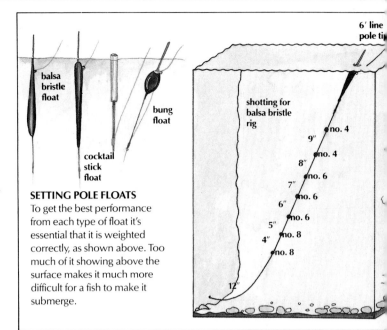

SETTING POLE FLOATS
To get the best performance from each type of float it's essential that it is weighted correctly, as shown above. Too much of it showing above the surface makes it much more difficult for a fish to make it submerge.

BALSA BRISTLE RIG – RUNNING WATER

It is worth taking trouble to space out the shotting pattern accurately, using progressively smaller shot towards the hook. This allows perfect control of the float, which can be held back hard, thus allowing the bait to precede it. Always use the minimum length of line between pole tip and float, and follow through smoothly as the float is drawn downstream by the flow. The float to choose for running water has its buoyancy towards the tip for stability and sensitivity.

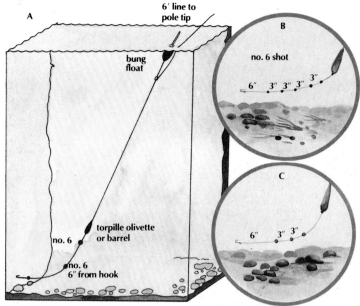

A

6' line to pole tip

bung float

no. 6

torpille olivette or barrel

no. 6 6" from hook

B

no. 6 shot

6" 3" 3" 3" 3"

C

6" 3" 3"

BUNG FLOAT RIG – RUNNING WATER

This rig, employing the German 'bung' float, is for running water when the balsa bristle pattern is unsuitable. Whichever of the three patterns you use, the olivette must never be fished more than 6 inches from the bottom. The 6 feet from float to pole tip gives maximum trotting distance in the swim. This float must be held back hard and inched along the swim if it is to fish correctly. Try position A first; this arrangement is the most efficient. With the float cocked so that only its antenna shows above the water, hold back with the pole as you inch it down the swim. Stop for one or two minutes, and if a bite doesn't result, repeat the pattern to the end of the swim. If this is unsuccessful, try pattern B, then C.

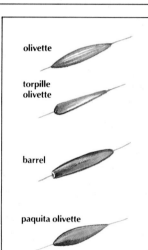

olivette

torpille olivette

barrel

paquita olivette

styl lead

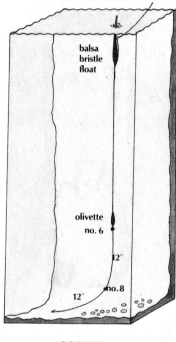

balsa bristle float

olivette no. 6

12"

no. 8

12"

BALSA BRISTLE RIG – SHORT LINE, STILLWATER METHOD

This rig, sometimes described as the classic pole tackle, is designed for bottom fishing still waters at a range of about 15 feet, with a flick tip and a short line. As an example, for a water depth of 6 feet at a range of 15 feet, the length of main line from pole tip to hook length should be about 9 feet – 2 feet from float to pole tip, 6 feet for the depth of the swim, plus the hook length on the bottom. The rig should be set up before fishing, so that you can check the balance of shot and float; only the bristle and the white collar of the float should be above the surface. In this example the stop shot is a number 6, and the number 8 is the unsuspended 'tell-tale' shot which registers the bite.

LONG LINE RIG FOR STILL WATER

Longlining means fishing with the float beyond the pole tip, as opposed to directly below it as in shortlining. For an average depth of, say, 6 feet, at a range of 15 feet, fishing with a 15-foot pole enables you to fish 24 feet out, where fish should take more boldly. This rig has other merits: set up this way it will take fish at all depths 'on the drop' from the surface to the bottom, and its self-cocking quality allied to quiet water entry is less likely to scare fish near the surface. Strike horizontally to avoid breakoffs with these fish, as they usually make off directly with the bait.

no. 6

no. 8

no. 8

SPINNING—1

Just as the loose term 'baitcasting' is used to describe casting artificial lures with a revolving spool (multiplier) reel, the term 'spinning' refers generally to all forms of artificial lure fishing with a fixed spool (spinning) reel, and not simply to fishing with revolving blade spinners.

The fixed spool reel is easy to cast with compared to the revolving spool, which demands a higher level of skill. For most situations, the simple underarm and over-the-shoulder casts (as used in float fishing) are fine for spinning.

The beauty of the fixed spool reel is that, unlike the revolving spool, it can be used on almost any rod except the trigger-type baitcaster. Short rods are favored for tossing artificials short to medium range, say up to 35 yards, with longer rods being good for casting up to 70 yards or more. Long, supple-actioned rods are also useful for flipping little jigs or worms into or over tall reeds for perch or crappies.

Choosing a rod is seldom easy, but while the keen angler may own a couple or three different rods to cast a wide range of lures, a medium-fast action rod of between six and nine feet will be enough for most purposes.

For the constant casting which spinning involves, always choose the smoothest reel you can afford. It should have a large diameter, smooth-lipped spool for long effortless casts, a silent antireverse, and be capable of holding 200 yards of, say, 8, 12 or 15 pounds test line, depending on the size of fish you're after.

The slipping clutch should be smooth and there should be a non-grooving roller on the bale arm. For ultralight spinning the choice should be a small model holding 4 to 5 pounds test line.

One of the most important factors in fishing with a lure is the depth at which you work it. It's no good retrieving a lure two feet below the surface if the fish are ten feet down in thick weed, or hugging the bottom in even deeper water because the temperature's very low.

So think in terms of horizontal 'layers' of water when presenting artificials. At various times of the season, fish will live at different levels according to the temperature and/or where the bait fish shoals are gathered.

The spoon, due to its weight and shape, is one of the best lures for finding the right level because it can be 'counted down'. On your first cast, leave the bale arm open during the time it takes the spoon to flutter down to hit bottom and the line to fall slack.

As the line slips through the rings, count the spoon down in seconds, an average of one foot per second being a reasonable descent rate to assume. This will give you a rough idea of how deep the water is at that point, and on your following casts you can count the spoon down to whatever depth you want before you start the retrieve.

The retrieve should be slow at first, using the spoon's inherent vibrations to attract a fish, but if there's no response to this then it's time to work the lure more. Always imagine that a fish is

When using spinners, plugbaits, or spoons, it's likely that you will need to make several changes of lure to find the bait for the day. A rig incorporating a snap link swivel in the leader permits changes to be made quickly. The leader is either mono or, for sharp-toothed prey, wire.

WORKING A FLOATING/DIVING PLUG

reel line

swivel

wire leader

snap link swivel

plug

lure's depth is controlled by the rate of retrieve

path of lure

With imaginative use the floating/diving plug can be made to perform nearly every trick in the book. The faster the retrieve the steeper the dive. With a stop-start retrieve the plug will rise and dive in a lifelike way.

DIVING VANES

deep

the angle of   shallow
the diving vane will determine
how shallow or deep a lure goes

ANTI-KINK VANES

celluloid anti-kink vane

plastic anti-kink vane

Hillman weight and swivel

the Hillman weight
with hole on one side,
groove on the other

half-moon or fold-over weight

No single swivel, however
efficient, will eliminate line
twist without the aid of an anti-
kink device.

*Above Spinning with artificial lures
is an ideal way to fish for
predators such as pike, which will
also readily take a properly
mounted deadbait fished on a
spinning outfit.*

following the lure, then you can
visualize how it will be reacting to
the movements of the lure.

Try suddenly speeding up the
retrieve for a few turns of the
handle, then give the lure a sharp
twitch and stop winding
altogether. Now the spoon will be
fluttering downwards, and if it's
being followed the fish will
probably go down after it; pike
especially respond to this. Now
suddenly zoom it upwards again,
and that's when the fish is most
likely to strike.

Always keep the rod pointing
towards the lure during the

retrieve, with only a slight
sideways deviation for twitching
and jerking, otherwise the hooks
may not be driven home on the
strike.

Some fish, such as large trout,
hit a lure hard and swim off all in
one movement, which really
hooks them well. Others, though,
particularly bass, walleye, pike
and perch, open their mouths,
grab the lure and stop swimming.
These really do have to be hit with
a heavy upwards strike to force
the hooks in. Then, throughout
the early stages of the fight, keep
the rod well bent with as much
torque on as you dare.

Much of the general technique
of presenting spoons also applies
to sinking plugs, which can also
be counted down to the desired
depth. But unlike spoons, which
are always angled upwards from

the first turn of the handle, plugs
with deep diving vanes (or lower
protruding lips) will stay deep
and fish more or less at the same
level throughout the retrieve.

Many plugs, particularly the
throbbers and rattlers, have such
good built-in action and vibration
due to body shape and vane angle
that little jerking or twitching is
required from the rod tip. The
rate of retrieve is, again, most of
the secret.

When clipping on a new lure
(use a wire leader if you're after
toothed predators) always make a
few trial pulls through the water
close to the boat or bank to
familiarize yourself with its
action. Unless you know just
what a lure can do, you'll never
really use it to its full advantage.

Fishing with surface plugs such
as crazy crawlers, jitterbugs or

concave-headed poppers, is
probably the single most exciting
part of all artificial throwing
because you can actually see the
strike.

But unlike deep divers with
their inbuilt action, these lures
have to be made to move in a
lifelike way and so soft-tipped
rods, which absorb all the action
you're trying to create, are out.
Movement can really only be
given to these surface lures with a
stiffish rod.

From the moment the lure
touches the surface, its movement
should be as varied and unusual
as you can make it. Twitch it,
leave it static for a few seconds,
then twitch it again. Make it
gurgle by slamming the rod tip
down to the surface, jerk it, pause,
gurgle again and so on. Anything
that will give action to the lure

SPINNING—2

should be tried, because the way a fish will respond to a particular movement cannot be forseen. The time of day, changes in subsurface visibility, the availability of bait, fish shoals and the presence of other predators are all influential factors.

Surface lures invariably work best close to natural features or snags because that's where fish are hiding up, either waiting for predators or prey to pass by, or just holed up for a rest. So never consider a spot unworthy of a throw or two just because of vegetation or because the chances of extracting a hooked fish seem remote. Slam the hooks home first, and then worry about landing the fish. As likely as not,

by the time a fish has caught up with the lure it will have had to leave its hideaway to give chase anyway. Even so, it's always wise to use weedless lures where the vegetation's likely to cause problems.

A stiff, snappy rod is also the tool for plastic worms in heavily reeded waters on fish such as bass. With the worm weedfree rigged and the hook point buried so that it slips easily through the vegetation, the stiff rod helps strike the hook home through the rubbery worm and into the fish's hard mouth.

To present artificials such as plastic worms, newts or twisters in deep water, use a weighted head directly in front of the lure.

Then it can be counted down like a spoon. Worms seem to produce more interest when retrieved in a twitching and darting movement along the bottom, over boulders or through weed.

Large, live worms can prove a deadly bait for many species. In shallow, still water, hook the worm once only through the middle and simply freeline it to the bottom. Leave it there for a few seconds, then retrieve it in a series of short, sharp jerks, with a long pause between each so it starts to flutter down again. Expect a hit at any time during

the retrieve.

In flowing water, pinch a swan shot or two 18 inches from the worm and fish it in the same way, allowing it to bounce across the current as it drifts downstream. For very fast water, rig up a fixed link ledger and use a dipsey to either hold bottom or bump along as desired. With this rig you can take almost any river fish, from eels to salmon.

A well-balanced spinning rod and reel is the most sensitive outfit for presenting the whole range of spinning type lures such as spinner baits, revolving bar

Below *When you use a short, lightweight spinning outfit, whether from a boat or from the bank, playing and landing large fish is a real challenge, and even small fish can put up a good fight.*

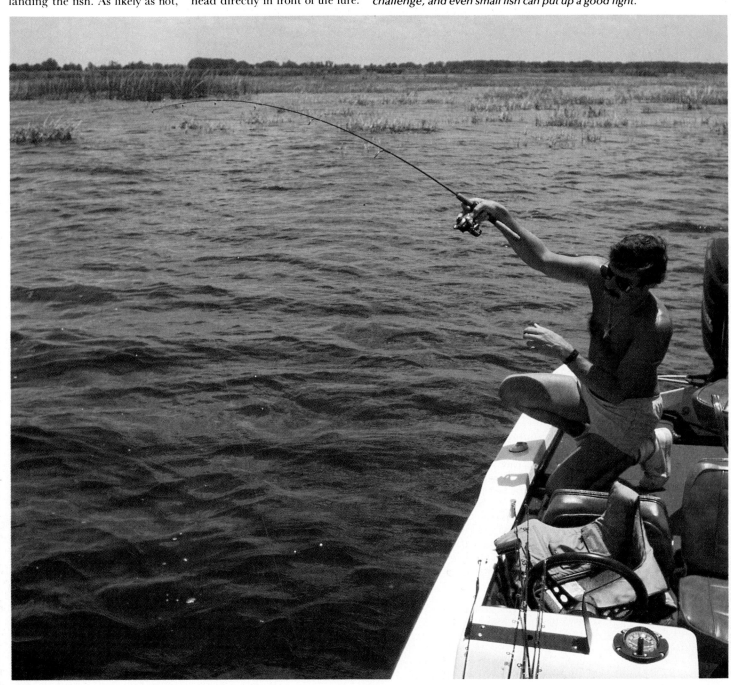

spoons or spinners, leadheaded jigs and other lightly weighted lures like attractor bugs.

With the larger spinners and spinner baits (don't forget an antikink vane to stop line twist) use a simple countdown retrieve to explore different water levels, as with spoons. Since most of the attraction comes from the fluttering skirt and vibrating blade, additional rod tip action should be minimized.

Use basic up-and-down and side-to-side movements and simply vary the retrieve with a pause or total stop every so often, allowing the lure to flutter downwards. Hits will often come the very second you start winding again.

There are two basic ways of attracting bites with leadheaded jigs or bugs on a spinning outfit. They can be jigged vertically up and down in any depth of water from a boat or down beside bridges or piers. Or they can be cast out from the bank or a boat and, after touching bottom, retrieved in an up-and-down nodding action, following the bottom contours or over weedbeds.

As you lift or wind, the jig's head pops upwards and towards the rod. Then as you ease on the retrieve or stop winding, down it goes again. It's this nodding action, plus whatever hairs, feathers or other attractors the jig has for a tail, that makes it so attractive to predatory fish.

You can also use a spinning outfit with small dead fishbaits mounted on special flights, or more simply on two size 8 trebles on a 15 inch swiveled wire leader (snap tackle). The term 'wobbling' perhaps best describes this technique because the bait creates most vibration if it's mounted slightly curved.

For a 5 inch bait, fix the trebles 2 inches apart and work two points of the top treble into the bait's eye sockets, with two points of the lower treble inserted along the flank. In very shallow water, or to work the bait at the surface, no extra weight should be added, but to take the bait down quickly to deeper areas, fix two to four swan shots immediately below the swivel.

Once the bait hits bottom (watch out for bites on the drop), retrieve it in an erratic, sink-and-draw style with plenty of jerks, pauses and twitches. When a fish takes the bait, strike quickly and hard and keep the rod well up so that the hooks go solidly home. Some species, especially pike, are notorious for throwing the hooks at this stage, so keep plenty of torque on them.

Because constant casting tends to smash up fish baits, a good supply of fresh deadbaits is necessary. This method will, on occasion, actually out-fish lures or livebaits, particularly in colored water where visibility is poor.

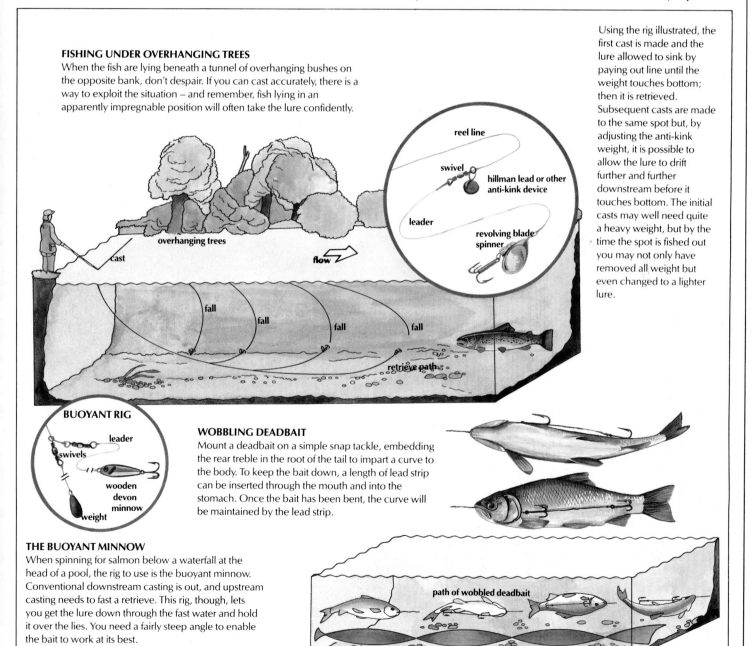

FISHING UNDER OVERHANGING TREES
When the fish are lying beneath a tunnel of overhanging bushes on the opposite bank, don't despair. If you can cast accurately, there is a way to exploit the situation – and remember, fish lying in an apparently impregnable position will often take the lure confidently.

reel line
swivel
hillman lead or other anti-kink device
leader
revolving blade spinner
overhanging trees
cast
flow
fall
fall
fall
fall
retrieve path

Using the rig illustrated, the first cast is made and the lure allowed to sink by paying out line until the weight touches bottom; then it is retrieved. Subsequent casts are made to the same spot but, by adjusting the anti-kink weight, it is possible to allow the lure to drift further and further downstream before it touches bottom. The initial casts may well need quite a heavy weight, but by the time the spot is fished out you may not only have removed all weight but even changed to a lighter lure.

BUOYANT RIG
leader
swivels
wooden devon minnow
weight

WOBBLING DEADBAIT
Mount a deadbait on a simple snap tackle, embedding the rear treble in the root of the tail to impart a curve to the body. To keep the bait down, a length of lead strip can be inserted through the mouth and into the stomach. Once the bait has been bent, the curve will be maintained by the lead strip.

THE BUOYANT MINNOW
When spinning for salmon below a waterfall at the head of a pool, the rig to use is the buoyant minnow. Conventional downstream casting is out, and upstream casting needs to fast a retrieve. This rig, though, lets you get the lure down through the fast water and hold it over the lies. You need a fairly steep angle to enable the bait to work at its best.

path of wobbled deadbait

SURFCASTING AND SALTWATER SPINNING

Surfcasting can be great fun, and on days or nights when the fish run inshore to feed, it can also be a highly productive sport. Bass, cod, flatfish, bluefish, skate and rays are the most likely fish to be taken by surf fishermen.

Under most circumstances a 12 foot beachcasting rod capable of casting 2 to 4 ounces is ideal, but in areas subjected to strong tides a rod made to throw 4 to 6 ounces may be needed. The choice of reel depends on your personal preference and casting ability; many anglers use a multiplying reel, while others prefer a large fixed spool.

To get maximum results from a surfcasting session, a good working knowledge of the area to be fished is essential. Knowing the topography of an area is nine tenths of the battle, as fish are seldom spread out evenly along an entire beach. Like people, they congregate in places where food is most accessible.

Rocky outcrops, deep gullies and beds of shellfish are the places to find fish in a feeding mood, shellfish beds being of the most importance. Having discovered the whereabouts of such features, trial and error will teach you the most productive time of day to fish and the stage of tide most likely to bring results.

Keep your terminal tackle as simple as possible. For example, multi-hook tackle seldom catches more fish than a single hook. Worse, the multi-hook rig has a tendency to tangle on just about every cast.

The choice of bait depends on the type of fish you expect to catch. Flatfish and small bass fall best to worms, crab, squid strip or shellfish bait, but larger bass and skate or ray prefer whole or cut fish or squid.

Once you've made the cast and dropped the bait in or close to a likely area, you have to wait and watch for a bite, so most experienced surf anglers use a single-leg or tripod style rod rest; a few prefer to hold the rod.

Surf fish tend to bite decisively, the bite normally registering as a series of hard preliminary knocks on the rod tip. This is usually followed by a hard, slow dragging pull caused by the fish moving out with the bait. You should strike the second the rod tip drags down, then play the fish out and beach it rather than use a net.

Very often, you'll get better results fishing at night than in the day. This is particularly true if you're fishing for cod, skate, striped bass or bluefish species preferring to feed during darkness.

Saltwater spin fishing is a neat, clean way of taking fish. A box of lures can be carried easily in a pocket, and with only a light rod and reel to carry it's possible to cover several miles of coastline in

Right *Surfcasting from a shingle beach; the rods in use here are fitted with multiplier reels.*

THE PENDULUM CAST

This cast is used where rocky ground or the surf make an off-the-ground cast impracticable.

A. The starting position is the same as for the off-the-ground cast, but with the rod sloped upwards by 30°. Hang the sinker on a 4-foot leader drop. Using minimum rod movement, swing the weight in a pendulum arc parallel to the line of cast, until the leader is parallel to the ground. Practice this swing to a count of four, with the weight reaching maximum height on the outswing at one and three, and the backswing at two and four. With the weight at maximum height on the backswing (four), begin the cast proper.

B. Start the swing, sweeping your left hand smoothly up to eye level. From this point on, the remainder of the cast is similar to the off-the-ground cast which is described below.

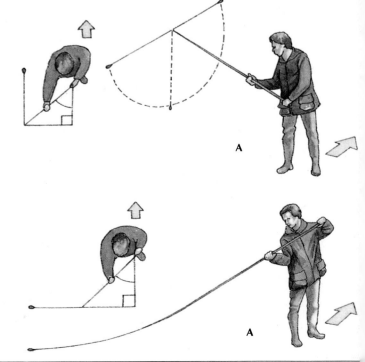

OFF-THE-GROUND CAST

A. Stand with your shoulders parallel to an imaginary line out to sea, with your toes touching the line and your feet comfortably apart. Hold the rod level, a foot away from your chest, with your hands at shoulders' width apart. With your left hand at eye level, slope the rod down 30° to the right. The swing your shoulders 45° to the right, and bend at your waist and right knee to dip your right shoulder.

B. Keep your arms in position relative to your shoulders, and straighten up and swing your shoulders back parallel to the imaginary line. Continue the swing until your chest faces almost down the line.

C/D. As your shoulders parallel the line, push your left hand forward and up, then down to your left hip, punching forward with the right. Stop the rod dead, with no follow through.

a day's fishing. Rocky areas lend themselves well to this style of angling, although in summer, when the mackerel shoals move inshore, even beaches are worth trying.

Rocks, however, provide the best venue. A rocky coastline attracts a wide variety of fish, many of which fall readily to artificial lures. A good plan is to stick to a selection of, say, twelve lures, for instance two surface plugs (preferably one-piece), a pair of shallow-diving jointed plugs, and eight varied spinners. These should include bar spoons, wobbling spoons, and a couple of heavy German Sprat type lures.

The plug baits are ideal for use in wide, rocky gullies. They work particularly well in the throat of a gully where the water is agitated. Big fish such as bass and pollack often hang out in such rips and races, picking off bait fish caught in the swirl of breaking water.

For long casting from headlands or out across sandy bays, spoon baits work best. Being made of metal they cast well, and when retrieved at speed they give the impression of a solitary, panicked fish heading for the pool cover. Big predatory fish seldom resist such an obvious lure.

Very occasionally, though, a wary fish will follow a lure only to turn away at the last second. When this happens, cast the lure out again in the direction taken by the retreating fish. Often the lure will be hit within seconds of touching the water.

Although many types of sea fish will take a lure retrieved in a straight line, most experienced spin fishermen prefer to vary their rate of retrieve and also to use the rod tip to swing the bait on and off course. A bait retrieved in this way must look very much like an injured fish – a very tempting target for a predator – and using this technique will normally catch more fish per session than a lure that swims on an even keel.

LOOP KNOT

reel line

loop stiffened by plastic tube

BASIC PATERNOSTER RIG

For a basic paternoster rig, the leader is tied to a loop knot formed by taking a loop of the main line, looping it around the line 4 or 5 times, and pushing the middle of the loop through the centre.

B

B

C

D

TROLLING — FRESHWATER

Trolling, or trailing as it's sometimes called, is fishing by pulling an artificial lure or mounted fishbait behind a moving boat. As the intention is to give predatory fish the impression that the trolled bait is alive, moving at the right speed, with a suitable lure fished at the correct depth, is the combination which leads to success.

The simplest form of trolling is to trail the lure behind a rowed boat. Where the bottom shelves down deep, you row slowly so the bait can work deeper, and where it shallows you row quickly to bring the bait up, so that it doesn't foul the bottom muck or become stuck in snags or weeds.

If you're trolling alone, use just one or two rods, angled outwards from either side of the boat in rod holders close to the stern. Then when you get a bite, you ship the

oars, possibly drop the anchor, and grab the rod to play the fish.

Some anglers like to trail with a sliding float on the line, set well overdepth beneath a stopknot. The float gives early indication of a predator's attack on deadbaits, and is especially useful with trailed livebaits, a deadly effective method for catching species like pike, muskies or walleye in still water or slow-moving rivers.

Other baits which can be trailed behind a rowboat, with or without a motor, are teams of flies or single large streamer-type flies, fished deep down with a lead-cored line on large lakes or reservoirs.

To troll from a motorboat for trout or pike, use a large-lipped, deep-diving plug with the boat moving at one to three knots. Even heavy spoons can be trolled at depths of several feet on basic

tackle, as long as trolling speed is kept slow to prevent the spoon from surfacing.

Treble hooks should always be kept really sharp, and for all motor trolling use a revolving spool (multiplier) reel which can be put in or out of gear quickly.

Exactly how far behind the boat to troll the lure can never really be defined. A good starting distance would be 50 to 60 feet, but you should try increasing this if you're not getting any bites.

There are various ways of getting a lure down deep and keeping it trolling at that depth. Some anglers use wire-based or lead-covered lines, but others favor heavy, vaned trolling weights fixed well ahead of the lure.

There is, however, nothing to match the simple, effective, all-round control of the downrigger,

which keeps the lure trolling at exactly the depth you want regardless of trolling speed, an impossible feat with all other methods.

Although computerized down-riggers with auto winch facilities are widely used, a simple manual downrigger will cover most fishing situations in both still and running waters.

A crank handle centerpin winch, which holds the downrigger cable, clamps to the stern or the side of the boat close to the stern. On top of the winch housing is the tubular rod holder, and protruding from the center is a 24 inch boom with a pulley at the end through which the cable feeds down to the water.

At the end of the cable is the downrigger weight itself, a lead ball weighing 3 pounds or more (depending on trolling depth and

168

TROLLING WITH OARS

boat direction

boat is rowed
at speed to suit
bottom contours

MOTOR TROLLING WITH SONAR

boat direction

path of bait

TROLLING WITH DOWNRIGGER

rod is bent under tension

boat direction

downrigger
line

reel
line

deadbait

THE DOWNRIGGER IN ACTION

rod rest

butt
restraint

fixed spool
reel

winch
reel

line looped
over reel
handle to
lock reel

60 lb
line

wooden block
clamped to stern

wool depth
markers

to rod rest

reel line

wool depth
markers
1 metre
apart

3-way
swivel

to bait

light line
breakaway
link

3 ft

1-1½ lb
weight

FRESHWATER TROLLING

When trolling under oars, the rod or rods are wedged beneath the rear thwart. The bait's depth is controlled by the length of line out and the rowing speed of the boat.

By skilful use of the motor the fisherman can alter the depth of his trolling bait to closely follow the bottom contours as shown on the sonar readout.

As the downrigger line is lowered it takes line from the rod reel against the check. At the desired depth the downrigger is locked as shown. Depth is altered according to the sonar readout.

These drawings show the basic components of a simple downrigger. Unlike other methods which incorporate additional weight, when a fish takes the bait on a downrigger the breakaway link snaps giving a direct weight-free contact with the fish.

Above Freshwater trolling can involve simply trailing a lure behind a rowed boat, or, as here, using several lines fished from the stern of a large, powered boat.

speed). The weight is finned, and a quick release clip which holds the rod line is fixed to it by 4 inches of cable.

The line is clipped in to fish the lure at anywhere from two to a hundred or more feet behind the boat, and the downrigger lowered by the winch to the required depth. Literally any depth can be fished (if the cable and line are long enough), with the lure following horizontally behind the downrigger weight.

The reel is left out of gear, with the ratchet on, for lowering the weight down to trolling depth and for raising or lowering it at any time during the troll. When the lure is set at the trolling depth, the reel is thrown into gear and the preset clutch helps to set the hook and avoid a break when a heavy fish grabs the lure.

The reel line is wound up tight so the rod tip takes on a tight bend. It then quickly straightens and springs up if a fish pulls the line from the quick release clip. With the reel line free of the downrigger, the fish is played in as normal.

Using a downrigger in conjunction with sonar, lures can be trolled up and over obstacles such as submerged treetops, through steep-sided gullies and over shallow bars and weedbeds. Some sonars have color display screens which show what lies beneath the boat – the depth, the bottom contours, obstacles and even the fish.

It's all a far cry from simply walking along the bank, tossing out a lure and cranking it back in. But for trolling on large waters, where the fish could be literally miles away, fitting your boat with equipment that can locate the fish electronically can save you much time and trouble.

READING THE WATER

Being able to 'read' the water for signs of where a shoal or even an individual fish might be lying is an art that successful anglers use to great effect; others rely more on luck. Luck certainly plays its part in angling, as it does in any other human activity; the ones that get away may do so for reasons completely beyond your control. But an understanding of the habitats preferred by the fish you're after means that you can use a methodical approach which will swing the odds in your favor. At the very least, it'll make it unlikely that you'll waste time fishing a stretch of water when the fish are elsewhere.

This approach applies to all forms of fishing, from creeping up on a wily old brown trout lurking in an awkward run among thick weed, to trolling blue waters for billfish. Being able to read the water and make the most of any opportunity is far more important than owning a rack of expensive rods. Fishermen who produce results – whatever the species and wherever the location – do so through observation, not luck.

They look to see if the water is clear or colored, and how far into it they can see. This gives them an idea of what kinds of fish might be present, where, how and when they're likely to be feeding, and how close to them the lure or bait must be before they can see it.

Observant anglers also note how fast a river is flowing, and whether it's running at normal height, low, or in full spate. They study the current patterns, not just for a second or two but for several minutes. Then, like the fish which feed on food brought down by the current, they too have an idea of where that food will be deposited – and they know where to put the bait.

If they have time, they study the water at dawn and at dusk, and at other times during the day, watching the feeding and resting habits of the fish. They are constantly aware of the wind direction across still waters, knowing that micro-organisms such as planktons drift with the waves until they come to rest against a shore, when the fish that eat them will gather there, followed by the predators that feed on them in their turn. Observant anglers also watch for tiny, almost imperceptible movements in what is otherwise a totally flat, calm surface, and invariably, except in all but the coldest conditions, they see something which gives them a clue to the location of the fish.

The tools of the trade, apart from keen eyesight, are a pair of good-quality polarized sunglasses to cut through light reflected from the surface, and a good pair of binoculars. The binoculars should be reasonably powerful (8×30 is an ideal format) but light enough to hold steady with just one hand, so you won't have to put your rod down when you use them. Binoculars help you to spot distant clues, such as tails or dorsal fins breaking the surface, or the delicate twitches of reed stems when fish move between them, something almost impossible to see with the naked eye at even comparatively short distances like 30 or 40 yards.

When you're fishing at sea, binoculars will help you to see the signs – such as feeding seabirds, a shoal of bait fish being pushed up, changes in water color, or a fin cutting the surface – that can lead you to a good catch. To find features below the surface, like reefs, dropoffs and wrecks, good charts and a sonar are essential, as they also are on large, deep lakes.

Sea fishing, especially for big game, usually involves a lot more searching than does fishing on all but the largest fresh waters. Out at sea, there's usually very little aquatic vegetation and obviously no bankside trees or shrubs or marginal reeds to guide you to where the fish are likely to be. For the freshwater angler, knowing the various aquatic plants and the depths of water that they grow in, and which fish are attracted to them and why, is an essential part of reading the water.

There are, of course, many other (and far less obvious) signs to watch for in freshwater fish location, so the angler who is constantly on the lookout and who treats observation as a key to success will catch fish, while others waste their time in a barren area, patiently enjoying nothing but the scenery. Patience is a virtue the angler often needs, but successful fishermen are also alert and watchful. They are always watching for indications of fish showing on the surface – fish jumping, snatching flies, creating bubbles or disturbing the vegetation.

Even the appearance of a sudden flat of smooth water on the surface is reason enough for some anglers to head for the spot. It could be simply the result of a 'wind knot', but it could equally well be caused by a big fish turning over just beneath the surface, an action which for a few seconds irons out even quite strong waves.

ESTUARIES

An estuary is the tidal mouth of a river where it opens into the sea. All estuaries are worth fishing because the inflow of fresh water into the sea attracts and holds the attention of many species of fish.

Some estuaries are created by short, narrow yet strong little rivers that carve their way through steep-sided valleys and high cliffs before passing out into salt water. In deep, narrow estuaries of this kind, the ecological system varies considerably from the upper section of the estuary to the lower section.

The upper section often consists of shallow mud or sandbanks, many of which become exposed at low water. In this section, small ragworms, shrimps and shellfish of the clam type often abound. This natural abundance of small food items is particularly attractive to shoaling mullet and hunting flounder. Bass will also visit the mud banks, but normally confine their activities to the deeper water in the lower section of the estuary.

Where the mud/sand banks finish and the water rapidly deepens, the nature of the bottom changes dramatically. The mud gives way to tiny sand patches and mixed rock and shingle. The higher density of the salt water in this lower section promotes the growth of seaweed, in particular spiral wrack.

This weed, and the natural cover provided by the larger stones, gives ample shelter to colonies of green shore crab, and the sand patches are equally attractive to shoaling sandeel. These food creatures, plus larger worms, in turn attract other, often larger fish, some of which take up semipermanent residence in the lower section of the estuary. Conger, thornback ray and wrasse are typical examples of fish which often become semiresident in deep estuaries, while other fish such as bass and mullet are regular visitors.

Apart from in-running and semiresident sea fish, many estuaries are run by salmon and sea trout, spawning fish on their way inland to shed their eggs in the gravel shallows of the parent river and its tributaries. In some areas, the tiniest inflow of fresh water is enough to attract and hold migratory fish, and sea-run brown trout in particular will stay for long periods of time in the vicinity of such a stream outfall. Fly fishing and spinning on a rising or full tide will often produce excellent catches.

Many anglers overlook the angling potential of estuaries. This is wrong, for estuary fishing is often good and it allows the angler to fish in many different ways. In deepwater estuaries it is often possible to fish from rocks, docks and even roadways as well as from a boat.

Fishing style and baits depend a great deal on the fish you hope to catch. Conger, for example, are often found in the deep marginal areas where they find rich pickings amongst the trash, fish and fish guts dumped there by local fishing boats. For conger, a heavy beachcaster and wire leaders are essential. The bait can be a whole or half fish, cast out only a few yards. Skate and bass may take the same sort of bait, but they are normally found well away from the shore in the deeper gullies. A lighter beachcasting rod, and the ability to cast 80 to 100 yards, are essential if you want to fish for these species.

Further upriver, where the deep water shallows over mudbanks, mullet and flounders are the main angling species. The mullet normally swim and feed in large shoals, which can be attracted by attaching a chunk of stale bread to a length of string and a suitable stone. The length of string depends on the depth of the water at high tide, the idea being to anchor the bread so that it floats on the surface.

With luck, the feeding mullet shoals will find the bread and begin to feed around it. Once you see the fish feeding, you can use a piece of bread, worm, sweetcorn, banana or part-cooked macaroni as hookbait, fished on a freshwater float fishing outfit.

In all estuaries, flounder can be taken on static baits, such as worm or peeler crab, or on a traditional flounder spoon rig. Originally devised by J P Gerrard, the technique of fishing a trailing worm behind a large plastic or metal flounder spoon is still recognised as one of the best ways to catch flounder of all sizes.

The single hook is baited with a ragworm and the spoon and bait are cast out and allowed to touch bottom. Then the spoon is retrieved very slowly so that it ploughs through the top layer of mud and silt. Hunting flounder see and investigate the disturbance, finding what is apparently a small flounder making off with a large, juicy worm. Naturally, the larger fish

tries to steal the worm and gets itself hooked in the process.

The trick to this sort of fishing is to ignore the first few twitching bites and wait for the rod to pull hard over as the taking flounder finally swallows the bait. This technique can also be used from an anchored boat, or by trolling the spoon and bait behind a slowly moving boat.

The mobility of dinghy fishing is a great advantage in estuaries, allowing you to change position quickly and to explore side creeks and saltwater lagoons. Dinghy fishing also scores over shore fishing where the estuary is wide and the river splits into many separate channels running between sand or mudbanks. At low tide, these channels are difficult to reach by boat and too far out to be cast to from the

shore. At this stage of the tide, though, the flow of water through the channels is swift and they contain little natural food to attract fish. It's only during high tide that fish will move into these channels, so as to get to the surrounding mud and sandbanks where they find worms and other foods that live in the slacker water.

At the mouths of these channels, where the fresh water meets the salt water, the flow is slowed and any food being swept down by the freshwater current is deposited there. This can make it a rich feeding ground which attracts many small species, and these in their turn attract larger fish such as flounder, dogfish and bass. Fishing from a dinghy on the seaward side of these channels can be very productive.

In other wide estuaries, the

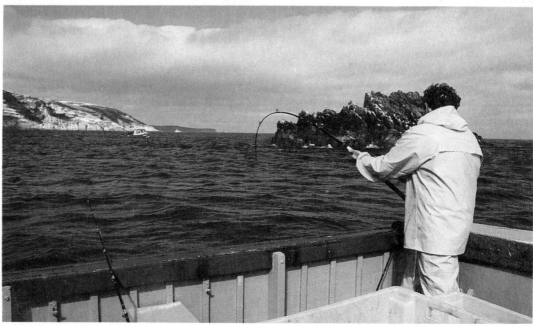

Above *In the lower section of an estuary where the bottom changes from mud or sand of higher up the river to shingle and rock, you can find conger, wrasses, small rays, mullet and other small species.*

Right *Fishing from a boat in a large estuary lets you get to the deeper waters, and gives you more mobility than you could hope to get when you're fishing from the shore.*

outflow from the river is gentler and not split into deep, separate channels. The water flow is shallow and gentle, and provides a favourable habitat for many food creatures such as plankton, crabs, shellfish and worms. These create an abundant food supply for flatfish, bass, pollack and mullet, which gives good, productive fishing to both shore and dinghy anglers.

OFFSHORE WATERS — TEMPERATE

Offshore waters, in this context any water beyond the casting range of shore fishermen, can be fished close-in from a small craft or further out from a large boat.

Small-boat anglers can often find good fishing in the most unlikely places, such as shallow sunk mud or sandbanks. These flats are usually scarred by deep gullies carved out by the prevailing tidal flow, and being deeper than the surrounding flats the gullies act as food traps. Live and dead crabs, worms and small fish all wash across the exposed flats until they reach and drop into a gully.

This plentiful supply of food and the added security of the deep water draws many species of fish into the gullies. Bass, small cod, flatfish, shark and stingray all use gullies as feeding areas, so it pays to learn where these gullies are. The simplest way is to use an echo sounder to locate each natural dropoff. In areas where the mud or sand isn't prone to shifting, once you've found where the gullies are you can use shore marks to guide you to them on future expeditions. In areas subject to exceptional runs of tide, certain places act as natural holding points for fish feeding on small fish and eels trapped in the strong tidal flow. These holding points can normally be located on the downtide side of any projecting rocks or small islands.

As the main flow of the tide races by on either side of the rock, it creates a downtide slack water area practically devoid of movement. Fish use this slack water both as a resting area and as an ambush point. By taking up station a yard or two from the heavy run of water, they can wait in comfort for food to be swept past them in the tide. Then, with a flick of the tail and fins, they shoot out, nail the fish or eel, and dart back into the slack area to wait for the next meal to be swept within range. A bait or lure cast to fall on the edge of the tide run should produce instant results.

In areas where giant common skate are known to exist, you'll often find them in deep water on the downtide side of an island. Another good skate holding point is in between two adjacent islands. Provided the islands are close enough together, they'll act as a natural barrier which funnels the water through the gap between them. This rush of water will scout out a deep hole on the sea bed into which all manner of edible matter will fall, and skate will normally take up permanent residence in this natural food trap

Further offshore, rock pinnacles and submerged rock ledges are well worth investigating. Two distinct types of fish inhabit this sort of ground: true bottom feeders, like conger, and lethargic bull huss live in or on the rock itself, while bass, pollack and coalfish swim above. The bottom dwellers can only be caught by anchoring over the rock pinnacle or ledge and fishing a bait hard on the bottom. The free-swimming fish are better taken on small, trolled lures, livebaits or feathers.

Offshore sandbanks are extremely good places to catch flatfish such as flounder, turbot, brill and plaice, and various members of the ray family. These sandbanks are normally formed by tidal action, and the fish take up feeding positions on the downward slope of the bank. This means that most offshore banks are only fishable at one stage of the tide, some on the ebb, others on the flood, depending on the position of the bank.

Most of the fish present on offshore banks feed almost exclusively on sandeel, and for this reason natural live or dead eels make the best bait, although a simulated eel cut from a fillet of mackerel may also provide good fishing.

The different types of fish on the bank tend to take up distinct feeding positions. Free swimmers like bass normally hang out just below the lip of the bank; flatfish like turbot and brill frequent the middle bank section, while at the base of the bank you're most likely to find skate, ray and monkfish. Additional angling interest is provided by tope and the occasional porbeagle shark, which stage lightning raids in search of small flatfish and the free-swimming mackerel shoals that prey on sandeels.

The best terminal tackle to use for bank fishing is a straightforward running ledger which incorporates an 8 to 10-foot leader. This extra-long leader is essentially an aid to better bait presentation. Sandeels on the move are active fish, so a live, dead or simulated eel must be allowed to move about in the tidal flow. To help the appearance of the bait, use a smaller than normal hook – size 2-0 or 4-0, but

Left *Fishing close-in from a small boat lets you get to spots beyond the reach of the shore angler, and you can find good sport in the gullies between shallow mud or sandbanks, or waters next to small islands and rocky outcrops. Using an echo sounder is a good way to find the gullies when you're fishing sandbanks, especially where the sand is prone to shifting.*

Above *A flock of seabirds, such as gulls, feeding on a shoal of baitfish, often indicates the presence of larger, predatory fish that have chased the baitfish to the surface.*

Below *Sonar and navigational aids essential for safe and successful wreck fishing, along with accurate and up-to-date charts.*

no larger. A big hook may have a better chance of hooking a big-mouthed bass or turbot, but its weight may well cause the bait to work unnaturally.

Always carry a spare rig of heavy tackle in case shark appear. Normally, the first indication of a shark in the area comes when bites abruptly cease or when a hooked fish is chewed up on its way to the boat. Under these circumstances, a bait of one or two fresh mackerel dropped over the lip of the bank will normally get results.

Sunken wrecks can be very productive marks to fish. In many areas the seabed is littered with the casualties of two world wars and thousands of long-forgotten storms. The vast majority of such wrecks are located a long way from land in depths of 150 feet or more, so to locate them and fish them properly you need an electronic navigation system, accurate hydrographic charts showing their positions, and an echo sounder.

A wreck is, in effect, a man-made reef which becomes a haven for many kinds of fish. Within the hull and superstructure of the wreck you will find, for example, conger and often shoals of sea bream. Just above the wreckage live cod and huge ling, and higher still hang the shoals of more active pollack and coalfish.

Wrecks can be fished from an anchored position or by repeatedly drifting over the wreck. When conger are your main target, anchoring is the only practical way to get a bait to the fish, but for all other species, drift fishing with natural baits or artificial lures – or a combination of both – will bring the best results. On a recent wreck which hasn't been heavily fished, catches may run to thousands of pounds in weight, the total bag being made up of mixed fish of a large size. Wreck fishing is a hard-work sport which requires sturdy tackle and equally sturdy anglers, but it almost guarantees large catches of big fish.

OFFSHORE WATERS — TROPICAL

Offshore fishing in tropical waters is one of the most fascinating forms of angling. The diversity of fish, their size, colours, habits and the methods needed to catch them add immensely to this fascination. Offshore tropical fishing ranges from bonefishing on coral flats to reef fishing in medium depths and fishing the open ocean ranges for giant game fish.

True coral flats are formed of coral sand or marl, and can stretch for miles without the water reaching more than waist deep. Such places hold stocks of bonefish, barracuda, permit, small sharks and rays. The larger species, such as the sharks and rays, are seldom fished for in these waters, but the smaller species make a perfect target for the light-tackle angler.

Most coral flat fishing is done from flat-bottomed boats or by actually wading in the water. It's vital to know where on the flats to find the fish, and for this you need to understand their movements over the apparently featureless coral sand.

An obvious place to find fish is on the very edge of the flats where the shallows cease and the deep water begins. This is a great place to find barracuda, which take advantage of the deep, dark water to lie in ambush for the shoals of bait fish. Barracuda also hunt across the flats, and they can often be found amongst bonefish in ankle-deep water.

Such channels are easy to see, as the normally glass-clear water tends to take on an oily, slightly opaque look as the water deepens. Large permit also follow these deep troughs, although they normally confine their activity to the edge of the gully where they are most likely to find crab or prawn in reasonable numbers.

Any tiny island of sand on the flats is worth investigating, as it usually indicates a stronger than normal tidal flow. Fish use the barrier of sand as a temporary resting and feeding place, lurking in the lee of the island ready to rush anything edible washed past in the tide flow. Bonefish use such places regularly, feeding head-down and giving away their positions by showing their tails above the surface. A bonefish that has its tail up like this is actively feeding and can normally be induced to take a bait.

Reef fishing is very different from coral flat fishing. Reefs may begin in only 25 feet of water,

Above Coral flats, which are formed of coral sand or marl, often extend for great distances from the shore before the water reaches more than waist deep. Such flats are prime areas for bonefishing, and good places to find barracuda, permit and small sharks. Bonefish often betray their presence by 'tailing', feeding nose-down in shallow water with their tails sticking up above the surface.

Left Dropoffs, channels and gullies attract predators such as sharks and barracudas, which lurk in the deeper, darker waters and prey on shoals of baitfish and other unlucky victims such as snappers and groupers.

Above *Tarpon often gather in small schools to surface feed , and can then be caught by casting to them from an anchored or drifting boat.*

gradually deepening away until they reach depths of over 100 feet. Fishing a tropical reef is one of the greatest of angling experiences; from the moment the bait touches bottom there's the chance of hooking something out of the ordinary.

The places to look for on the shallow parts of the reef are the sunken coral heads. These grow like huge mushrooms and provide all kinds of reef fish with food and protection. Groupers, yellowtail snappers, queen triggerfish and a host of lesser though often equally beautiful fish are the main inhabitants of a coral head. These in turn attract the predatory king mackerel, barracuda and small shark.

Beyond the shallow section of the reef, where it drops away sharply into deep water, the boat can be anchored or allowed to drift. Here, the electronic weaponry of the boat may be used to find the best places to fish. A good echo sounder quickly pinpoints the unseen rock pinnacles

or deep gullies between jagged coral walls.

These are big boat grounds, where fish can weigh up to 100 pounds or more. Giant groupers and huge barracuda are the main species, but such a place can also produce amberjack, shark, and a host of smaller but exotically-marked groupers. This is no place for light tackle fishing, because the instant a fish picks up a bait and feels the drag of the line and rod tip it will bolt for cover – cover that may be less than a yard away.

In this type of fishing, if you hesitate you'll lose. Strike, heave and crank the reel handle all at the same instant, and with luck the fish will swim up into open water; but make a mistake, and it's goodbye fish, goodbye end tackle.

When deepwater fishing for species such as sailfish and blue or white marlin, the 600 foot dropoff line is the place to find, using the boat's echo sounding equipment. Once located, the dropoff should be followed, for it's over this depth of water that billfish like to feed.

Water temperature is another very important factor in marlin fishing. The higher the water

temperature, the more likely you are to find marlin, so the boat should have a digital water temperature gauge giving constantly-updated readouts as the boat covers the likely area. It's surprising how much the water temperature can rise or fall in less than 100 yards. The sea has warm currents that flow through it like rivers; find these, and you'll find the fish.

Floating weed is another place to find billfish, along with dolphin (dorado). After storms, huge rafts of weed will appear on the surface and pack together, forming floating weed islands which on occasions will stretch for mile after ocean mile without a break. This weed becomes a sanctuary for crabs and small fish, which attract the interest of billfish and dolphin. A bait trolled along the edge of a weed raft usually produces a strike very quickly. To see a giant blue marlin burst out of the weed and nail a lure in an explosion of white spray is one of the most thrilling sights in angling.

When dolphin are on the move, it's advisable to use smaller lures, as this species seems to be more attracted to them than to larger

patterns. Dolphin are a very popular sport fish because they strike hard, fight well, and indulge in displays of aerobatic ferocity that have to be seen to be believed.

Dolphin are attracted to just about any sizeable floating object they come across. Many boat skippers put out anchored buoys to attract these fish, and it's worth fishing thoroughly around any flotsam such as an old oil drum or a raft of floating rubbish. If a shoal of dolphin is in residence, sport can be fast and furious. Dealing out newspaper sheets like giant playing cards laid in a row, then returning to number one to fish the line of them, has been known to work, so powerfully are dolphin attracted to shade.

You should always check out any bird activity, as flocks of diving seabirds are a sure indication that bait fish are being harried by some sort of predator.

Even a single bird can lead to fish, if it's a frigate bird. This great, giant-winged bird will nearly always be trailing a big billfish. In the Bahamas, fishermen call it the marlin bird, and watch its every movement intently.

SHORELINES

The nature of the local shore can vary considerably from one section of coastline to the next. In some areas the shoreline is sandy, in others it's sand mixed with rocks, vast shingle banks, deep rocky gullies or high vertical cliffs.

Shingle beaches are normally found along exposed stretches of coastline, where wave action often heaps the pebbles up to form banks many miles long. Such banks are normally high, shelving sharply down into a good depth of water.

At first glance, a shingle beach looks a dull, uninteresting and rather barren place to fish. Few creatures can live among the constantly moving shingle, so there's little there to interest fish. Further out, though, the water deepens and the environment is normally much richer. The piled pebbles of the bank give way to a fairly level sea bed composed mostly of grit and fine sand, which provides a home for sandeels, crabs and often small fish on which the larger species feed.

Many anglers make the mistake of overcasting when they're fishing a shingle beach. The hotspot areas are normally within 20 to 50 yards of the beach; a cast of 100 yards or more simply places the bait out beyond the main feeding areas. Occasionally, when long periods of winter wind have caused the wave action to scour at the base of the shingle bank, long casting can be effective, but most times a short cast is the best way to put your bait into the major feeding areas.

Most shingle beaches are crescent-shaped, flanked at each end by a headland. This layout forms a natural haven for small, edible creatures and a rich feeding ground for large, predatory fish. At low spring tide it's sometimes possible to locate upthrust sandbanks which are normally covered by water. These usually occur 30 to 75 yards out, and between them and the beach, the wave action often scours out a deep hole which forms a natural

bait trap and so this area is usually worth fishing.

Of all the venues open to the shore angler, a rugged, rocky section of coastline is the most fascinating and often the most productive. The places to look for are the deep, sheltered gullies which half-empty on a falling tide. As the tide retreats, many small fish, prawns, crabs and shellfish die from exposure to the air. Later, as the tide begins to flood, these dead and dying creatures are washed out into the deeper water.

This natural groundbait attracts a great many kinds of fish into the mouth of the gully. Some fish, like wrasses and conger, are resident species. Others, including bass, pollack and codling, are marauding visitors. In gullies which have a wide mouth and a sandy bottom, it's often possible to catch flatfish.

From the outer edge of the rocks, the rough grounds may give way to deep water over sand or mixed sand and rock. Long

Above *Surf fishing from a sandy Atlantic beach. Surf beaches are at their best in conditions like this, when a strongish inshore wind is pushing the breakers ashore.*
Left *Deep rocky gullies below cliffs are good places to find a wide variety of species.*

casting from the rock spurs can produce tope and various types of skate and ray. Places to look for in particular are gullies divided by a sunken ridge of rock, and gullies which are thick with kelp weed. Kelp jungles hold a lot of big fish, while the rock ridges provide cover and feeding areas for the more active incoming predators.

To fish a surf beach on a day when the wind is whipping up the waves to send rollers crashing across the flat sand, is one of the most exciting of all styles of shore fishing. Shallow though the beach may be, the wave action digs out a great deal of food which the more vigorous predators like bass come inshore to feed on.

Most bass anglers like to drop

their bait out beyond the third breaker. This is a good ploy, because the inshore section of the beach may hold only crab and shellfish, but out beyond this relatively barren area, free-swimming shoals of bait fish provide the bass with an ample food supply. Even large plaice, flounder and small turbot can be caught from this part of the beach.

A surf beach normally fishes at its best when a strongish inshore wind creates large, powerful breakers. These surge inshore to produce a long, creamy surf, although if there's too much wind the breakers may become too high and ragged to fish. The perfect conditions come one or two days after a period of strong onshore winds, and the leftover ground-swell seems particularly attractive to the fish.

Natural shoreline features such as exposed rocks are worth exploring. The wave action is divided by the rock, and often scours out a deep hole which

many incoming fish will visit. On a flood tide, this hole will be on the beach side of the rock; later, when the ebb tide is well established, the inshore hole will fill and a new scour will appear on the seaward side of the rock.

Surf beaches seldom fish well in flat, calm conditions; flounders may be catchable, but little else will. Under such circumstances night fishing is worth trying, and may produce the odd bass.

In areas where the shoreline is made up of sheer or almost-sheer cliffs, the fishing can often be extremely good, and vertical cliffs usually fall directly into deepish water which is an ideal habitat for many species of fish.

In some places, anglers actually fish directly from the clifftops, while in others they scramble down narrow fissures and along rock ledges to reach fishable positions. Good though this fishing may be, great care must be taken to avoid accidents, which all too often prove fatal. Not only is there the danger of

falling, there is also the risk of being swept into the sea by a big wave. It's usually safer to fish from an anchored boat below the cliffs.

Piers, sea walls and jetties provide good, safe platforms for anglers wishing to fish into deeper waters. Most of these places provide good mixed fishing for a wide variety of fish. In a sandy area, fishing from a pier or from a sea wall will produce mostly flatfish, small ray or the occasional bass. In more rocky areas, conger, wrasse and mullet, plus the occasional shark or mackerel, will provide the main sport.

Piers can often be extremely good fishing venues. The weed-covered sunken pier supports provide cover for shoals of smelt and similar bait fish, which attract the interest of bass in the summer and cod in winter. The base of a pier support may well become a conger stronghold, so for anglers wanting a big fish, long casting isn't always essential.

STILL WATERS

S till waters range in size from ponds only a few yards wide to lakes tens or even hundreds of miles across. For the angler, these different waters provide a fascinating and varied range of challenges, and finding out what goes on beneath the surface is interesting in itself as well as being a great help when it comes to catching fish.

A good starting point is to get to know your local ponds, because what happens in ponds also happens in most other still waters, albeit on a much larger scale. Even the largest lakes have shallows around the shore lines, with bays, inlets and coves, where the vegetation and aquatic life can be much the same as in ponds or small lakes.

Whether a pond is deep or shallow, clear and weedy or colored like a bowl of thick pea soup (as many are), the food chain begins in the bottom silt or detritus. This silt, composed of accumulated rotting vegetation and other organic wastes, is broken down by micro-organisms to form a food supply for tiny creatures, which in turn are eaten by larger ones.

Colonies of small crustaceans,

Above *The rich green color of many small waters during the warmer months is caused by an abundance of green planktons.*

Right *Water lilies normally grow in depths of between 3 and 6 feet. Waters thickly covered with lilies are usually clear, because their shade prevents sunlight from stimulating plankton growth.*

such as scuds (freshwater shrimps), feed through the upper layers of detritus, while further down, in the more mature, finer-particled sediment, are the thread-like annelid worms and the larvae of aquatic insects. These creatures form an important part of the diet of many species of fish, including carp.

Carp feed from the bottom with their heads half-buried in the silt, probing with their barbules to locate their food. They suck in vast quantities of sediment, sift out the food, and blow the sediment out again. This behavior creates clouds of suspended sediment, which make it easy to locate feeding carp, especially in normally clear-watered ponds and lakes; it can also cause great damage.

Carp can, and often do, change the entire natural balance of even quite large waters. Their foraging in the sediment digs up beds of soft-rooted plants, and by muddying what was once clear water it cuts off the sunlight that the plants need. By destroying vegetation in this way, carp can make a water unsuitable for many other species of fish.

When bottom-feeding fish are nosing through the detritus, as well as stirring up clouds of silt they release bubbles of natural gas that are trapped in the sediment. During the peak feeding times of early morning and late evening, small groups of bubbles rising to the surface can denote the presence of shoals of fish working the bottom, while straight lines of bubbles usually mean that larger fish are ripping through the layer of rotting vegetation in search of scuds and other food.

Detritus gas bubbles also rise naturally, without being disturbed by fish, but while such bubbles are rising they usually break the surface at just one point, rather than moving around as they would if released by feeding fish. Another source of static patches of bubbles, which shouldn't be confused with those caused by fish, are springs which rise through the bed of a pond or lake.

Even a feeding pike can cause bubbles. As it rockets up from the bottom to grab its prey, its powerful tail action can release a great cloud of bubbles from the disturbed sediment.

In general, small waters can be divided into two groups: those with clear water and a lush growth of soft-rooted weeds, and those with colored water whose vegetation is mainly marginal reeds or sedges. These differences are the result of many factors, including the presence of phosphate and nitrate fertilizer residues washed into the pond from nearby farmland, the amount of sunlight reaching the water through the shade of any bankside shrubs or trees, and the numbers and types of fish present. Depth also plays an important part. Shallow ponds are usually warmer than deep ones, and so the growth of the plants and animals they contain is much quicker.

Sunlight, in conjunction with nutrients such as fertilizer residues, stimulates the growth of the tiny plant organisms known as phytoplanktons. During the warmer months, many waters turn a rich-pea-green color because of the presence of billions of these single-celled green planktons. These are the staple food of the animal or zooplanktons, such as daphnia (water fleas), and are also eaten by fish during the first few weeks of their lives.

In clear waters, where the numbers of phytoplanktons are kept low by the feeding of zooplanktons, clouds of daphnia can often be seen in the warmer shallows. At first sight, it seems as though the surface of the water has been sprinkled with orange-red brick dust, but closer inspection reveals billions of the upright-swimming water fleas, swimming frantically but wafted helplessly by the wind and water movements.

The balance between phytoplanktons and zooplanktons dictates whether the water is green or clear. A rich variety of aquatic plants, particularly the soft-rooted weeds, also helps to keep the water clear because they consume many of the nutrients which would otherwise be taken up by the phytoplanktons. In addition, where the surface of a pond or small lake is almost covered by plants such as water lilies, the water usually remains quite clear because the sunlight can't penetrate the depths and stimulate phytoplankton growth. However, any water with more than its fair share of carp will be permanently turbid because of the fine silt particles churned up by the fish and held in suspension in the water.

Patches of water lilies and other floating plants are good places to fish during hot, sunny weather, because many species love to rest in the shade they provide. They are also good spots to find predators such as pike, perch and black bass, which lurk among the underwater stems, waiting to rush out and grab any passing food.

Even when the surface is quite thickly covered with lilies or other plants, the stems below will be relatively sparse, enabling slim-bodied fish to pass easily between the stems without touching them. Broad-bodied fish, however, often brush against the stems as they grub about, betraying their presence by causing twitches and shakes in the surface foliage.

Bankside trees and bushes can also create good fish-holding areas. Overhanging branches provide the fish with cover, and food in the form of insects and grubs which fall into the water from them. Underwater roots, and lower branches which actually dip into the water, become covered in algae and attract snails and the larvae of many aquatic insects, so fish gather there to feed, as they do among the stems of marginal reeds.

In many reservoirs, fish are to be found among the submerged trees which grew in the valley before it was flooded. Sometimes these are marked by buoys, or shown on charts of the water, but if not, they can be located by sonar. Where the bed of a reservoir or other still water is virtually featureless, artificial fish-holding areas can be created

Above *Dawn is a peak feeding time for many species, which makes it one of the best times of the day for fishing.*

Right *Feeding fish often betray their presence by creating surface disturbances and bubbles.*

Left *Marginal plants are good fish-holding areas. Fish feed on the snails and insect larvae whch live among the plant stems, and on insects, grubs and caterpillars which fall into the water from bankside trees and bushes.*

by anchoring large rafts of cut trees and branches to the bottom. This is a common practice in North America, where the positions of these brush piles are usually shown by buoys or by shore markers.

If you're going to fish a really large water, it's a good idea to spend some time beforehand studying a chart of it. A good chart will detail all the obvious hotspots, such as shallows, sunken forests, plateaux, deep-water dropoffs along the marginal shelf, and deep gullies between islands.

Near the shore, the old ideas of always following the wind, or fishing into the wind, can often be very useful. This is because concentrations of plankton, caught in the surface layers, can be blown inshore by the wind. Shoals of bait fish fry are attracted to these buildups of plankton in the shallow waters, and small predators following the fry shoals attract the interest of large predators such as pike. Before long, a large patch of water which might have been competely empty of fish only the day before, when the wind direction was different, becomes full of life. You can often locate these gatherings of fish by looking out for flocks of fish-eating birds, such as gulls, grebes and cormorants, which are usually quick to find them.

Although some predators do roam considerable distances in search of their food, perch and the members of the pike family prefer to find a good source of food, such as a shoal of bait fish, and stay close to it. Good places to find resident bait fish shoals, and their attendant predators, include waters over rough ground, the edges of dropoffs, and the mouths of inflowing rivers.

In contrast, salmon, char and certain species of trout are lovers of deep, open water, and the only really effective way of finding them is by using sonar, preferably in conjunction with a subsurface water temperature probe.

Deep waters have three fairly distinct layers: the epilimnion (upper layer), the thermocline (middle layer) and the hypo-limnion (lower layer). During summer and in the fall, the thermocline separates the warm epilimnion from the much colder hypolimnion, while in winter the epilimnion is colder than the hypolimnion. The water temperature changes only slowly between the surface and the thermocline, and between the thermocline and the bottom, but it changes rapidly through the comparatively thin thermocline. This rapidly-changing temperature makes the thermocline easy to locate with a deep temperature probe.

As the epilimnion warms up at the beginning of summer, fish such as lake trout, which prefer cool water, must move deeper, to the thermocline or even below it. To help the angler find these fish, many of today's sonar units are sensitive enough to detect the denser water of the thermocline. There are also temperature probes which can be attached to the downrigger weight, or lowered manually from a drifting boat.

Modern electronics have taken much of the guesswork out of tackling vast, deep waters, and made fishing them far more productive. With the latest equipment it's a matter of reading the display, rather than the water.

STREARMS AND RIVERS

Apart from those which originate in lakes, most rivers – even the mightiest of them – start their lives as tiny creeks, fed by springs or the meltwaters of mountain snows.

The coldwater mountain streams, where small trout rule the roost, are certainly the most picturesque, though because of the low water temperatures they are nowhere near as rich as the lowland streams, and hold far fewer fish. In the upper reaches, invertebrate life is limited to insect larvae and scuds, which scuttle about among the smooth, worn rocks and stones on the bottom. As a stream widens and matures, it offers a greater variety of habitats, with bottom weeds, marginal plants and bankside trees providing food and shelter for an increasing number of fish species.

Along the course of a high, coldwater river, fish are nearly always found in pools. Not just pools beneath waterfalls, but also the deeper, slower pools carved out of the river bed by water funelling through narrows or between rocks. Pools offer a choice of fast or slow water, where fish like salmon can hold in the slower band just out of the full force of the current, waiting until they're ready to surge upstream over seemingly impossible obstacles to their spawning grounds.

Other species, like trout and grayling, wait in the pools for particles of food brought down by the current, and during the summer months, when insect life is at its most abundant, they need make little effort to secure a meal. In leaner times, they feed from the bottom among the stones, and on grubs and earthworms which are washed into the river during floods.

In lowland streams, an entirely different habitat of lush aquatic vegetation and bankside plants, plus additional general silting of the river bed between runs of sand and gravel, results in a far more complex environment. Food abounds, supporting large numbers of fish of many different species.

Whatever the type of river or stream you're fishing, it pays to know whereabouts the fish are likely to be. For instance, careful study of a boulder-strewn flood river when the water level is low will show you where the fish are likely to lie up when the river returns to its normal level. Look

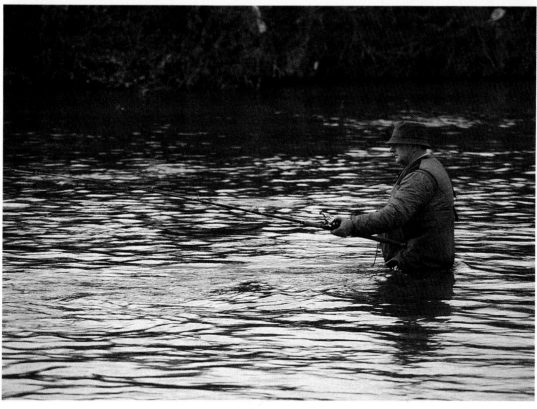

Left *Pools in rock-strewn upland streams are good places to find brown trout.*
Below left *To catch migratory fish such as salmon, you need to know when to be on the river as well as where to find them.*
Below *Insect larvae and small crustaceans are the main fish foods in gravel-bottomed streams.*

out for large rocks, because the areas of slack water which form behind them are favorite spots for salmon, trout and even pike. Many river keepers actually place large rocks in shallows to create this kind of shelter, and in deeper sections build wooden or steel stagings out from the bank to deflect the current, providing

enough slack behind them to accommodate a large fish or two.

Sunken trees and bridge supports also create areas of slower water adjacent to the main flow. Most species like to hold up in slack water, because it's much easier than continually facing the full force of the current, so such areas are always worth exploring

when you're fishing a river.

Confluences, where rivers meet, are great hotspots. Where both rivers are fast-flowing, fish rest in the slower water between the two courses, slipping out into the current from time to time to grab some passing food. Close into the bank, among the marginal reeds and rushes where sediment usually builds up, predators like pike will lie in wait.

At a confluence where one river is fast and the other is either much smaller or of a much slower flow, an eddy will form. The swirling water of the eddy will carve out a depression, often quite deep, which is much to the liking of bottom-feeding species. During times of heavy flooding, you can expect to find most species just into the secondary river where the flow is much quieter. Such retreats very often hold both predators and prey, holed up together in even tiny areas because their normal living quarters are under threat.

Islands are also great fish attractors. Predators lurk where trees overhang or the lower branches actually submerge, and any grasses or sedges fringing the island provide fish with cover as well as a large stock of aquatic and terrestrial insects. This food potential, combined with the cover, means that islands are likely to be surrounded by large numbers of fish, so if you're going to fish an unfamiliar river, an island is a good place to begin.

Another place where large numbers of fish are often found is in a weirpool. These pools are perhaps the most interesting and productive of all river features, and a large one might hold practically every species of fish found in the entire river system, from tiny minnows to huge catfish.

Fast water species, such as salmon and trout, will occupy the main white water flow areas where oxygen levels are highest, while in the back eddies, well away from the full current, species like perch, bream, chub and roach will be found. Pike like to lie in wait close to the bank, and in the deepest water, amid the debris which has accumulated over the years, other predators such as eels and catfish will take up residence. Finally, if the river is clean, the very tail end of the pool is a good place to find plentiful stocks of crayfish, one of the deadliest of natural baits for most species.

The presence or absence of crayfish is a good indication of the health of the river, because they

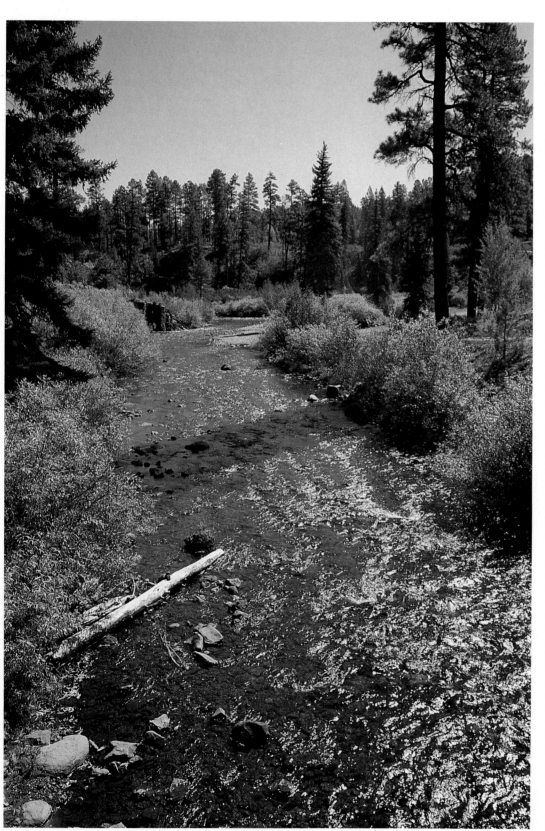

have a low tolerance of pollution. When a river becomes contaminated, either by farm chemicals leached in from the land or by industrial pollution, species like crayfish, and the little brook lampreys which cling to the stones with their sucker-like mouths, are the first to suffer.

In really fast, wide sections of river, where the bottom is rocky and uneven, study the surface patterns for a guide to the bottom topography. For instance, huge boils and vortexes on the surface are areas where several currents are merging around a submerged obstacle, usually a particularly large boulder or a high, packed rock outcrop. However, down below, on either side of the obstacle, things are invariably much quieter and fish could be holed up there, so it's worth fishing through the turbulence.

Broken water also occurs over shallow rock plateaux and even, in the case of winter currents, over the remains of the previous summer's reed or bullrush stems.

There is nearly always a tiny slack immediately behind these natural barriers where fish shelter from the full force of the current.

Old, well-established millpools and little overshoot pools where water is diverted from the main stream for irrigation are wonderful features to explore. As in the much larger weirpools, trout are to be expected wherever there is a strong pull of white water tumbling over the sill from the river above. Further down, at the tail end where the bottom shelves up to hard gravel and beds of weed, surface feeders will compete with the trout for hatching insects.

Irrigation ditches are usually worth exploring, especially where they've been neglected and become overgrown with a wealth of vegetation, such as lilies, reeds and rushes. In Britain, these ditches are usually the home of rudd, tench and bream, while in North America they are good places to find largemouth bass.

Where irrigation ditches are

connected to swampy tropical or subtropical coastal river systems, as they are in Florida, the hard-fighting snook and tarpon may be found. These fish, which occur in the inshore coastal waters, also travel quite far inland, even into fresh waters. The prime hotspots for them, though, are brackish inlets, bayous, creeks and canals where lush and dense vegetation creates a maze of food-rich hideouts for them.

Dams, built across rivers for flood control, hydroelectric power, irrigation systems or to create reservoirs, can also be well worth exploring – not just the stillwaters behind them, but also the often turbulent waters below.

The typical dam wall has a concrete apron over which low-water currents tumble into the huge pool below. When water levels are higher, however, such as in early spring, excess water cascading down from the spillways carves out a very deep hole, called 'a washout hole, in the bottom of the pool.

Most species can't tolerate this kind of violent water movement, so they seek refuge further down the tailrace, usually behind the wing dams. These are manmade rock piles that jut out from the shoreline and are designed to stop bank erosion by deflecting the current back into the centre of the channel. When the water is really high and fast-running, the sheltered water on the downstream side of a wing dam, or any similar patch of slack water, is

Below left *An area of quiet water in an otherwise turbulent river is where fish like to rest.*

Below *Reed and rush beds provide many species with shelter and a good supply of insects and other food, but you can't always fish them from the bank.*

Right *Chalk streams are excellent trout waters, but a careful and stealthy approach is essential to avoid spooking the fish in the crystal-clear water.*

where you'll find the fish.

When the water returns to its normal, lower level, the fish move back into the mainstream and the pool itself. Though these pools can be massive, they're really only very large versions of the lovely little pools you might find along the course of an upland stream.

Many of the biggest rivers have a deep, often swiftly-flowing main channel which is kept turbid by the high number of boats which use it. This turbidity suits many bottom-dwellers such as eels and catfish, but species which prefer clear water and a roof of aquatic vegetation over their heads will keep to the margins or choose an off-river backwater.

These off-river locations often offer habitats virtually identical to those found in still waters; if so, you should treat them as such. Search areas such as dropoffs, patches of weed, beds of rushes or reeds, around bluffs and in sunken timber, and at cove entrances where fry are gathered.

Another type of location where many river species occur, not always voluntarily, is the oxbow lake. Oxbow lakes are formed in flat country, where the river flows in horseshoe-shaped loops or meanders. The outer banks of a loop are eroded by the current, while silt is deposited along the inner banks. In time, this erosion narrows the neck of the loop so much that the river breaks through it, usually during a flood, cutting a new channel that bypasses the loop.

The ends of the loop become silted up, cutting it off from the river and creating an oxbow lake that still holds some of the species found in the river which formed it. In addition to these species, many oxbows contain others which have been deliberately introduced to create new fisheries.

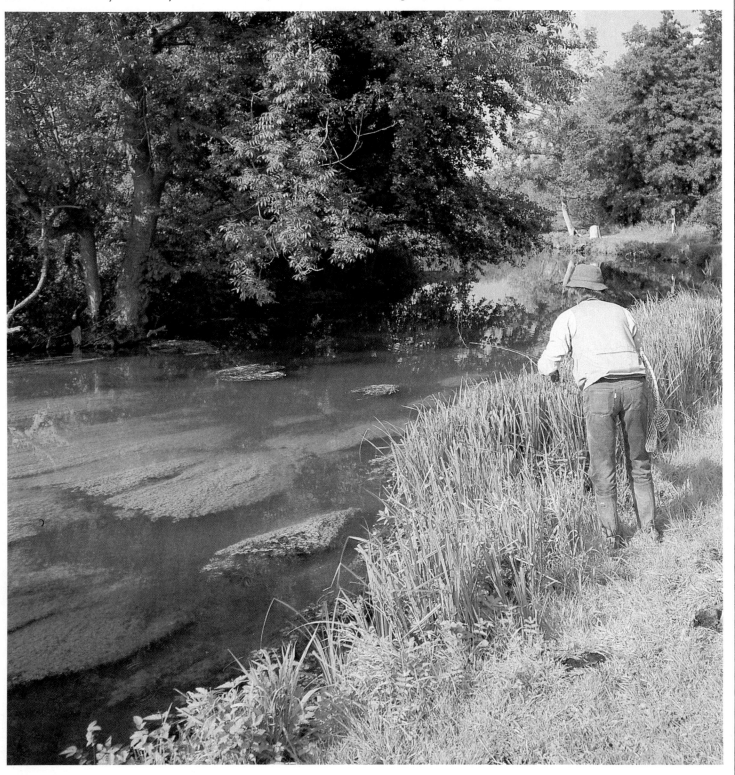

Index of Scientific Names

CREDITS

Authors:
Trevor Housby
Arthur Oglesby
John Wilson
Additional material by
Colin Newman

Editorial:
US Consultant A.J. McClane
US Editor Keith Gardner
UK Editor Ian Wood
Assistant Editors Nigel Flynn,
Tessa Carias
Art Director Steve Leaning

Photography:
Main studio photography
Theo Bergström
Additonal studio photography
John Darling, Peter Gathercole
Location photography John
Darling, Peter Gathercole,
Trevor Housby, Arthur Oglesby,
Graeme Pullen, Mike Millman,
John Wilson

Artists:
Fish species Colin Newman
Other artwork Nigel Bass,
Lyn Cawley

Manufacturers and suppliers:

Abu Garcia Inc,
21 Law Drive,
Fairfield,
New Jersey 07006.

Bruce and Walker Ltd,
Huntingdon Road,
Upwood,
Huntingdon,
Cambridgeshire PE17 1QQ,
England.

Daiwa Corporation,
7421 Chapman Avenue,
Department C-A,
Garden Grove,
California 92641.

Peter Drennan,
Leopold Street,
Oxford,
England.

Gardner Tackle,
2 Pepperbox Lane,
Palmers Cross,
Bramley,
Surrey GU5 0LW,
England.

Hardy (USA) Inc,
10 Godwin Plaza,
Midland Park,
New Jersey 07432.

Leeda Tackle Ltd,
14 Cannon Street,
Southampton SO9 2RB,
England.

Ryobi America Corp,
1158 Tower Lane,
Bensenville,
Illinois 60106.

Shakespeare Fishing Tackle
Division,
Drawer S,
Columbia,
South Carolina 29260.

Sparton Fishing Tackle,
Sileby,
Leicester,
England.

Taylor and Johnson Ltd,
Broad Ground Road,
Lakeside,
Redditch,
Worcestershire B98 8YP,
England.

Woody's of Wembley,
565 High Road,
Wembley,
Middlesex,
England.

Detailed credits

Pages 10-11: *tackle picture* Bergström, supplier Hardy; *inset photograph* Millman, *photograph* Housby
12-13: *tackle picture* Bergström, suppliers Abu, Daiwa, Ryobi; *photos* Oglesby (12), Darling (13)
14-15: *tackle picture* Bergström, suppliers Daiwa, Ryobi, Shakespeare; *photo* Millman
16-17: *tackle picture* Bergström, suppliers Daiwa, Shakespeare; *photo* Millman
18-19: *tackle picture* Bergström, supplier Drennan
20-21: *tackle picture* Bergström, suppliers Leeda, Ryobi, Shakespeare; *photo* Gathercole
22-23: *tackle picture* Bergström, suppliers Bruce & Walker, Hardy, Ryobi, Shakespeare; *photo* Darling
24-25: *tackle picture* Bergström, *illustration* Cawley
26-27: *tackle picture* Bergström, supplier Woody's
28-29: *tackle picture* Bergström, suppliers Abu, Hardy
30-31: *tackle picture* Bergström, suppliers Daiwa, Ryobi, Shakespeare; *photo* Millman
32-33: *tackle picture* Bergström, suppliers Drennan, Ryobi, Taylor & Johnson, Woody's
34-35: *tackle picture* Bergström, suppliers Shakespeare, Woody's; *photo* Millman
36-37: *tackle picture* Bergström, suppliers Drennan, Gardner, Hardy, Shakespeare

38-39: *tackle picture* Bergström, suppliers Bruce & Walker, Hardy; *photo* Gathercole
40-41: *tackle picture* Bergström, suppliers Hardy, Woody's
42-43: *tackle picture* Bergström, suppliers Daiwa, Shakespeare; *photo* Darling
44-45: *tackle picture* Bergström, supplier Woody's
46-47: *tackle picture* Bergström, supplier Ryobi
48-49: *tackle picture* Bergström, suppliers Abu, Daiwa, Hardy
50-51: *tackle picture* Bergström, suppliers Daiwa, Ryobi; *photo* Gathercole
54-55: *tackle picture* Gathercole; *illustration* Cawley
56-57: *tackle picture* Gathercole; flies tied by Gathercole, and Steve Parton (Sparton Fishing Tackle)
58-59: *tackle picture* Gathercole; wet flies tied by Gathercole and Parton, salmon flies by Bill Coe
60-63: *tackle pictures* Bergström, suppliers Abu, Hardy
64-65: *tackle picture* Bergström, suppliers Abu, Hardy
66-67: *bait picture* Bergström; *illustration* Cawley
68-69: *bait picture* Bergström
70-71: *tackle picture* Bergström, suppliers Drennan, Woody's; *photo* Wilson
72-73: *bait picture* Darling; *illustration* Cawley
74-75: *photos* Millman

78-127: *all illustrations* Newman
130-131: *illustrations* Bass; *photo* Pullen
132-133: *illustrations* Cawley; *photos* Housby
134-135: *illustrations* Bass; *photos* Gathercole (134), Millman (135)
136-137: *illustrations* Bass; *photo* Darling
138-139: *illustrations* Cawley; *photo* Housby
140-141: *illustrations* Bass; *photo* Gathercole
142-143: *illustrations* Bass; *photo* Gathercole
144-145: *illustrations* Cawley; *photo* Oglesby
146-147: *illustrations* Bass, Cawley (147); *photo* Gathercole
148-149: *illustrations* Bass; *photo* Pullen
150-151: *illustrations* Cawley; *photo* Gathercole
152-153: *illustrations* Cawley
154-155: *illustrations* Bass; *photo* Darling
156-157: *illustrations* Bass; *photo* Pullen
158-159: *illustrations* Bass; *photo* Housby
160-161: *illustrations* Bass; *photo* Darling
162-163: *illustrations* Bass; *photo* Wilson
164-165: *illustrations* Bass; *photo* Pullen
166-167: *illustrations* Cawley; *photo* Darling
168-169: *illustrations* Bass; *photo* Pullen

172-173: *photos* Millman
174-175: *photos* Millman (174, 175 bottom), Darling (175 top)
176-177: *photos* Housby (176 top), Millman (176 bottom, 177)
178-179: *photos* Darling (178), Millman (179)
180-181: *photos* Millman (180), Wilson (181)
182-183: *photos* Pullen (182, 183 top), Darling (183 bottom)
184-185: *photos* Darling (184 top), Millman (184 bottom), Pullen (185)
186-187: *photos* Pullen (186 left), Darling (186 right), Housby (187)